S0-BBC-582

PORTUGUESE
LANGUAGE

Life

&
CULTURE

PORTUGUESE
LANGUAGE

Life

& CULTURE

Sue Tyson-Ward

TEACH YOURSELF BOOKS

For Mum, Dad, and Ed.

For UK order queries: please contact Bookpoint Ltd, 130 Milton Park, Abingdon, Oxon OX14 4SB. Telephone: (44) 01235 827720. Fax: (44) 01235 400454. Lines are open from 9.00–18.00, Monday to Saturday, with a 24-hour message answering service. Email address: orders@bookpoint.co.uk

For USA order queries: please contact McGraw-Hill Customer Services, P.O. Box 545, Blacklick, OH 43004-0545, USA. Telephone: 1-800-722-4726. Fax: 1-614-755-5645.

For Canada order queries: please contact McGraw-Hill Ryerson Ltd., 300 Water St, Whitby, Ontario L1N 9B6, Canada. Telephone: 905 430 5000. Fax: 905 430 5020.

Long-renowned as the authoritative source for self-guided learning – with more than 30 million copies sold worldwide – the *Teach Yourself* series includes over 200 titles in the fields of languages, crafts, hobbies, sports, and other leisure activities.

British Library Cataloguing in Publication Data
A catalogue entry for this title is available from The British Library.

Library of Congress Catalog Card Number: on file

First published in UK 2002 by Hodder Headline Plc, 338 Euston Road, London NW1 3BH.

First published in US 2002 by Contemporary Books, a division of the McGraw-Hill Companies, 4255 West Touhy Avenue, Lincolnwood (Chicago), Illinois 60712–1975, USA.

The 'Teach Yourself' name and logo are registered trade marks of Hodder & Stoughton Ltd.

Copyright © 2002 Sue Tyson-Ward

Typeset by Transet Limited, Coventry, England.
Printed in Great Britain by Cox & Wyman Ltd, Reading, Berkshire.

Impression number   10 9 8 7 6 5 4 3 2 1
Year   2006 2005 2004 2003 2002

CONTENTS

Acknowledgements

The author would like to thank the following for their help in the
preparation of this book: Phil Turk, the series Editor, and Sue Hart
and Rebecca Green at Hodder & Stoughton for their help and advice.

Maria Gilham and especially Francisco Fernandes for their
invaluable suggestions as Readers, and students at the Adult College,
Lancaster for their contributions. Brenda Wright for her invaluable
typing when things got desperate!

Many thanks, also, to the many people and organisations who so
kindly offered information, opinions and advice, amongst them
Paulo Lobo, Jackie Meikle, David and Maria Fremlin, Jeff Stokes,
Alexandra Aragão, Rita Marnoto, and in particular Maria Amélia
Estrela at the Coordenação do Ensino de Português in London, for
her endless support and steady stream of resources.

INTRODUCTION

This book is designed to give you as full a basic overview as possible of the main aspects of Portugal: the country, its language, its people, their way of life and culture and what makes them tick.

You will find it a useful foundation if you are studying for examinations which require a knowledge of the background of Portugal and its civilization, or if you are learning the language in, for example, an evening class and want to know more about the country and how it works. If your job involves travel and business relations it will provide valuable and practical information about the ways and customs of the people you are working with. Or if you simply have an interest in Portugal for whatever reason, it will broaden your knowledge about the country and its inhabitants.

The book is divided into three sections:

- **The making of Portugal**

  Chapters 1 and 2 deal with the forces – historical, geographical, geological, demographical and linguistic – that have brought about the formation of the country we know as Portugal and the language we known as Portuguese. Chapter 2 also takes a look at the role of Portuguese outside the immediate frontiers of Portugal.

- **Creative Portugal**

  Chapters 3 to 8 deal with the wealth of creative aspects of Portuguese culture from the beginnings to the present day. These chapters take a look at the main areas or works of literature, art and architecture, music, traditions and festivals, science and technology, fashion and food and drink, together with the people who have created and are still creating them.

■ **Living in Portugal now**
Chapters 9 to 12 deal with aspects of contemporary Portuguese
society and the practicalities of living in present-day Portugal:
the way the political structure of the country is organized,
education, the environment, the workplace and how people
spend their leisure time. The Postscript looks at the country's
political, economic and social relations with the wider world,
and takes a glance at the future.

Taking it further
Each chapter ends with a section entitled 'Taking it further', where
you will find useful addresses, websites, suggested places to visit
and things to see and do in order to develop your interest further
and increase your knowledge.

The language
Within each chapter you will encounter a number of terms in
Portuguese, whose meaning is given in English when they are first
introduced. If you wish to put your knowledge into practice, we have
provided in each chapter a list of useful words and phrases to enable
you to talk or write about the subject in question. Where English
spellings of Portuguese places exist, these are generally used.

We have been careful in researching and checking facts, but please
be aware that sources sometimes offer differing information. Of
course a book of this length cannot contain everything you may
need to know on every aspect of Portugal. That is why we have
provided so many pointers to where you can find further information
about any aspect that you may wish to pursue in more depth.
We trust that you will enjoy this introductory book, and that it will
provide leads to further profitable reading, listening and visiting.

Phil Turk
Series Editor

1 THE MAKING OF PORTUGAL

São bem-vindos a Portugal, a um país com uma história de muitos séculos, uma língua de muitos povos, uma cultura de muitos horizontes ... uma nação que deixou marcas e memórias em todos os continentes ... (Welcome to Portugal, to a country with a history of many centuries, a language of many peoples, a culture of many horizons ... a nation that has left behind marks and memories in all continents ...) – Jorge Sampaio, President of Portugal, *Guia Oficial, Expo 98*

Portugal: the magnetic country

Port wine, sardines, tea-towels, Carnival and Samba, coffee, Pelé, dessert wine, land-mines, flood appeals, Formula 1, golf, football and the spectacularly expensive legs of Luís Figo: all these are images and icons from the Portuguese-speaking world – and of course there's more, much more. But mention Portugal in conversation and many people instantly conjure up warming memories of sun-filled days in languid enjoyment of the increasingly popular holiday destination – the Algarve. In 1999, 27 million people visited Portugal, almost 12 million of these as holiday tourists (outnumbering native inhabitants of the country!). The vast majority of visitors come from the UK, now accounting for almost 2 million annually, Germany and Spain, and a steady influx from the USA (around 3 per cent of visitors), Canada and Brazil.

A huge 48 per cent of all tourists to Portugal stay in the Algarve (and indeed many go on to make their homes there). With average sunshine rates of 8.6 hours a day, and an almost-guaranteed year-round warm climate, it's no wonder the southern coastline is a PR person's dream commodity. For those who have ventured beyond the foreign, ex-patriot enclaves of the Algarve (even by a mere 5km or so), Portugal has offered much more than sun, beaches and pool-infested villa-land: a varied landscape, a fascinating history, good food, family values, a calm lifestyle (frustratingly so for some), and above all, the warmth of its welcoming people – a true hand of friendship and a feeling of belonging.

For those about to embark on the voyage of discovery for the first time, *bem-vindos*, welcome aboard!

Although we shall be concentrating on Portugal itself, the inextricable links with the rest of the Portuguese-speaking world cannot be ignored, and where relevant, reference will be made to points of interest relating to the remaining Portuguese-speaking countries, namely: Brazil, the African countries of Angola, Mozambique, Guinea-Bissau, Cape Verde, São Tomé and Príncipe, as well as East Timor and Macau in Asia (recently handed back to China) and of course the autonomous regions of Madeira and the Azores sitting in the Atlantic. A fuller picture of the early global dominance by Portugal is given on page 17, and on the map on page 16.

Landscape and climate

Sitting where it does, on the westerly edge of Europe, with a coastline of around 800km, and extending approximately 500km down through predominantly Atlantic climes towards a more Mediterranean atmosphere, Portugal has a vastly differing landscape, which has not altered greatly since the initial establishment of prehistoric features such as the imposing granite deposits in the northern and central highland areas, and the soft rolling plains of the south. Although it has a natural border with Spain in the form of a line of mountains and long rivers (such as the *Guadiana*), Portugal actually shares many geographical and geological features with its neighbour. It has been claimed that a more natural division of the whole Iberian peninsula might have been in three main sections cutting across from east to west; the Atlantic hills and mountain ranges of southern France, down across the central plains, and finally the Mediterranean coastal area. The climate changes too, in the same way as it does in Spain: from the wetter northern atmosphere, with concentrated rainfall in the fertile hilly and coastal regions (the most northern coast is called *Costa Verde* – the green coast), down through protected central areas, whose summers are relentlessly hot in contrast with freezing winters, and whose soil suffers as a consequence, and finally to the idyll of the south coast, whose mild climate is so coveted by northern Europeans. The capital, Lisbon, has variable weather, which has become increasingly unpredictable, although you can always be sure of a gentle breeze wafting in from the river Tagus. As world climates generally continue to change, even the Algarve has provided unsuspecting visitors with surprise downpours in the middle of hitherto sacrosanct warm periods.

Mountains (*montanhas*)

The highest land lies to the north and east, bordering Spain, and covers quite a substantial area, with the largest concentration of high ground in the regions of Alto Alentejo, Beira Alta, Trás-os-Montes and the Douro valleys. The *Serra da Estrela* (lit. the mountain range of the star), at 1992m, is the highest mountain range, and hosts a winter ski resort and spa (see map, p.4) In general, the hills are a popular destination for walkers, hunters (particularly for wild boar, *javalí*), and nature lovers. Madeira and the Azores are also high land-masses, all volcanic islands, with the *Pico* range in the Azores the highest point at 2351m.

Rivers (*rios*)

The two rivers of prime importance in Portugal are the *Douro* running through Porto, and the *Tejo* (Tagus in English) in Lisbon. Both have their origin in Spain, as the Duero and Tajo, and run down from the higher hilly regions out to the west and into the Atlantic. Both are highly influential sources of commerce – the Douro feeding the wine-growing areas of the north, and the Tejo watering the agricultural areas east of Lisbon, and providing important docking and transport links for the capital. Additionally, the river *Guadiana*, which flows through Spain and then runs north to south along much of the border, has played its part historically in the division of the two countries. Despite EU open frontiers, it is still randomly patrolled by Customs police, particularly in the

The Autonomous Region of Madeira
900 km south-west of Lisbon

Porto Santo

Madeira

Funchal

20 km

The Autonomous Region of the Azores
1700 km west of Lisbon

Corvo

Flores

Graciosa

São Jorge   Terceira

Faial

Pico

São Miguel

Fonta Delgado

Santa Maria

20 km

extreme south, in an effort to contain and prevent further misuse of the river as a smuggling route from North Africa. In the North of Portugal the rivers *Minho*, spanning the border with the Spanish province of Galicia, and *Lima*, with its beautiful bridge at Ponte de Lima, are the most well-known. Whilst on the theme of waterways, north of Lisbon is the fascinating town of Aveiro, Portugal's own Venice. Built around a network of waterways/canals, the town shelters a huge lagoon which is worked for its fertile seaweed, or *moliço*. The men who gather the stuff on their flat-bedded boats, and the boats themselves, are called *moliceiros*. Although numbers working this trade have dwindled, the seaweed itself is a prize commodity for enriching the agricultural land round about.

The coast *(a costa)*

Despite being in southern Europe, Portugal's coastline is Atlantic and experiences the wind and temperatures associated with those waters. The northern coast offers endless stretches of white beaches (the main coast is called *Costa de Prata* – silver coast), unspoilt and mostly unpolluted, and popular with holidaying Portuguese. In the Algarve the coast is dominated by fantastically shaped crags and rock formations *(rochas e falésias)*, yellow and golden remnants of the original coastline. Erosion of the cliffs is an on-going problem here, with recent highlighted cases of properties, including holiday complexes, in precarious positions on crumbling cliff-tops. In a number of resorts initiatives are now underway to strengthen and improve the line of sea defences. This powerful destructive force of nature does not deter visitors to the miles of glorious sandy beaches and fascinating coves along the Algarve.

The coast is not just about tourism though, however important that now is to Portugal. Throughout history the sea has provided a large part of the staple diet, in a variety of seafood and fish, as well as furnishing the impetus for external, distant exploration. Both of these themes will be visited later. Along the expansive coastline are a number of estuaries which provide natural breeding grounds for birds, with habitats of rare flora and fauna. Some of the larger ones have been formed into protected nature reserves, such as the *Alvor* and *Ria Formosa* reserves in the Algarve, and the Tagus and Sado Estuary reserves near Lisbon.

The regions (*as regiões*)

Portugal today has five administrative regions: *Norte*, *Centro*, *Lisboa & Vale do Tejo*, *Alentejo*, and *Algarve*. These represent areas of the country with distinct characteristics, from the industrial north, with the highest number of the population, encompassing the wine-growing lands but also the isolated mountainous areas, down through the rugged and coastal central part running into Lisbon and environs, the second largest region in terms of population. As the capital, Lisbon is a thriving cosmopolitan city with a wonderful mix of ancient and modern, making it a popular destination for visitors and investing businesses alike. From the Tagus valley the country opens out into the sprawling plains of the Alentejo – the predominantly agricultural, albeit poor, region, the largest region in land-mass, yet housing only a fraction of the population. The final area is the Algarve, with its tourist developments on the coast. The small number of local inhabitants (fewer than half a million) is swelled during the year by the millions of foreign visitors the region accommodates. In addition, Portugal counts as its territory the two autonomous Atlantic island groups of *Madeira* and the Azores (*Açores*). Mainland Portugal is further divided into 18 administrative districts, with smaller municipal and parish districts within them (see p.187).

However, ask a Portuguese person where they are from, and it is highly likely they will refer to the province from which they originate. The country was originally divided into 11 such provinces, the names of which are still used by inhabitants and still appear in many tourist information and guide books. As the provinces themselves vary in geography and culture, so too the people who live there differ in appearance, character and background. Portugal's most famous contemporary writer, José Saramago, famously stated in the BBC's series on 'Discovering Portugal', that he could not define the Portuguese, as each province offered such different characteristics: 'I'll probably die without ever knowing', he claimed. What is interesting, in the same series, is his description of a journey he once made by train in Europe, in the same carriage as a number of EU officials, who spent an inordinate amount of time trying to work out his nationality.

Despite giving them a number of clues about Portugal and the language, the officials exhausted all possible choices before asking with incredulity if he might be Portuguese!

Perhaps this is indicative of a lack of knowledge or interest in Portugal over the last couple of decades (apart from the tourist trade), but certainly Portugal is becoming an increasingly prominent player on the European stage, and this book will show you how much it has to offer across a variety of spheres.

The 11 provinces (*as províncias*)

O Norte

The North comprises the provinces of *Minho*, *Douro* and *Trás-os-Montes*. The Minho borders onto Galicia in northern Spain, and there are many overlaps, in culture and language across the frontier. It is one of the lushest areas in Portugal, with a climate and landscape similar to that in a damp, northern European country. It's no wonder its coastline is called the Costa Verde. The area produces the popular 'green wine' (young wine) – *vinho verde*, which is starting to make its way onto foreign wine-shop shelves. The *Minho* houses the country's biggest National Park, *Peneda Gerês*. The North in general is steeped in traditions, very religious, and hard-working. To the east, the *Minho* is flanked by the mountainous region of *Trás-os-Montes* (lit. behind the mountains). This is an area isolated geographically from the rest of the country, rugged in landscape, very poor in monetary terms, and whose towns and lifestyles are reminiscent of Medieval Europe; its people, however, are fiercely proud of their heritage, more Celtic in nature than much of the country, a legacy of northern invasions.

The main industrial area in the north is the *Douro*, whose river runs down from Spain (917km from source to coast), providing the vital font of life along the long valley from the surrounding hillsides down into Porto and the wine lodges (*caves*) on the riverfront at Vila Nova de Gaia. There are many links with the British, most of which are still visible today in the city of Porto, the country's second largest (Oporto is the anglicized name for it, it is in fact *O Porto* = the port). About 1.3 million people live in and around Porto, participating in the many busy commercial activities of the area which, in addition to viticulture, also include the production of ceramics, cotton goods, sardine-canning and some farming. The coastline stretching from the Douro southwards is popular with holidaying Portuguese, although Atlantic winds keep temperatures to a less tolerable level than in the Algarve at certain times of the year.

O Centro

The central provinces include the three Beiras (*beira* means edge or riverbank) – *Beira Alta* (higher), *Beira Baixa* (Lower) and *Beira Litoral* (coastal). Of these, Beira Litoral is home to a number of towns of great historical interest, including the beautiful city of Coimbra, Portugal's equivalent of Britain's Oxford or Cambridge. With a population of around 80,000, it is one of the largest cities in Portugal (only Greater Lisbon and Greater Porto count over one million residents), but is well-known for its university, founded in the 13th century, and its cape-clad student singers of the doleful Fado song. On the coast itself are various traditional fishing towns, whose fishermen still use oxen to pull their brightly coloured boats up the beach, and whose inhabitants still indulge in numerous rituals to accompany the blessing of their boats. The interior of the region is built predominantly from granite, some towns rising up out of some of the most magnificent boulders you will ever see. There is some small-scale farming here. The *Serra da Estrela* divides *Beira Alta* from *Beira Baixa*.

Lisboa

Around Lisbon, the provinces of *Estremadura* (Lisbon and the coastal area), so called as it was considered the 'extreme' part of the Roman Empire and *Ribatejo* (along the bank (*ribeiro*) of the river *Tejo*), sit shoulder to shoulder, supporting the capital and Greater Lisbon catchment area where approximately two million people live (almost one million in Lisbon itself). Lisbon has shot to popularity as a location for business investment, and now is home to many well-known foreign businesses, including hi-tech companies, such as Siemens, in a growing number of business parks. It is also highly rated as a spot for city breaks, especially amongst the affluent young in search of a lively nightlife. Lisbon is fashionable and in more than one way is the real hub of the country. The *Estremadura* area encompasses the lands surrounding Lisbon, taking in the breathtaking environs that are the setting for the picturesque towns of Óbidos (rated the most typical Portuguese town, because of its preserved cottages and town walls) and Sintra (adored by Lord Byron), as well as the popular resorts of Cascais and Estoril, once-fashionable summer destinations of European aristocracy. These were also the meeting places for many a spy during the two World Wars and in the Cold War period it is said that the character of James Bond was created by a chance meeting at the casino in Estoril. Beyond these, to the west, juts out the Cabo da

Roca, Europe's most westerly point, and the crashing Atlantic waters host world windsurfing contests. To the east of Lisbon, the province of *Ribatejo* stretches up along the Tagus valley, a highly fertile land where the fighting bulls are bred for Portuguese bull fights, the home too of the exciting Fandango dance.

Alentejo

Ribatejo falls down into the immense provinces of the *Alto* and *Baixo Alentejo*. These rolling plains of *oliveiras* (olive trees) and *cortiça* (cork), and vast expanses of open land are sparsely populated – a staggeringly low 20 people per sq km, compared with approximately 278 in the Lisbon region, and 166 in the north. The *Alentejo* ('away from the Tejo') has always suffered as a region, despite its dominance in size. The land itself is not particularly fertile, and has been a struggle to farm, although the area is known as the *Celeiro de Portugal* (the granary of Portugal), due to its cereal production. It is also here that cork is grown to supply most of the world's demands. Prior to the 1974 revolution (see p. 22) the area was divided into large estates, called *latifúndios* (latifundia) owned mostly by absentee landlords, worked with outdated methods by the locals. After the revolution in 1974 the estates were taken over and run by workers' cooperatives, but EU subsidies are still needed to help out the large rural communities existing there. Marble (*mármore*) is a valuable commodity quarried in and around the capital of the region, the historical town of Évora, and particularly at Vila Viçosa. Some of the small neighbouring towns produce some of the best red wines you will ever taste, and the town of Arraiolos has found worldwide fame for its hand-made tapestries and rugs (*tapetes*). The Alentejano people are extremely hard-working, in spite of adverse conditions on the land – groups of women as well as men are often seen on the backs of trucks taking them out to the fields. Sometimes seen as dour by outsiders, and often lampooned outside the region, they are, nevertheless, very welcoming when people make an effort to get to know them. The whole area, especially the *Baixo Alentejo*, has had historic links with Communism – in fact it was from here the 1974 revolution was instigated – and tends to be less fervently religious than in the north. The lower hills roll over into the rural *Algarve*, and houses become more typically Moorish, white, than in northern Portugal. Here, golf courses continue to flourish, and the building of dams has been encouraged (see Chapter 12).

Algarve

The *Algarve*, so named by its Moorish invaders *Al Gharb* (the west), is not as totally given over to tourism as the mention of its name in brochures suggests. The holiday complexes dominate the coast for a thin strip, stretching across approximately four-fifths of the region. The far eastern and western parts remain largely untouched and are areas of outstanding beauty, with important nature reserves. The coast of the western *Algarve* particularly, runs up into a wild Atlantic environment, with ideal walking areas. The southern Portuguese are slightly darker people, a throw-back to their Arab invaders who dominated there from the 8th to the 13th centuries. Houses are mostly white, as in the rest of the Mediterranean, and vestiges of both Moorish and Roman occupation can be seen in architecture (flat roof-top terraces), water irrigation channels, citrus fruits and *amêndoas (*almonds), and place names (*al* = Arabic for 'the') e.g., Alcoutim. Many people are employed in the intense tourist trade – in hotels, cleaning and related services, culinary work (food outlets, bars), and work alongside foreign residents in real estate, entertainment, and car-hire for example. Very easy-going, with good language skills, most of them are a contributing factor to the great holidays visitors enjoy in the *Algarve*. Of course the other main factors are the high number of hours of sunshine, beautiful, safe and clean beaches, spectacular rocky cliff-tops, and easy access direct to the main airport, Faro, recently upgraded and extended.

But the *Algarve* is not simply about holidays: from about 6km inland from the coast the landscape emerges (without the constriction of the villa complexes) as wonderfully wild and rural, protected by the high ridge of the Monchique hills. A haven for nature lovers, the area produces the ubiquitous 'fire-water', *Medronho*, from the wild strawberry bush, some wine , rice, carob (*alfarroba*) and almond-based sweets. The pace of life is languid, hot in the summer, and sometimes uncomfortably damp in the winter as few houses are set up with adequate heating.

Madeira and the *Açores*

Built on volcanic outcrops, and each home to about 250,000 people, these two groups of islands are autonomous regions of Portugal. *Madeira* has long been a popular holiday destination particularly of the British, who enjoy its quiet splendour, especially in Spring when the island blooms with myriad colourful flowers. Walkers take advantage of the challenging routes up the *levadas* (irrigation channels), and others simply sit back and accept the pampering in some of the elegant top hotels, such as the world-renowned Reids. *Madeira* produces the famous dessert wine, bananas and exquisite hand-made embroidery.

The *Açores*, named after the hawks (*açor*) seen circling the island by explorers, probably attract fewer mainstream visitors, being more untamed in nature, but offer a unique experience of local living. Tours have become popular for whale watching, an eco-tourism project developed from the traditional lifestyle of whale hunting. Some towns have been awarded UNESCO world heritage status (e.g. Angra do Heroísmo) as important sites of architectural and cultural interest. Many families from the islands move to Jersey and the Channel Islands to work in the hotel industry, as this offers opportunities for a better quality of life.

History

So, what events and people have shaped the country we know as modern Portugal and its inhabitants? Why are the Portuguese generally considered more gentle and unassuming, less exuberant, than many of their Spanish neighbours? And why is there often still a frisson of unease between the two nations? What is the origin of the old Portuguese saying '*De Espanha nem bom vento nem bom casamento*' (from Spain comes neither fair winds nor good marriages). To find out how it all began, let's first go back to the prehistoric times of *Ancient Lusitânia*.

Early history

Portugal is one of the oldest nations in Europe, with a rich prehistoric culture still evident in large numbers of megalithic sites.

In the second millennium BC, tribes lived in scattered *castros*, or hill-top fortified settlements. The area was visited by various travelling cultures, such as the Phoenicians, then in the 8th century BC by Greek trading settlements. In the 6th century BC the Carthaginians had control, but then lost it to the Roman Empire. The Romans called the peninsula (Spain and Portugal) *Hispania Ulterior*. During their conquests of these lands, the most difficult of the local tribes they encountered were the Lusitani, who lived north of Lisbon, and after whom that land was originally named. One of the myths of the time is that a Roman commander had enormous trouble convincing his soldiers that the river Lima, in northern Portugal, was not the mythical river Lethe (the river of forgetfulness, destined to take away the memory from anyone who crossed it). The only way he managed to get his men to cross in the end was to go through himself first, and call out all their names to prove his memory was still intact! In 60 BC Julius Caesar made his capital at *Olisipo* (Lisbon), and from there carried out his progressive development of the country, whilst still facing rebellions against the dogma of Christianity.

By the 5th century AD, barbarians from the northern countries were also making their mark on Portugal – the Alani, Vandals, Suevi and Visigoths, but it was the southern invasions which were to have most impact. The Moors arrived on the southern coast in 711. These Arab invaders settled well in the warmer climes of the south particularly, introducing farming methods, new crops (citrus fruits, almonds), cooking vessels and a relatively calm way of life. Their influence was felt northwards too, but in the far north local groups first started to push for a Christian Reconquest. In the 8th century Portugal, known by then as *Portuscale*, was under the rule of the Spanish kingdom of Leon, and by the 11th century, the Spanish ruler Alfonso VI had declared himself Emperor of the kingdoms of Leon, Castile, Galicia and Portugal.

It was time the inhabitants of the land of Portugal felt they deserved their own kingdom, ruled over by their own people. The opportunity came in 1128 in the form of the 18-year-old Afonso Henriques, the son of a French knight who had established his family in Portugal. In 1139 Afonso fought a great battle against the Moors in the Battle of Ourique, and started to call himself *Rei*

(King), and in 1143 the Treaty of Zamora signed between him and the Spanish ruler agreed that he could indeed be called King, in exchange for feudal loyalties to Spain. However, it was not until 1179 that there was papal recognition of the Portuguese kingdom to Afonso who by then was aged 70. As many travelling knights joined up to sweep southwards across Europe and fight the Arab infidels, groups such as the Knights Templar and Hospitallers embraced the crusades and joined Portuguese counterparts in a number of battles against the Moors. One of the most famous of these resulted in the construction of the Abbey at Alcobaça as a sign of thanks from Afonso for success on the battlefield. Then, in 1170 at the Battle at Badajoz, the Portuguese found themselves fighting an army consisting not only of Moors, but of Spanish troops too. Afonso broke his leg in action, was captured, and ultimately was forced to hand over the lands to Spain and the Moors. Nevertheless, his monarchy had given birth to a country which was to rise again and re-establish its independence on a firmer footing.

The birth of a nation

The *Reconquista* (12th-century reconquest) was now considered a western Crusade, with numbers of passing crusaders – the Knights Templars, the Hospitallers, the Knights of Calatrava and of Santiago – adding to the cause. For many of them, their motives for battle were predominantly to do with inheritance (ancestry and claims to the land), not wholly religious. Within Portugal the internal frontiers began to push southwards. In 1249, under Afonso III, the western Algarve and Faro had been taken back from the Moors and in 1256 the capital moved from Coimbra to Lisbon. Finally, in 1297 the boundaries were recognized by Castile, in the Treaty of Alcañices. Certain social transformations started to take place. The establishment of the *Cortes* (local assemblies of nobles, clergy, and the mercantile classes) was to prove important, as was a greater social mobility, especially with a resettlement of the labouring classes. North–south differences were smoothed over in this amalgamation of peoples, although you can still find variations from one end of the country to the other. The Church by now enjoyed great riches and power, and proved a threat to the monarchy, which made many unsuccessful attempts to stop its acquisition of land.

However, with Dom Dinis, the farmer–poet king, came a period of relative stability. Dinis was very keen on learning and literature. Under him, in 1288, the first university was established, first in Lisbon, then transferred to Coimbra. The minstrels' culture pervaded European courts and Dinis himself was an accomplished poet (see p.54). This atmosphere coincided with political progress which culminated in peace with Castile in 1297. Castles were built, and maritime organization set in place. The year 1308 saw the original friendship pact with England. Trade fairs were popular, but industrial production lagged behind. Then the country was rocked by a number of economic crises under Afonso IV. The black plague in 1348–9 decimated the country, whilst migration to the cities from the poor rural areas resulted in economic stagnation.

Once again the fear of Castile was thrust upon the Portuguese through ill-fated royal intermarriages. The most famous of these, the story of which was to spawn a host of literary and musical interpretations, was the tragedy of Pedro I and Inês de Castro. Inês was a Spanish lady-in-waiting to Pedro's Portuguese wife, and Pedro had the misfortune to fall in love with her. Their affair was a truly passionate one, with Pedro considering Inês to be his real queen. Unfortunately, Pedro's father discovered the affair, and fearful for the country (Inês belonged to an influential Spanish noble family), sent a pair of his henchmen to kill her. By now Pedro had installed her in her own palace, and had had children by her, his own wife having died, and the fatal visit to her by the two hit-men is movingly described in the poignant play, *A Castro*, by António Ferreira. When Pedro found out about her death, he vowed vengeance on the perpetrators and on his own father, and became known as *Pedro O Cruel*. The footnote to the story is that some years later, Pedro had Inês' body exhumed, dressed in fine clothes, and sat her by his side on the throne; he made all his courtiers kiss her hand as the ultimate recognition of his true queen.

Fernando I had ambitions to unite Portugal and Castile once more, and by the 1370s there were again hostilities between the two countries when he claimed the then vacant crown of Castile. But during his reign (1367–83) the ruling dynasty ceased to represent the national will. It was not long before João I (the illegitimate son of Pedro I) launched into civil war for the Portuguese throne and he was chosen as King in 1385. João (John) represented the Portuguese middle classes, by now tired of a lack of solid leadership. He was able to call upon the aid of English archers against the Spanish in the battle of Aljubarrota, through his links with England (he married Philippa of Lancaster, the daughter of John of Gaunt, Duke of Lancaster). Many legends grew up around these skirmishes with the Spanish, one of the more interesting being the miraculous help João was given in one important battle, which resulted in his vowing to have a monastery built at Batalha, just north of Lisbon. The story goes that he fired an arrow, saying the monastery would be constructed where it landed; he must have had a fantastic aim, since from the battlefield to where the monastery was built is a fair few miles! As disputes with Castile wound down again, and the Treaty of Windsor was signed in 1386, making the Anglo–Portuguese Alliance the oldest link of friendship in the world, it looked as though Portugal could settle down once more into a period of positive growth.

The building of the Portuguese Empire

Early voyages

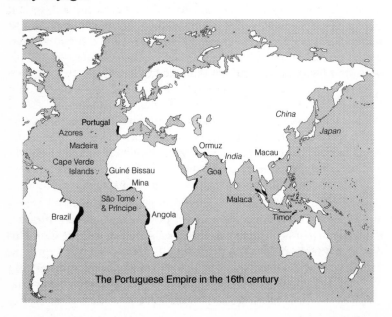

The Portuguese Empire in the 16th century

Under João 1 (1385–1433) trade and exploration were initiated, mainly it must be said, to occupy the nobility and boost commerce, but it was with João II , some years later, that overseas expansion really began, although it was never systematic at this point. Charting the world always seemed a secondary matter to the potent mixture of crusading ideals and romantic curiosity. It was a time of stories and legends about what lay beyond the edge of the known world: one of these legends was about Prester John, a mythical priest and king said to abide in darkest Africa. Despite these mythical characters who exerted a huge influence on the early explorations, the shortage of gold in Europe was the main factor behind these voyages – together with the benefits of the Crusades which were sanctioned by Rome. Shipbuilding was quickly learned from the technically adept Moslems and Italians, and the wide-hulled Portuguese *caravela* was created, ideal for carrying back heavy booty from long trips. Navigational equipment such as compass and charts were developed, although most voyages were jealously guarded and maps not freely bandied about.

One of João's sons, Prince Henry, became Master of the Order of Christ (the Portuguese branch of the Knights Templars), a position which enabled him to muster considerable support for the navigational cause. He set up the Sagres school of navigation, endowing much financial support but he himself did not participate to the extent that his (English) title of 'the Navigator' suggested. In fact the furthest he travelled was to North Africa.

The era of exploration

This is an era of the epic heroes of popular history, such as Afonso Sanches, who, having landed on an uncharted western coast, is supposed to have shared a log book with a Genoese navigator going under the name of Columbus!, and Gil Eanes, who, despite the tales of the horrors of the south seas and the Cape Bojador promontory off west Africa, in 1434 sailed on down and was to discover the legendary *Rio d'Ouro* (River of Gold). Not long afterwards another Portuguese, Bartolomeu Dias was to round the *Cabo de Boa Esperança* (Cape of Good Hope).

By now Spain was also in the full throes of exploration, and subsequently the Treaty of Tordesillas, signed by the two countries in 1494, divided the world between them. The demarcation line was set about 370 miles west of the Azores; Portugal laid claim to all lands to the east of this line, and Spain to the west. Portuguese expansion was now incredibly prolific, with heavyweights such as Vasco da Gama in 1497–9 getting through to Calicut, Pedro Álvaro Cabral discovering Brazil in 1500, and one of Ferdinand Magellan's ships, albeit in the service of Spain, circumnavigating the world in 1519–22 (sadly he himself did not make it to the end of the journey). In India and the East there were battles to establish trading posts, and constant wars with the Arabs; nevertheless, under the auspices of Afonso de Albuquerque – the Governor-General and founding father of the Portuguese Empire in Asia – Goa, Malacca, Ormuz and Macau were taken under the Portuguese flag. The *caravelas* were

now bringing back spices from the Indies, gold from Sudan and Africa, sugar and wine from Madeira and sugar and dyestuffs from Brazil. These all contributed to building a stable economy, but not really a rich one, as so many individuals – particularly the monarchy – took the lion's share of the new-found wealth.

Caravela

Economic problems

At first little manpower was needed to run this new Empire – size did not matter, but later more and more was needed. Also, the absence of a middle class meant there was a lack of educated planners, pilots, and administrators. It was not surprising, then, that Portugal began to run into problems. Whilst expansion had been undertaken as a Crusade initially, the explorers, in their haste to convert the peoples they encountered on their travels to Christianity, often neglected to set up the necessary structures and links for commerce. With deflation in Europe and the Portuguese Crown in debt, together with a shortage of manpower in domestic agriculture (all able-bodied men were now involved in the explorations), efforts were spent on maintaining Brazil.

The Renaissance

At this time contacts with Italy, France and Spain brought fresh exchanges of ideas. A printing press had been established in Lisbon in 1487, and by the 16th century a rush of new cultures and teaching methods gave the country a renewed feeling of vigour. Under João III control of education was handed to the Jesuits. The whole of Europe was living through full Renaissance, with the Portuguese contributing hugely in the fields of navigation, astronomy, maths and geography. Unfortunately, the *Inquisição* (Inquisition), with its religious fanaticism, was a strong feature of this period, in Portugal as much as in Spain. The main target were those Jews known as New Christians – mostly from middle-class mercantile families. This intolerance could only lead to the death of commerce and culture, and on Sebastião's ascent to power in 1568, the Inquisition gained even more power.

By 1560 the Casa da India (the national trading corporation) had become bankrupt. Sebastião was only 14 when he took the throne and in a number of early crusades against the Moors in North Africa he showed himself to be a bad military leader. In the fateful Battle of Alcácer Quiber, almost all of the 18,000 men were destroyed, only 100 escaping. Sebastião was lost in battle, but the subsequent rise of *Sebastianismo* – the hope of his return – was to keep the Portuguese flame burning during further acts of atrocity by their neighbours. To this day the Portuguese talk of Sebastianismo, as though they are still waiting for a youthful saviour – and many think he is there in waiting, in the guise of the Duke of Bragança, the Pretender to the throne. In 1580 Philip II of Spain invaded Portugal and within a year had installed himself as Philip I of Portugal. The Portuguese were back under the yoke of the Spanish.

Restoration – the House of Bragança

Amid the uncertainty surrounding the loss of Sebastião, there were several false claims to the throne (which have continued unabated over the years), and with the newly imposed Iberian Union adding to the woes of the nation, Portugal's treasury soon emptied. The economy was shored up by Spain, but this was an ill-at-ease alliance, which continued to cause problems with the new monarch, Philip II (III of Spain). His bungling of relations allowed the Portuguese monopoly of the seas to fade, as Dutch and English explorers grabbed strongholds around the world, including the Dutch in Brazil in 1630, and a few years later in Ceylon. It was not until a coup on 1 December 1640, when the Spanish governor was deposed, allowing a rather reluctant leader, the Duke of Bragança, to become King João IV, that a Royal House was re-established which would continue in situ up to the 20th century.

João immediately came up against problems in that France, Britain, Holland and the Pope all refused to confirm Portugal's independence, despite his attempts to form diplomatic ties in Europe. He decided to switch the external emphasis from the Indies to Brazil. Happily, during the reign of his successor, Afonso VI and the brother who usurped his throne, Pedro II, European links were cemented when in 1661 Catarina of Bragança married Charles II of Britain and in 1668 Spain officially recognized Portuguese independence.

Unfortunately, these momentous links were not mirrored by the situation within Portugal itself. Pedro found himself ruling a country in economic depression, its maritime commerce dissipated with the lucrative spice trade now almost completely outside its control. Luckily gold pouring in from Brazil was able to support the economy, and the state wisely began to back small industries, such as glass, textiles, tiles and pottery, which would prove to be Portugal's future when the Empire and its riches began to shrivel. Portugal entered a period of relative stability, ironically not reflected in the life of its monarch, João V, who from his coronation in 1706 spent large amounts of gold on buildings, the arts and education. Nothing wrong in that, but his penchant for visiting brothels and convents in Lisbon resulted in an undisclosed number of illegitimate sons – some born to nuns!

Lisbon earthquake

During the reign of the next king, José, the country was hit by a devastating earthquake (*terremoto*) on All Saints Day in 1755. The epicentre hit Lisbon just as Mass was being celebrated, killing around 5000 people instantly, but many thousands more were killed as church candles sparked off a widespread fire, and a tidal wave that came up the Tagus swamped many more. The strength of the earthquake was such that it even damaged villages in the Algarve, and in the aftermath it is estimated that possibly 40–50,000 lost their lives. The tatters of the capital were rebuilt on a Neo-classical grid plan which is called the *Baixa*, or downtown Lisbon today, thanks to one man, the Marquis of Pombal, a canny statesman and diplomat. He declared 'Close the ports, bury the dead, feed the living', and miraculously the city was reconstructed without depleting the state treasury. Unfortunately, the next monarch, Maria, found Pombal guilty of crimes against the state, and had him confined to his estate. She herself was soon declared unbalanced and power passed to her son, another João, in 1816.

The Peninsular War and afterwards

From 1801–20 there was a spate of wars all over the Peninsula. In the War of the Oranges Portugal lost the border town of Olivença to Spain, and in 1807 Napoleon demanded that Portugal declare war on England. As the French advanced into Spain, in what was to become the Peninsular War, the Portuguese royal family fled to Brazil. In the famous battle at the Torres Vedras lines, north of Lisbon, with British aid the Portuguese finally routed Napoleon. However, a spate of assassination plots and an uprising in Oporto, caused by the unease of the power Britain then seemed to hold in Portugal, not only gave rise to the Liberal movement within Portugal, but forced the return of the king from Brazil, which had been declared a kingship on an equal footing with Portugal in 1815. The next 90 years were to witness a succession of shaky monarchies, with constant tussles between republicans and absolutists under the rule of Maria II (1834–53). By the 1860s England was dictating external affairs, particularly through its stronghold in the wine industry, but Portugal still held on to its African territories, pouring money into their maintenance. In 1892 Portugal was declared bankrupt, which led to a backlash of corruption and anti-monarchy feelings nationally. This culminated in 1908 with the King, Carlos I and his son being assassinated in 'Black Horse Square', Lisbon. The Royal House of Bragança finally fell under Manuel II, who had also been wounded in the attack. The current Duke of Bragança is one in a line of pretenders to the throne, should there ever be a recall of the monarchy.

Revolution through to developing nation

Throughout the 19th century, Portugal felt the influence of the rest of Europe in the arts and literature, and as the process of rebuilding the nation continued, politics came to the fore in the writings of authors such as the historian Alexandre Herculano, and in the critical essays and drama of Almeida Garrett (see p.62). With this background to the current state of the nation, it was hardly surprising that socialist undercurrents began to be felt. This was clearly manifest in what became known as the Coimbra Question, a division of the scholars between the older generation desperate to maintain the status quo, and the 'Generation of 1870', who called for intellectual and spiritual values to be reassessed. The Republicans proved themselves incapable of steady leadership, failed to introduce much-needed financial reforms, and with the gloom surrounding the 1920s Depression, lost much of their popular support. During World War I Portugal initially maintained a neutral stance, then joined the Allies under Britain's influence, who called upon their old alliance as a conscience pricker.

In 1932 President Oscar Carmona named his Finance Minster António de Oliveira Salazar as Prime Minister, a position he would retain until his death in 1968 (see Chapter 9 for details of the dictatorship and its overthrow). With Salazar's demise, his successor, Marcelo Caetano, tried to make some changes, but in the face of mounting opposition, felt obliged to slide back to the oppressive ways of the old regime as his only means of exerting power. However, the movement for change had set in and there was an underlying growing discontent, especially among the army. In 1973 the formation of the *Movimento das Forças Armadas* (MFA) – Armed Forces Movement – was to prove instrumental in the overthrow of the yoke (see p. 182).

Since then, Portugal has continued to progress on many fronts, participating fully within the European Union, and hosting large-scale conferences and events such as the successful Expo 98. Although many parts of the country remain underdeveloped, today's younger generations of Portuguese can look forward to a wider range of opportunities than ever before. It has often been said that Portugal has finally started to look inwards and towards

Europe again after such a long history of external exploration and neglect of its neighbours. Other chapters in the book will investigate to what extent that is true.

Portuguese kings and heads of state – a summary

Up until the 12th century, the land was ruled in various ways by the leaders of the invading peoples who settled there, including the Celts, Romans and Moors.

House of Burgundy	**House of Bragança**
1139 Afonso Henriques (Afonso I)	1640 João IV
1185 Sancho I	1656 Afonso VI
1211 Afonso II	1683 Pedro II (Regent from 1668)
1223 Sancho II	1706 João V
1248 Afonso III	1750 José I
1279 Dom Dinis	1777 Maria I / Pedro III
1325 Afonso IV	1816 João VI (Regent from 1792)
1357 Pedro I	1826 Maria II
1367 Fernando I	1826 Pedro IV
	1853 Pedro V
House of Avis	1861 Luís I
1385 João I	1889 Carlos I
1433 Dom Duarte	1908 Manuel II
1438 Afonso V	
1481 João II	**Republic**
1495 Manuel I	(Provisional government)
1521 João III	1910 Dr Teófilo Braga
	(President)
House of Hapsburg	1911 Dr Manuel de Arriaga
1557 Sebastião	45 governments up to 1926
1578 Henrique	1926 General Carmona
1580 Felipe I (Philip II of Spain)	1951 Gen. Craveiro Lopes
1598 Felipe II (Philip III of Spain)	1958 Rodrigues Tomás
1621 Felipe III (Philip IV of Spain)	1974 Gen. Spínola
	(Provisional governments)
	1974 Costa Gomes
	(Provisional governments)
	1986 Mário Soares
	1996 Jorge Sampaio

GLOSSARY

o país *country*
a nação *nation*
a terra *land*
a serra *mountain range*
o clima *climate*
o rio *river*
o mar *sea*
a costa *coast*
a região *region*
a paisagem *landscape*
a história *history*
descobrir *to discover*
invadir *to invade*
conquistar *to conquer*
os Romanos *the Romans*
a reconquista *reconquest*

fundar *to found*
estabelecer *to establish*
a civilização *civilization*
o reino *kingdom*
o rei *king*
a guerra *war*
há...séculos / anos ... *centuries/years
   ago*
há pouco tempo *not long ago*
ao norte/sul/este/oeste *in the north,
   south, east, west*
as descobertas *discoveries*
a restauração *restoration*
a dictadura *dictatorship*
a revolução *revolution*
a democracia *democracy*

Taking it further

Suggested reading

The Portuguese: the land and its people, Marion Kaplan (Second
   Revised Edition), Penguin, 1998
Portugal: a companion history, J.H. Saraiva, Carcanet, 1997
Prince Henry 'the Navigator' – a life, Peter Russell, Yale
   University Press, 1999
Cultural links between Portugal and Italy in the Renaissance, Ed.
   K.J.P. Lowe, OUP, 2000
A New History of Portugal, H.V. Livermore (Second Edition)
   CUP, 1976
The Christian Century in Japan 1549–1650, C.R. Boxer,
   Carcanet,1993
The Portuguese Seaborne Empire 1415–1825, C.R. Boxer,
   Carcanet,1973
Portugal's Struggle for Liberty, Mário Soares, Allen & Unwin,
   1975
Off the Beaten Track – Portugal, Nick Timmons, MPC, 1992
Insight Guides – Portugal, Ed. Alison F. Hill, APA, 1989

Eyewitness Guides – Portugal with Madeira and the Azores,
Dorling Kindersley, 1997
Backwards out of the Big World: a voyage into Portugal, Paul
Hyland, Flamingo paperback, 1998

Places to visit

Parque Arqueológico do Vale de Côa – the world's largest
collection of open-air Stone Age engravings. Avenida Gago
Coutinho 19a, Vila Nova de Foz Côa. Tel: 079-76 43 17
Citânia de Briteiros – Iron Age settlement and archaeological site.
15 km north of Guimarães, Minho. Tel: 053-41 59 69
Conímbriga – largest excavated Roman site in Portugal, with
beautiful mosaics. South of Coimbra, Beira Litoral.
Tel: 039-94 11 77
Gabinete de Estudos Olisiponenses – History of Lisbon, Estrada
de Benfica 368, 1500 Lisboa

All guide books list other places of historical and natural interest.

Websites

ICEP – Portuguese Trade and Tourism Organisation,
www.portugal-insite.pt

Beaches – information, **www.infopraias.com**

Instituto Meteorologia – the weather, **www.meteo.pt**

Portugal-info – information for travellers, esp. from USA,
www.portugal-info.net

CPHRC – Contemporary Portuguese Politics and History
Research Centre, University of Dundee, UK,
www.dundee.ac.uk/politics/cphrc

Oporto Town Hall – local information, **www.cm-porto.pt**

Lisbon Town Hall – local information, **www.cm-lisboa.pt**

Algarve information, **www.algarve.com**

List of Portuguese sites, **www.portembassy.gla.uk/portpages.html**

Portugal Virtual – lots of links, has an English version,
www.portugalvirtual.pt

Portugal na Rede – general, cultural and commercial links,
  www.interacesso.pt/lugares/portnet/htm

Portugal em linha – links with the Portuguese-speaking world,
  www.portugal-linha.pt/

Countrywatch site on Portugal very useful on all aspects.

Portuguese search engines

SAPO, **www.sapo.pt**
TERRA VISTA, **www.terravista.pt**
PORTUGALNET, **www.portugalnet.pt**
BUSCANET, **www.busca.net**
PORTUGALWEB, **www.portugalweb.pt**
PORTAL DE PORTUGAL, **www.portal.pt**

2 | LANGUAGE

A nossa magna lingua portugueza de nobres sons é um thesouro. (Our great Portuguese language is a thesaurus/ treasure of noble sounds) – Fernando Pessoa, 1930

An important world language

Out of the main Latin-based (or Romance) languages, it is probably fair to say that Portuguese is one of the least well known outside the spheres of the Portuguese-speaking world. For those visitors to Portugal who try and pick up some of the lingo, it represents a confusing rapid-fire babble interspersed with 'ooshes' and 'shushes'; it has been claimed on numerous occasions that it sounds like Russian or a similar Eastern European language, and certainly the intonation bears a resemblance, even though the written form is more akin to a mixture of French and Spanish. What the vast majority of people do not realize is that Portuguese is a very important world language indeed, not simply the language spoken in their holiday destination; it is a wonderfully rich and diverse idiom spoken across four continents by almost 200 million native speakers. In global terms, it is the third most widely spoken European language in the world, behind only English and Spanish, and overall in the world league-table lies sixth or seventh (the debate still goes on about the top two or three, but without doubt it is far more widely spoken than French, German or Italian). The next section will explore how it comes to hold such a lofty global position.

The Portuguese in general are justifiably proud of their language and for those non-natives privileged enough to have learned it, it is a beautifully sonorous way of talking, with expressive intonation, making it sound very 'sing-song'. To many native speakers it represents their whole cultural heritage, and its prolific spread is linked to their early world expansion and domination. The importance of these cultural and linguistic ties are evident in the fact that Portugal's National Day is named after their most famous 16th-century poet, Luís de Camões, who wrote an epic poem (*Os Lusíadas*) based on Vasco de Gama's famous voyage to India. One of Portugal's ambassadors is quoted as saying:

> *A data nacional de Portugal não é a de uma batalha, de um gesto, de um triunfo ou de um acto constitutivo; é a data em que o destino arrancou à vida um poeta que soube elevar aos píncaros o culto da sua língua.* (Portugal's National Day is not the date of a battle, of a gesture, of a triumph or of a constitutional act; it is the date on which destiny dragged into life a poet who discovered how to lift to its pinnacle the worship of his language.)

Instituto Camões

Despite the high number of Portuguese speakers in the world, there has been a growing fear in recent years that the language was increasingly having to fight to resist attack from other languages in those countries where Portuguese was the official language of communication, especially throughout the emigrant communities. With the preservation, and also expansion of the language in mind, in 1992 the Instituto Camões was set up, initially under the auspices of the Ministry of Education, and from 1994 within the remit of Foreign Affairs. The Institute acts as a Portuguese cultural and linguistic promotional body, supporting work around the world undertaken by embassies and educational institutions. It sees as its main priorities the 'promotion and defence of Portuguese language and culture, through the stimulation of its teaching and through the importance given to the Portuguese presence in the world'. This is particularly vital, given the large number of Portuguese emigrants living and working in other parts of the world, who feel their language is devalued as it is merely the 'language of immigrants'.

History and influences

Before the invasion of the Romans, the (present) Spanish and Portuguese regions had been inhabited by various races, (see Chapter 1). Two of these were most notable – the Celts and the Iberi, the latter of which gave their name to the peninsula – *Iberia*. Despite initial resistance, the peoples of the regions succumbed before the military might of Rome, and later came to assimilate the language and customs of their conquerors. To this assimilation of culture and language the term Romanization was given. The assimilation of the language was not determined by decree; it resulted rather from an imposed necessity. Latin was the official language; through it all public and official contracts were made; it was also the language of the most prestigious class, a fact which competed to put down the other spoken languages of the region. So the peninsula was finally totally Romanized, and importantly, from the Latin, after a series of transformations, the Portuguese language emerged.

The diversification of Latin

Latin was the language spoken in the central region of Italy. The reasons which brought about the division of Latin into various other languages are multiple. Here are the main ones:

- Latin was dispersed throughout European regions by the Roman conquerors and with time it became the language of the conquered peoples, including the Iberian peninsula. The dominated peoples, speakers of the Latin brought to them, little by little started to gain independence from Rome's dominance and to form their own nations.
- However, the breaking up of the Roman Empire does not explain on its own the upsurge of 'neo-Latin' languages. Another probable reason is the fact of Latin having entered into contact with a group of greatly varied languages of those conquered peoples. Before the Roman conquests there was not just one language, but many. This evidently contributed towards the later diversification of Latin itself.

■ A third cause is that the very language of the invaders already came divided into various dialects, as Latin was not spoken in a uniform way by all Roman citizens. The language taken by them to various European regions developed in diverse ways. The Latin implanted in the conquered regions was not Classical Latin, eminently cultured and literary, but Vulgar Latin, the normal speech of those people considered less cultured.

Barbarian linguistics

In the 5th century the pensinula suffered a new invasion, that of the many groups of barbarians who did not come from just one place and did not possess a uniform language. The barbarians did not manage to implant their civilization or language on the conquered territories. But after these invasions the Latin language throughout the region underwent alterations, above all in its sounds and vocabulary. So much so that even today there are examples of many words of Germanic origin brought by these barbarian races, mostly words designating arms and clothing, such as:

dardo (dart/spear), *espora* (spur), *estribo* (stirrup), *guerra* (war), *elmo* (type of helmet)

The Arabs

The domination of the barbarians which lasted three centuries was succeeded by that of the Arabs. In spite of certain cultural influences, the Arabs too did not manage to impose a totally new language or culture, with the exception of a small group who assimilated their customs (known as *Mozarabs*). The Arabs tried to impose their language as the only recognized one, but the dominated people resisted, continuing to speak Vulgar Latin, at this time now quite altered from its original form. Arab influence on the language of the Portuguese region in particular manifested itself in the vocabulary, incorporating words designating plants, jobs, measurements and instruments:

alfaiate (tailor), *algarismos* (digits), *alface* (lettuce), *alfinete* (pin), *alcatifa* (large carpet)

(the Arab prefix *al-* means 'the')

By the 12th century, when Afonso Henriques was proclaiming himself first king of Portugal, two linguistic branches had implanted themselves in the Portuguese region, quite distinct from what was spoken in neighbouring Castile. In the north the Galician language or Galician–Portuguese – Galicia is that part of Spain which sits above the northern border of Portugal (the Spanish call Galician '*la lengua de los gallegos*' – the language of the Galicians); in the south another, perhaps with Arab influence, from which no documentation remains.

Further changes

Slowly Galician–Portuguese spread throughout the south. There was later a progressive differentiation between Portuguese and Galician (*Galego*). In the 9th century Portuguese forms start to appear in documents, but it is only from the 12th century that whole texts in Portuguese are registered. The travelling troubadours from France contributed to the spread of linguistic forms and ideas, and home-grown minstrels with their own style of poetry and songs were encouraged by Dom Dinis, the poet king (see p.54). It is possible, with a bit of help, to interpret the language of early Portuguese into its modern equivalent, as Chaucer and Shakespeare can be translated from the originals. In more recent times the language has evolved with influences from English, especially in technology and business spheres, and from within the Portuguese-speaking world itself, with Brazilian soap-operas accounting for a new range of expressions throughout Portugal.

The spread of Portuguese

So, where do all these 200 million speakers of Portuguese come from? Apart from all the communities worldwide where the language is spoken by immigrant Portuguese, and not forgetting the former colonies of Macau and East Timor where vestiges of Portuguese remain, the official 'heavyweight' Portuguese-speaking countries are:

	Population 1998
Portugal	9,900,000
Brazil	165,900,000
Angola	12,100,000
Cape Verde	401,000 (est. yr 2000)
Guinea-Bissau	1,200,000
Mozambique	18,900,000
São Tomé and Príncipe	160,000 (est. yr 2000)
	208,561,000

The language in mainland Portugal is pretty uniform, due in part to the relatively early establishment of the country's borders, and the fact that Portugal has been little affected by the many political turmoils seen elsewhere in Europe. The two main factors contributing to the extraordinary spread of Portuguese elsewhere are its maritime explorations and colonial establishments in the 15th and 16th centuries, and emigration at that time and later in the 19th century and over the last two decades.

In 15th-century Africa, Portuguese was often the language employed down the west coast for dealing with the local people. Though Portuguese was somewhat of a 'lingua franca' here for trade particularly, simplifications of it led to Creole (a mixture arising from a combination of European and Negro influences) and a pidgin version (simplified or jargon-influenced language between people of different nationalities). These variations were to spread across to eastern coasts, and make their way towards Asia, the Indian Ocean and the Caribbean. In the smaller African countries of Cape Verde, São Tomé and Príncipe and Guinea-Bissau, Portuguese exists alongside other Creole and local African languages, though it is still the 'official' language of those regions. You will also come across Creole of Portuguese origin in parts of Senegal, Equatorial Guinea, and Benin.

Brazil is the place where Portuguese became most widespread, and consolidated much earlier than some of the African countries. The descendants of the indigenous peoples who inhabited the Brazil discovered by Cabral still speak a variety of languages, but the language of the settlers prevailed, although over time local accents and vocabulary moved towards what is now the variant referred to as Brazilian Portuguese. Remember, it is not 'Brazilian', as many people still erroneously call it, including a number of native speakers who claim '*Falo brasileiro*' – I speak Brazilian. However, that is far more acceptable than the popular belief that they speak Spanish in Brazil. It's a good fact to get right, particularly if you end up on a TV quiz show!

On many Asian–Pacific islands, and around the East African, and Indian coasts, Portuguese was to remain the common language of all trading and settling developments from the 16th to 18th centuries, despite the arrival on the scene of the English and Dutch explorers, who were to usurp the Portuguese as the key players in this part of the world. Nowadays, apart from a few Portuguese Creoles in places such as Sri Lanka, Macau, Java and Singapore, few people actually speak the language in Asia.

The other major factor in the spread of Portuguese is emigration. Although some people accompanied the explorers in the 15th and 16th centuries, and set up their lives in distant lands, emigration on a large scale really took place around the 1850s (by then the Portuguese royal family had established itself in Brazil, having gone there at the time of the Napoleonic invasions) until the time of the revolution in 1974. These emigrants, in some cases in huge numbers, took their customs and more importantly their language, to places as distinct as France and Switzerland, the UK (particularly the Channel Islands), USA and Canada, South Africa and South America. It is estimated today that there are almost five million Portuguese emigrants worldwide who are contributing their language to local environments.

Considering the size of Portugal itself, it is testimony mainly to the overseas expansion that its language has enjoyed such a prodigious spread.

What's different about Portuguese?

Portuguese falls into the group of languages referred to as 'Romance', or 'neo-Latin', as it is predominantly Latin in origin. Along with it, French, Spanish, Italian, Romanian (and regional languages such as Catalan, Andorran and the language of the Spanish Balearic islands) all share either similar language structures or vocabulary. This means that, for anyone with a background in any of these languages, Portuguese is not so difficult to grasp. However, it is said that Portuguese has probably remained structurally closest to Latin, which is certainly obvious from some of its grammatical features, and it is totally alien to its main cousins in pronunciation. For absolute novices to the language, it can pose a few problems initially, but as the many tourists to Portugal who try to learn a few phrases will bear testament, it is perfectly possible to learn at least some basics. For those with knowledge of other Romance languages, it is a wonderfully fascinating idiom, which offers the challenge of a complex verbal system and tricky pronunciation, the delights of which, once mastered, can be totally absorbing!

Pronunciation

Whilst you may be able to recognize much of the written language, especially if you know some Spanish, Portuguese sounds nothing like its Latin relatives. It has been claimed many times that although the Portuguese can understand Spanish, the reverse is rarely true. Most Portuguese towns bordering Spain pick up Spanish TV channels, and the residents quite happily understand what they are watching. In market towns, such as Elvas in the Alentejo, many Spaniards come over from nearby Badajoz to shop (as it's often cheaper), and quite unabashed speak their own language to local Portuguese shopkeepers, who can communicate well enough with them in Spanish to relieve them of their money!

Portuguese pronunciation is generally characterized by:

- the 'shushing' sound on the end of many words in the plural, such as:

    os carros (the cars) = oosh carrosh

- nasal sounds, eg those designated by a ~ (til)
  - *-ão* (ow), as in *não* = no
  - *-ães* (eyesh), as in *pães* – loaves
  - *-õe* (oi), as in *põe* – puts
  among others, plus
  words ending in *-m*, or plural *-ns*, e.g.:
  bem (well), *homens* (men), *sim* (yes), *tens* (you have)
  The letter *m* at the end of a word is not pronounced as it would be in English, as in 'ham', where the lips come together and almost force the letter from the mouth; in Portuguese the sound is much more at the back of the mouth and is made at the top of the nose, as if you had a cold.
- There are also the tricky letter combinations of *-lh* (like the lli in 'million'), and *-nh* (like the ni in 'onion'), and like the Spanish ñ, but often more difficult to get the tongue round. *Ch* in Portuguese is 'sh', not 'ch' as in Spanish.
- Final *-o* is invariably 'oo'
- Final *-l* is almost like a 'w'
- *-rr* can either be gently rolled (not as much as in Spanish), or pronounced from the back of the throat in a sound similar to loudly raising some spit (or like the Scottish 'lo*ch*', depending on how graphic you choose to be!)
- there is no 'lisp' sound in Portuguese, unlike in some parts of Spain
- the Portuguese *d* is generally harder than in Spanish, but often *de* is inaudible, e.g. *uma sandes **de** queijo* (a cheese sandwich), where the *de* sounds rather like a fleeting 'd'.

Despite what appears to be a complex sound system, Portuguese is in fact classed as a 'phonetic' language, i.e. it is pretty much pronounced as it looks. Many of my own language students reckon it all becomes much easier after a bottle of wine anyway – and I wouldn't argue with that. It certainly helps to have a 'looser' tongue to speak it, as many of the sounds rely on your tongue moving liberally from one bit of your mouth to another. It is a language with a very melodic sound, and sing-song intonation, softer than Spanish, and has led to some comparisons with Welsh, in particular in the intonation for questions.

So, the Portuguese 'sing' their language, but they also sound as if they do it at great speed, because, to a lesser (or greater) extent they slur the start and finish of words, so that everything runs together. This can be cause for great consternation, even to someone well practised in the language, as you then need to rely heavily on context and guesswork to decipher what you think you've heard. It is a particular trait of the Algarvians to do this, so that expressions such as *Boa tarde* (good afternoon) often become *Bo tard*; *escudo* (the pre-Euro currency) becomes *scud*; and *Até logo* (see you later) is simply *t'log*. On a recent visit to a local restaurant in the Algarve, one of my students was asked if he wanted *vin tint, vin bran* (= *vinho tinto, ou vinho branco* – red or white wine)!

On a more widespread scale, words beginning with *es-* generally lose the *e* in speech, hence *escola* (school) becomes *shcola*, and *espanhol* (Spanish) becomes *shpanhol*. The *e* itself faintly lingers at the back of the mouth as the *s* takes over.

For Brazilian pronunciation see p.48.

The structure/ grammar

As a Latin-based language, Portuguese shares much of its structures with other Romance languages, and differs from English in a number of ways:

- It has an extensive verbal system where endings change. There are six (five commonly used) verb endings, which matter, as they tell you exactly who is carrying out the action, and at what point in time. The words for I, you, he etc. are not necessarily used, e.g., *falamos* = we speak, *falei* = I spoke, *falavas* = you were speaking.
- Nouns and adjectives also change their endings according to gender and number (i.e. there are the concepts of masculine and feminine and singular and plural), but the number of endings are fewer than in the original Latin, or in German (known as 'cases'). Another difference from English is that the normal place for an adjective is after the word it is describing, hence 'the black cat' would become *o gato preto* (the cat black).

But how does it differ from its cousins?

Verbs

The Portuguese system is more complex than others in the Latin group, as it has certain features now lost, or not developed in the others. As many people come to Portuguese after learning some Spanish, there are some important differences:

- A future subjunctive, to express actions in the future after certain expressions such as 'if' (*se*) and 'when' (*quando*), where in English we would use the present tense (If I see you next week..../ When we win the lottery....).

- A personal infinitive, for use especially in sentences where there may be more than one action being carried out by different subjects – the personal infinitive can more easily pinpoint the subject of a particular action. e.g. *Depois de pormos a mesa, eles sentaram-se* = After **we** laid the table, **they** sat down. *Pôr* is the ordinary infinitive for 'to put/lay'.

- Conveying the *-ing* form in continuous tenses, Portuguese differs from Spanish in that whereas Spanish uses the verb 'to be' (*estar*) + gerund, e.g., *estamos hablando* (we are talking), Portuguese employs *estar* + *a* + infinitive – *estamos a falar* (except in Brazil where the gerund *-ando* is used more widely in these tenses).

- The perfect and preterite tenses in Spanish and Portuguese fulfil different purposes. Take the verb 'to buy' (*comprar* in both languages):

	Perfect	Preterite
Spanish	*He comprado* = I have bought	*Compré* = I bought
Portuguese	*Tenho comprado* = I've been buying (recently)...	*Comprei* = I bought/ have bought

The American expression, 'Honey I shrunk the kids' would be 'I've shrunk the kids' in British English, but both would be translated in Portuguese using the preterite tense: *Querida, fiz encolher às crianças.*

■ *Ser* and *estar*, the two verbs meaning 'to be', in Portuguese are almost identical to the Spanish, except that for locations of buildings, towns and places you use *ser* in Portuguese (or an alternative verb *ficar*, to be found), whereas *estar* is used in Spanish. In Portuguese *estar* can only be used for temporary states, situations, positions.

Other features

Portuguese has maintained a Latin 'neuter' (neither masculine nor feminine) in words such as:

todo (m), all every	*toda* (f)	*tudo* (everything)
este (m), this (one)	*esta* (f)	*isto* (this thing)
esse (m), that (one)	*essa* (f)	*isso* (that thing)
aquele (m) that (one) there	*aquela* (f)	*aquilo* (that thing)

There are no apostrophes in Portuguese, apart from in a few surnames, or place names, such as D'Ávila, but a number of contractions take place involving the definite articles (the words for 'the') and indefinite (the words for 'a/an/some'). The contractions have come about over the years to make certain combinations of words easier to say, and have now evolved into an integral part of the language, e.g.:

de (of, from) + *o* (the) = *do*
em (in, on) + *uma* (a) = *numa*
por (by, through, for) + *as* (the, plural) = *pelas*
a (at, to) + *os* (the) = *aos*

Guessing at Portuguese words

With a little bit of background assistance anyone with some knowledge of French, Spanish or Italian can quite easily read written Portuguese.

■ Perfect, or near-perfect cognates (words with similarity in other languages) exist across the board. Look at the following table of nouns to note the similarities:

Portuguese	Spanish	Italian	French	English
pão	pan	pane	pain	bread
mês	mes	mese	mois	month
mãe	madre	madre	mère	mother
novo	nuevo	nuovo	nouveau	new
noite	noche	notte	nuit	night
três	tres	tre	trois	three
cereja	cereza	ciliegia	cerise	cherry

Spelling differences between Spanish and Portuguese. Some of the most common variations include:

■ Spanish *ie* is usually *i* or *e* in Portuguese, and Spanish *ue* becomes *u* or *o*:

Spanish   *cierto*   Portuguese   *certo*   = sure, certain
          diez   *dez*   ten
          puerto   *porta*   door

■ Spanish *bl* and *pl* often become *br* and *pr* in Portuguese:

blanco   *branco*   white
plato   *prato*   plate

■ Initial *h* in Spanish is often *f* in Portuguese:

hablar   *falar*   to speak
horno   *forno*   oven
hormiga   *formiga*   ant

■ Spanish *z* is often *ç* in Portuguese:

azúcar   *açúcar*   sugar
caza   *caça*   hunt

■ Speakers of Spanish can also hook onto slight differences where a single letter has been lost over time. Common examples include:

	Spanish	**Portuguese**
Plurals losing l	*pasteles*	*pastéis*
~ for a lost n	*sano* (safe)	*são*
Dropped N	*luna* (moon)	*lua*
Similar endings	*-able > razonable*	*-ável > razoável*
-ll > -ch	*llover/llorar*	*chover/chorar*

For those approaching Portuguese from scratch there are also features to look out for in spelling to get you nearer the English equivalent:

■ words ending in *-ção* usually correspond to words in English ending in -tion/ -sion: eg. *estação* (station), *informação* (information)
■ with words starting with *es-*, often if you drop the *e* (as so often happens in speech) you should be closer to the English: *escola* (school), *escala* (scale), *estudante* (student), *Espanha* (Spain)
■ *ph* is replaced by an *f*: *farmácia, telefone, fotografia*
■ *-mente* is the ending of words which usually have -ly in English: *lentamente* (slowly), *rapidamente* (quickly)

It's all a case of deciphering the puzzle by using whatever references you have to hand, and many people find that with a few hints such as those above plus whatever else they add from their own findings, they can, and do, start to read written Portuguese relatively comfortably.

The Acordo Ortográfico

For a number of years now the Portuguese-speaking nations have been working towards a common agreement on spelling. There are various differences, particularly with Brazilian Portuguese, and although the differences usually do not impede understanding, it has been a cause of unease that the spelling of the variants remains non-uniform.

Written accents

Without entering into all the intricate details of accentuation, suffice it to say that the following written accents are in use:

´ (acute) used to denote where a word is stressed

` (grave) used predominantly to show where a contraction has taken place, and only used on seven words in Portuguese

^ (circumflex) closes a vowel sound and denotes stress

~ (til) nasalizes and usually denotes stress

, (cedilha) – makes a c soft – ç

There are some difficulties for learners of Spanish, in that identical words in both languages may succumb to a different rule of accentuation, hence *pastelería* (cake shop) in Spanish, but *pastelaria* in Portuguese.

Confusions

One thing most people find when listening to Portuguese (whether in full-flight or slow-motion) is that certain combinations of sounds, or even individual words, appear to mean something entirely different. Now of course this happens in English too; imagine a foreigner listening to here/hear, bear/bare, so/sew, etc. You have to rely heavily on the context and sensible guesswork to sort it out. Here are some 'funnies' I have collected along the way:

■ In Brazil once, a Brazilian friend of mine rang her local newspaper to check on a prayer she had requested to be published in memory of a family member. The newspaper receptionist asked '*Que oração?*' (what prayer?), but Lu thought she heard '*Que horas são?*' (What time is it?) and told the person the time! And this between two native speakers!

■ On a recent trip to the Algarve, Bill met up with a friend (Guy) who was making his life out there in the building trade. Guy told Bill that when he met up with all the builders in the morning the Portuguese greeted each other by saying 'It's a shovel' – *É pá* – a word Guy had learned (correctly) as a tool of his trade. But, what they were actually doing is employing a frequently used colloquial expression of greeting or banter – *Eh pá!* , meaning something akin to 'Oi mate'. The *pá* here comes from the word *rapaz* (boy/lad). A case of not calling a spade a spade!

Forms of address

Portuguese forms of address (how you call someone 'you') are a
sensitive minefield, laden with traditional forms of respect. Your
choice of form is dependent on how well you know the person,
what your relative ages are, and the status of that person. The
following should give you an idea:

Tu	Used with family members, very good friends, children and pets. Rarely used in Brazil, apart from certain areas. Has its own verb endings.
O senhor (O sr.) *A senhora (a sra.)*	Polite forms, used with strangers, older people
O / a + first name e.g. *O João*	Not as intimate as *tu*, but used between colleagues, friends of equal standing
Você	Originally comes from *vossa mercê* = your grace, used as the main form in Brazil, and now more widely in Portugal
(a) Dona + first name (woman) *(a) Sra. Dona* + first name	Respectful forms, used with older, or married women particularly
O menino/ a menina	Used with boys, girls and young women, often with the name, e.g. *a menina Susana* (as I am still called by one family in Lisbon!)

O sr. Dr/ Prof./ Eng A sra. Dra/ Prof./ Eng	With people who have notable professions or high levels of education, such as medical, academic, or engineering
Vós	The old, original 'you plural', now rarely found outside church language, speeches and in remote villages
Os senhores (os srs) As senhoras (as sras)	Polite you plural
Vocês	General form for plural you

Additionally, for people in the highest positions in society, such as the president, or politicians and judges, etc., you would be expected to use the title *Vossa Excelência* (Your Excellency), with the corresponding plural form *vossas excelências* to a group of honoured people. In letter-writing there are also various other conventions with traditional origins.

To add to this, many of these forms take the same verb form as the third person (he, she and it), as the illustration below indicates:

falar (to speak)

Singular		Plural	
eu falo	I speak	*nós falamos*	we speak
tu falas	you speak	*vós falais*	you speak (rarely used now)
ele/ela fala And also:	he/she speaks	*eles/elas falam*	they speak
você fala/ o senhor fala		*vocês falam/ os senhores falam*	
A senhora fala/		*as senhoras falam/*	
a Ana fala, etc.		*Você e a Ana falam*, etc.	

When visiting Portugal and meeting people for the first time, it is always prudent to err on the polite side and use *o senhor/a senhora*, and the forms with *Dona* for older women. Politeness and respect mean a lot to the Portuguese, and this is just one of the ways by which that can be manifested. As always, take your cue from what is being used around you, and if you eventually get on to the *Tu* mode with your friends there, you'll know you've been accepted on extremely pally terms!

Vocabulary

Portuguese words in use in English

There are a number of words or expressions we use in English which owe their origin to Portuguese at some point or other. Did you know, for example, that the 'vindaloo' curry you enjoy on a Saturday night came from the Portuguese via their Indian explorations? *Vinho* (wine) and *alho* (garlic) were the two main flavourings of the dish *vindalho*. How about accompanying it with a good cup of char? The Portuguese word for tea is *chá*, the taste for which was, again, brought back from the East (the word is originally Chinese), and the word used in India for the drink is 'chai'. On the same topic of food, 'marmalade' comes from the Portuguese word for quince (*marmelo*), introduced to Portugal by early invaders (the Ancient Greeks ate quince preserves and the Romans called it *melimelum* – honey apple, because the apples were preserved in honey).

Place names also depict Portuguese influence: Natal in South Africa, so called as it was discovered by Portuguese explorers at Christmas (*Natal*), the Cameroon in Africa, again explorers found an abundance of shrimp there (*camarão*), and the Flores islands in Indonesia, named after the wealth of flowers encountered there. The full extent of Portuguese exploration is shown in further linguistic infiltration, as in the word in China for the ruling power, and the language spoken by those in authority – Mandarin – comes from the Portuguese *mandar* (to lead, command) – courtesy of the Latin *mandare*!

English words in use in Portuguese

There are also examples where English has managed to infiltrate Portuguese, a number that is growing rapidly. Foreign words in use in Portuguese are known as *estrangeirismos* (foreign-isms). Words which have been borrowed and 'Lusonified' are said to have been *aportuguesadas*. They include:

um lanche/ lanchar (a snack/ to snack), probably originally from lunch
os jeans (obviously)
champô (*xampu* in Brazil) – shampoo
um fax/ um email (*correio electrónico*). *Emilio* which the Spanish now use has not caught on in Portugal
o futebol / râguebi
stop – used on road signs
o check-in – at the airport
está OK – it's OK
o surf
hi-fi
traveller's cheques
o marketing/ o interface

Loans from France include: *charcutaria* (delicatessen), *soutiã* (*soutien* in Brazil) (bra), *ecrã* (screen), *robô* (robot), and from Italy comes the omnipresent *ciao* (bye). Some wonderful words also remain which are undoubtedly Latin, such as *quotidiano* (everyday) and *longínquo* (distant).

Slang and colloquialisms

Portuguese has its fair share of colloquial and slang expressions (*calão* or *gíria*), enough to fill a separate book. This aspect of any language changes constantly as new words and expressions fall in and out of fashion. Mainland Portugal is highly influenced by the power of the mighty Brazilian soap-operas (*telenovelas*). The Portuguese are as hooked on these (and they are myriad throughout the day) as the British once were on the Australian onslaught. But it's thanks to Brazil that expressions such as: *tudo bem?* (OK?), *tchau* and *tchau-tchau* (bye), from the Italian *ciao* (large Italian communities in places like São Paulo), and *Oi* (Hi) are now in wide circulation in Portugal. In turn, the Brazilians consider 'cute' the Portuguese use of *pois* (well, erm, er) and often make fun of them by referring to them as '*pois pois*'!

Here is a small selection of common colloquialisms in circulation, including some widely used expletives (of a more benign nature!):

Bestial!	Fantastic!
gajo/ gaja	bloke, guy/ slag (difference in rules for the sexes)
Isso é canja	It's a piece of cake (literally chicken soup)
Porreiro!	Bloody good! Brilliant!
Que droga!	Damn! Blast!
Bora aí	Let's be off
flipar	to flip, go loopy
Vá à fava!	Get lost!
Bolas!	Nonsense! (words of annoyance)
Vá para o diabo/ o inferno!	Go to hell!

False friends – *amigos falsos*

We have said a lot about using what you know to guide you in your language learning, but sometimes a word you think **must** be the same as one you already know in another language, turns out to be a red herring and can throw you off tack completely. Here are just a few to show you what I mean:

English	French	Spanish	Portuguese
Tea	Té	Té	Chá
Train	Train	Tren	Comboio
Monday	Lundi	Lunes	Segunda-feira

Portuguese concepts

Some thoughts and concepts do not travel across linguistic borders. This is starkly illustrated in the Portuguese notion of *saudade*. Loosely translatable as 'nostalgia/ homesickness/yearning', it cannot be adequately transposed into a different language. *Saudade* is the deep feeling portrayed in the Fado music (see Chapter 5), and has been explained as the heart-felt yearning for distant places, peoples and times.

Diminutives and augmentives

The Portuguese widely use diminutive forms of vocabulary to create words that are smaller, cuter, and friendlier. The main forms are the suffixes *-inho/-zinho* .Thus the word for cat (*gato*) becomes the word for kitten as *gatinho*; a house (*casa*) becomes smaller as *casinha*; *obrigado* (thanks) is turned into *obrigadinho* to sound even friendlier. Even people's names are affected: *José* > *Zé* > *Zezinho* = Joseph > Joe> little Joe/ Joey. And greetings too: *Adeus* (goodbye) > *adeusinho*, *tchau* (see you) > *tchauzinho*.

There are also augmentive forms to make words bigger, or stronger. Although not as commonly used as diminutives, there is still a lot you can do with suffixes such as *-ão/ona*: *garrafa* (bottle) becomes *garrafão* (demi-john), *carta* (letter) becomes *cartão* (greetings card, credit card, cardboard), and *mulher* (woman) becomes a large woman as *mulherona* (which can also be used pejoratively).

Regional differences

The language on the Portuguese mainland is pretty uniform, unlike in neighbouring Spain. Accents in Portugal differ slightly from north to south, as you might expect in any country, and some areas tend to speak with a greater or lesser clarity and speed. The clearest Portuguese is considered to be that of Coimbra, but, in contrast, for the many visitors to the Algarve, the problem is that of contending not only with a fairly strong local speech (Algarvese), but also with slurring! Local or regional dialects have all but died out apart from a fascinating pocket of *Mirandês* in the isolated Trás-os-Montes region, a local language somewhat akin to Vulgar Latin, and in the southern border town of Barrancos, a strange mix of Spanish and Portuguese is uttered by locals, known as *Barranquenho*. In Madeira and the Azores local pronunciation is more drawn-out, initially making it difficult to understand.

In Galicia the regional language, *Galego*, is a very close relative of Portuguese proper. The two are so alike that travellers in Galicia would be able to make themselves understood in Portuguese, and would have few problems comprehending the Galego around them.

One aspect where you do find regional variation is in the words for everyday items, again a feature present in any language. Take the terms for bread products – even in English we have huge variation: rolls, baps, barm cakes, cobs... So, too, in Portugal: *pãozinho* (bread roll) in most places can also be a *papo-seco* (a slightly smaller roll), particularly in the Algarve. *Broa* (corn bread) is more common in the north, and *pão-de-forma* (packaged sliced loaves) may be unheard of in some isolated areas. You will doubtless come across others on your travels.

Portuguese around the globe

In Brazil, the vast majority of its approximately 166 million inhabitants speak Portuguese, albeit a variant of the language which differs in pronunciation, vocabulary and some grammar. In this respect it could be said that the differences between the two are on the same lines as those between British and American English. In most cases understanding is not impeded, apart from a few items of vocabulary. Pronunciation-wise, some of the main differences include: *-te* pronounced as *-tche*, *-de* as *-dge*, final *-o* as in o and not *-oo*, and much more open vowel sounds. Often it is easier to latch on to what Brazilians are saying purely because they tend to open their mouths wider to let the full sounds of words escape. There are also around 250,000 indigenous peoples left in Brazil, said to speak 170 languages. In some of the more accessible tribes projects are underway to preserve the local language as a written language (many of them are purely oral languages), with the aid of anthropologists and teachers. Thus they are also introduced to Portuguese in the process, although in a manner totally unlike that of the earlier missionaries who tried to force western civilization upon them. Brazil has been an instigating force in the setting up of the organisation *CPLP*, *Comunidade dos Países de Língua Portuguesa*, or Community of Portuguese-speaking Peoples.

In Africa too there is an umbrella term for the Portuguese-speaking countries of the former Portuguese empire: *PALOPs – Países Africanos de Língua Oficial Portuguesa* (African Countries with Portuguese as Official Language).

Although there are also local languages in the African countries, the main Portuguese language spoken by the majority differs little from that in Portugal, mostly in vocabulary.

A glance at the following table will give you an idea of how general vocabulary may vary between European, Brazilian and African Portuguese:

English	Portugal	Brazil	Africa
Youngest son	(Filho) Mais novo	Caçula	Candengue (Angola)
Breakfast	Pequeno-almoço	Café da manhã	Mata-bicho
Train	Comboio	Trem	Comboio
Bus	Autocarro	Ônibus	Machimbombo

In the East, in what remains with ties to Portugal, the strength of the language is fluctuating. In East Timor, where a 20-year battle to relieve the country of its Indonesian oppressors has recently resulted in victory of sorts, Portuguese is still spoken and will become the official language. In Macau, now back in the hands of China, Chinese and Portuguese are both deemed 'official languages', although Portuguese is hardly used now outside the civil service. Most of the ethnic Portuguese population of the island had been expected to leave at the time of its hand-over. Plans to open a new Portuguese-curriculum school in Macau, to maintain the language and culture beyond the hand-over, have run into criticism at a time when most schools there have been turning to Cantonese and English as the media of learning. Local legislators have complained that the proposed new school is not ambitious enough in its size and remit, despite a start-up capital of almost US$3 million, and that overall Portuguese will decline in the region, as both a native and a second language.

GLOSSARY

a língua *language*
o idioma *language*
falar *to speak*
escutar *to listen (to)*
ouvir *to hear*
escrever *to write*
o latim *Latin*
o árabe *Arabic*
a influência *influence*
o dialecto *dialect*
a gramática *grammar*
o sustantivo *noun*
o verbo *verb*
a adjectivo *adjective*
a ortografia *spelling*

o acento *accent (written)*
o sotaque *accent (spoken)*
pronunciar *to pronounce*
parecer *to seem like*
o vocabulário *vocabulary*
a língua falada *the spoken language*
a língua estrangeira *foreign language*
lusófono *relating to Portugal*
as palavras *words*
o sentido *meaning*
...quer dizer... ... *means ...*
o calão *slang*
a gíria *slang*
o crioulo *Creole*
bilíngüe *bilingual*

Taking it further

Suggested reading

História da Língua Portuguesa, Paul Teyssier, Sá da Costa, 1990
The Romance Languages, Martin Harris and Nigel Vincent, Routledge, 1997
The Loom of Language, Frederick Bodmer, Allen & Unwin, 1946
Dicionário Editora da língua portuguesa (good monolingual dictionary) Editora, New ed. 1994
Oxford-Duden pictorial dictionary (detailed visual/vocabulary) Oxford University Press, 1992
Michaelis dicionário práctico (bilingual English/Portuguese, both directions), Michaelis, updated regularly
Collins Portuguese dictionaries (various sizes)

Learning

BBC series – Discovering Portuguese, often repeated, and worth recording on video. Six programmes of background scenes of Portugal, and language, although parts need updating now.

Satellite TV, if you have access to it, will enable you to reach Portuguese TV; there is an international channel called RTPi.

On-line courses, such as that offered by the University of Glasgow (UK), called *De tudo um pouco*.

Dicionário Universal da língua portuguesa (CD-ROM version of Portuguese dictionary), Texto Editora. Visit their website at: **www.telepac.pt/texto**

Various Portuguese-learning CD-ROMs now available from good bookstores.

Enrol on language classes at your local college/ language school.

Try to speak with the Portuguese when you are in Portugal – they will be grateful you have made an effort, and will encourage your attempts.

Places to visit

Camões Institute, R.Rodrigues Sampaio 113, 1150-279 Lisboa. Tel: 213-109 100

Coordination of Portuguese Language Centres worldwide, Centro Coordenador dos Centros de Língua Portuguesa, Campo Grande 56, r/c, 1700-078 Lisboa. Tel: 217-956 113

Websites

There are many sites and materials in both English and Portuguese. Here are just a few ideas:

Camões Institute – language and cultural information, **www.instituto-camoes.pt**

Comunidade de Países de Língua Portuguesa – Portuguese-speaking communities, **www.cplp.org**

Portugal and the Portuguese language – **www.public.iastate.edu/~pedro/pt_connect.html**

The human languages page – materials, interesting links, institutions and information in the language of your choice, **www.june29.com**

King's College, London – Dept. of Portuguese and Brazilian studies, various links: **www.Kcl.ac.uk/depsta/humanities/pobrst/kclhp.htm**

Língua Portuguesa – key this into search motor AltaVista, and you should link to many more sites.

3 | LITERATURE

A verdade que eu conto, nua e pura
vence toda grandíloca escritura.

(The truth that I tell, naked and pure, beats all grand writings)
– Camões, *Os Lusíadas*

Portugal has a wealth of literature which is vastly underrated, mostly as a result of its relative inaccessibility, and consequent lack of promotion on the world literary stage, a problem shared to a certain degree with its Spanish neighbour. In part this may have been due, until recently, to a dearth of work in translation – very few people study the language to a sufficiently high level to be able to cope with literature, and what is only available in Portugal fails to spread beyond the realms of academia. In part, also, it is due to the seemingly Portuguese trait of not wishing to shout their heads off about their national treasures. Many people who have not even studied beyond a basic level in other languages, may still recognize names such as Hugo, Rousseau, Dumas, Goethe, Lorca, Cervantes etc. But mention the Portuguese greats such as Camões, Gil Vicente, Queirós and Pessoa, and most will draw a blank look.

Luckily things have started to change of late, and through the work of various cultural organizations alongside publishers and promoters, more Portuguese work is now available in translation. However, there is still a long way to go, despite the current access to writers such as the 1998 Nobel prize-winner, José Saramago, Portugal's finest contemporary writer, whose books are now widely on sale in translation, and the highly acclaimed Brazilian writer Paulo Coelho, who recently scored a hit with *The Alchemist*.

When considering the literature of Portugal, we should also not forget the stack of writing from Brazil and Africa in particular, and reference will be made later in the chapter to relevant writers from around the Portuguese-speaking countries who have shaped the Portuguese literary world.

Whilst people and events across Europe have influenced writing in various countries for hundreds of years, Portugal had the additional events of its era of explorations which resulted in some distinctive home-grown writing. A tour through Portuguese literature across the ages will give you some idea of the breadth and depth of work, from the earliest oral traditions right up to what the Portuguese like to read right now.

Early literature – the troubadours

The earliest literary communications of any kind date back to the oral tradition of storytelling that existed in all parts of the world and as a pre-writing tradition, has little documented evidence. However, this, along with the custom of chanting or singing to accompany work (as witnessed in African tribes still today, or in the old sea-shanties), was the environment which was to engender the rise of early epic tales of heroics and battles, long poems which were recited by heart, often in episodes over a period of time (the first soap-operas?), and which were eventually written down and passed into documented writing. But whilst Spain had its famous *Poema de Mio Cid* (*c*1140), later immortalized on screen by Charlton Heston, and France produced its equally eminent 12th-century *Chanson de Roland*, Portugal's epic, *Os Lusíadas*, was only to appear much later.

In the meantime, throughout the 12th and 13th centuries, what Portugal embraced and gave its own slant to, was the tradition of poem-songs, taken across Europe by wandering minstrels or troubadours. Mostly originating from Provence, these court entertainers travelled from country to country, telling tales of love and adventure, mostly to courtly audiences. Many of them made their way down from southern France into Iberia and the tradition was particularly seized upon by Galician–Portuguese poet musicians, who developed two very distinct strands of these so-called *Cantigas*.

Cantigas de amor

The love poems often involved the theme of a young maiden pining for her so-called male 'friend' who has gone away somewhere, leaving her behind to wish for his return. These *cantigas de amigo* were surprisingly sensitive to the woman's point of view, despite all being written and performed by men. The other love poems, based on courtly love, usually portrayed some unrequited love – the poet setting his beloved on a pedestal from where she might scorn his advances.

Cantigas d'Escarnho e mal-dizer

The other strand of poems could not have been more different: a satirical look at love and the negative aspects of women's sexuality – bawdy, rude, full of gossip and a quagmire of double entendre! Often poets would also hurl invective at each other in the poems, not restraining themselves to criticism of a work or performance, but also pointing a blatant finger of ridicule at their rivals' bodily parts! Other people who did not escape criticism were the *ricos-homens* (decadent nobility), *soldadeiras* (women who accompanied bands of soldiers), homosexuals, and husbands cuckolded by their loved ones.

The *Cantigas* continued to travel the courts for some time, encouraged by the king, Dom Dinis, whose deep interest in education and culture helped to fire the literary imagination of the time. More than 2,000 poem-songs have survived, mostly in songbooks known as *cancioneiros*.

The chroniclers

During the 13th and 14th centuries, writing consisted mainly of translations from Latin prose, and adaptations of knightly legends, such as the *Lenda do Rei Rodrigo*, about the last Visigoth king who lost Spain to the Moors in 711, and the vast collection of Arthurian-type Grail Quest tales, *A Demanda do Santo Graal*. There were also chronicles of the lives of saints or noble personalities.

Fernão Lopes

The political upheavals in Portugal during the establishment of new central powers and ruling parties, from the late 14th to 15th centuries, were documented by the court writer and keeper of the National Archives (the Torre do Tombo), Fernão Lopes (born c1380). Lopes' task, instigated by his king, Dom Duarte, was to chronicle the happenings and characters of the reigns of the monarchs Dom Pedro, Fernando and João. Although Lopes himself stated that '*a estoria ha de seer luz da verdade e testemunha dos antigos tempos*' (history must be the light of truth and testimony to the times past), he was also constantly aware of the role of the historian in conveying history '*como uma escrita*' (as a written story). The result was not a consolidated documentary of events, but a subjective rendering of the truth. However, the fact remains that the material in the *Crónicas*, which cover exciting events such as the battles against the Spanish, the love story of Inês de Castro (see also p.58), and the heroic deeds involved in bringing the Master of Avis (Dom João 1) to the throne, is simply not always reliable. Despite this, Lopes is generally accepted as the first modern Portuguese historian, or as a later historical writer, Alexandre Herculano, was to call him – '*o pai da historiografia portuguesa*' (the father of Portuguese history writing).

Gomes Eanes de (A)Zurara

Lopes' successor at the Torre do Tombo was Gomes Eanes de (A)Zurara, whose view of history was quite an aristocratic one – that it essentially revolves around one great man and, for Zurara in particular, that was Dom Henrique, who in 15th-century Portugal was having to face the fact that a number of hopeless military decisions taken by him, and disastrous battles, had left the ruling class in the precarious position of being critically judged by its people. Zurara intended his historical works as a defence of the *senhores* from whom he received his patronage, and in his *Crónica dos feitos de Guiné* (Chronicle of the events in Guinea) presents Henrique as a cult hero, making sure that his sponsorship of exploration in Africa was duly recorded for posterity in a form acceptable to him. This is a far cry from the views of an eminent

16th-century historian, Bartolomé de las Casas, who was to denounce Henry as a common criminal and murderer of peaceful people in Africa! Whatever the motives for its existence, the *Crónica* contains some fascinating tales of encounters with savages (to whom the Portuguese did the favour of either civilizing or killing!), cat people, and the flora and fauna on their travels in 'Negroland'.

Early Renaissance

With the growing overseas expansion, and influences from Italy and the revival of the classics, the Renaissance in Portugal set the scene for a group of writers who were to make their mark, although writing in general did not move far from the established styles laid down by the troubadours. **Garcia de Resende** collated the *Cancioneiro Geral* (General Songbook) in 1516, which contained the work of 300 poets of the time. Resende himself won acclaim for his verse version of the love story of Pedro and Inês de Castro. **Bernadim Ribeiro**, whose sentimental writing is best exemplified by his novel – *Menina e Moça* (Child and Maiden), which came out under the original title of *Livro das saudades* (Book of Longings, 1554–7). A pastoral background and chivalrous ideals lend the book a distinctly lyrical air.

Francisco de Sá de Miranda (1488–1558) spent time in Italy, as part of a trend at the time to satisfy indulgence in all things Italian; on his return his bucolic poetry portrayed his deep love of the countryside and simple joys of the people who live there; however, his pessimism arising from his close observation of vices in society at court gave his writing a rather gloomy tinge.

Gil Vicente

By far the greatest poet to emerge from the group, and who became the founding father of Portuguese theatre, was **Gil Vicente** (*c*1465–1538). Vicente was a dramatist who worked in the courts of the Kings João II, Manuel, and João III. Working with equal competence in Portuguese or Spanish, his numerous plays – comedies, religious plays, tragedies and farces – span both languages. Many of them show a satirical observation of all that society has to offer, with all walks of life portrayed in them, at a time when Portugal was enjoying international prestige and huge wealth. They are also peppered with songs from Portuguese folk poetry. During the Inquisition some of his work was banned, as it contained too much critical satire for the liking of the zealots. Vicente's audience was made up of court people, often the same people from year to year. There was no advantage at the time in writing for the *povo*, the ordinary people, as writers depended on the patronage of the court. Printing of published works was still on a very limited scale even by the end of the 16th century in Portugal. The plays, usually performed by courtiers or servants, often celebrated some particular time of the year, such as Easter, but once the king had seen a performance, it would not need to be done again. Vicente, knowing that his audiences enjoyed his plays, had to recycle popular themes, with similar characters, but make each play slightly different. He is famed for his play on words, in many misunderstood asides between characters, in the same way as Shakespeare injected humour into his comedies; and, like Chaucer, many of the defects of his characters are alluded to through humour.

In his popular *Auto da Índia* (India Play/Farce), a woman whose husband has supposedly embarked upon a voyage to India is found crying by her maid. The maid immediately assumes her mistress to be in deep sorrow at the loss of her husband for the next three years. However, the truth of the matter is that the news that her husband is not departing after all has just reached the woman and she is distraught at the prospect of not being able to carry on certain illicit meetings behind his back!

Moça: *Jesus! Jesus! Que é ora isso?*	Maid: Now then, now then!
	What's all this about?
É porque se parte a armada?	Is it because the fleet is off?
Ama: *Olhade a mal estreada!*	Mistress: Just look at the silly fool!
Eu hei-de chorar por isso?	Would I be crying for that?

The best works include the morality, or religious plays, such as the *Auto da Alma*, and the three *Barca* plays (*Inferno*, *Purgatório*, *Glória*), and the farces and social satires, such as *Auto da Índia*, *Quem tem farelos?* and the *Farsa de Inês Pereira*.

The Golden Age

The next generation of writers continued some of the styles established by the 'humanists' (those writers influenced by classical studies, and devoted to human interests) – with comedies of manners, moralizing tales and dialogues, often on religious topics. One of the greatest works to be created at this time was the verse-play *A Castro*, based on the tragic love story of Inês de Castro and Pedro. The 'play' is done very much in the style of Greek tragedies, with a chorus warning of events, and commenting on the actions of the characters. It is extremely moving, particularly in the scenes where Inês is pleading to save the lives of her small children. It also draws the audience into the realms of kingship, and the responsibilities of the monarch, as Pedro's father tries to dissuade his son from the distractions of the woman, and turn his mind to future rule. In this part, it touches on the Machiavellian themes of deceit and cunning. (Machiavelli was a 16th-century Florentine philosopher, whose treatise on ruling, *The Prince*, advocated the use of often unscrupulous means to strengthen the state.) Although novels of chivalry remained popular, little other prose fiction emerged from the 16th century.

Chroniclers of conquest

The other main stream of writing, however, is interesting, as it encompasses the historical travel writing and chronicles of a number of writers, following the patterns set down by the earlier chroniclers, Lopes and Zurara. One of the most important historians of this time was **Diogo do Couto**, who continued the history of Portuguese overseas conquest started by **João de Barros** in 1552. The *Décadas da Ásia* was an ambitious investigation of the history and geography of the 16th-centruy Portuguese expansion in the East. It was not completed until 1615. The travel books of the time are full of the excitement, adventure and drama you might expect, given the era of exploration. One of the more accessible is the *Peregrinação (The Peregrination*, in translation), 1614, by **Fernão Mendes Pinto**, an anti-crusader hailed as the Portuguese Marco Polo. *The Peregrination* is a long, colourful work, written in descriptive diary form, of Pinto's adventures in

East Asia, where he was involved in trading and piracy, even at one point being enslaved himself.

Luís Vaz de Camões (1525–80)

Luís Vaz de Camões (Camoens in English) began his life as a poet and scholar attending the university in Coimbra. He was sent to Africa on military service after an affair with a noblewoman and subsequently banished to Goa after a skirmish with a courtier and a prison sentence. In addition, he lost an eye in Africa, was shipwrecked whilst trying to get home from Macau (where he had ended up from India), and on his death from the plague he was buried in a common grave. However, with all this romantic, adventure-filled backdrop that was his life, he was an accomplished poet, and under the patronage of the king, Dom Manuel, in 1572 he published his epic poem *Os Lusíadas* (The Lusiads – the sons of Lusus, mythical founder of Portugal, and hence 'The Portuguese') to instant acclaim and a royal pension. The poem was to establish him as Portugal's greatest writer, a hero of the country, whose work was to inspire and influence writers such as Milton, Byron, Lope de Vega, Goethe and the German Romantics. It is no coincidence that Portugal's National Day is named in his honour. So, what was it about that single piece of writing that brought Camões such posthumous fame?

'Onde a terra acaba e o mar começa (where the land ends and the sea begins)'

Os Lusíadas

Europe was in the full throes of Renaissance, with a heightened contact with the culture, art and literature of the ancient Greek and Roman civilizations. Influences from Italy were brought back to Portugal by travelling writers and scholars, and the discoveries were very much part of this new era of awakening. Portugal was in a slight lull after the initial frenzy of exploration, and the country seemed to be sliding backwards. In the poem, Camões shows his disappointment with the status quo, but by the end has his eyes set on the hope of seeing Portugal rise again to new glories. It is not surprising then, that the poem is dedicated to Dom Sebastião (who was later to be lost in battle in North Africa), whose young figure opens and closes the work, as the symbol of hope for the future.

The poem itself has a classical structure, and is on an epic scale, like Homer's *Odyssey* and Virgil's *Aeneid* before it. It shares many features with the *Aeneid*, including the dedication to the king, the supernatural elements (the 'gods' fighting for and against the protagonists), and a procession of the future line of rulers shown in great glory. Whilst visibly a tale of the heroic voyage of Vasco da Gama to India, the poem cleverly works in the entire history of Portugal, combining Camões' intense patriotism (his own long absences from his country served to strengthen his love for what he called his '*patria ditosa amada*' – his happy, beloved homeland) with dozens of exotic scenes, celestial influences, and poetic wizardry. He claims Portugal will be better than the Greek and Roman Empires: '*ser-lhe-á todo o oceano obediente*' (the whole ocean will obey her), and whilst exalting Italy as the metropolis of the Roman Empire, he says that Portugal is the crown of Europe.

The 17th century

Dialogues, letters and sermons

The trying times of yet another Spanish encroachment on Portuguese independence led to a general stagnation in all areas of society. The only shining star seemed to be Brazil, which was to furnish Portugal with great riches. Against this uncertain background, the writers of this period indulged in publishing dialogues commenting on current affairs, such as those produced by the aristocratic **Francisco Manuel de Melo** (1608–66). Melo suffered from great bouts of melancholy, particularly as he contemplated what he considered the mediocrity in society around him. Although he never married, he felt he knew enough to produce a book moralising on the subject! His *Carta de Guia de Casados* gave words of wisdom such as letting women do the housework to keep them busy, as men should worry less about this type of thing! Men should not go after other women, especially nuns or the maids in one's own house! Women only laugh to show off their teeth – they should only smile at home! The other writer of the time who became an international personality was the Jesuit preacher **António Vieira** (1608-1697), whose sermons are full of fire and brimstone, incredibly imaginative and bold beyond his time. They fill 15 volumes, and some of the most interesting are those he preached in northern Brazil to rouse the locals against attack by the Dutch.

The 18th century

Age of Enlightenment

Any enthusiasm for the excesses of the baroque period were sent into the shadows by the reclaiming of classical regularity, keenly and rigorously led by the French and Italians. In place of the flights of fancy afforded by poetic licence, literature of a more academic and educational vein crept in, in this era of social reform. However, in the midst of the stern treatises emanating from many writers, some managed to buck the trend, such as **António José da Silva**, who created a series of comical plays for puppets (*marionetas*). The puppet *óperas* offer a satiric glance at Portuguese society, and an opportunity to mock characters such as social climbers, lawyers and doctors. **Francisco Xavier de Oliveira** sent back letters from England, and through these *Cartas Familiares* (1741–2), established himself as the first Portuguese essayist. Meanwhile, **Manuel Maria Barbosa du Bocage** was a bohemian character, who indulged in the excesses of life and perhaps wasted much of his talent. His philosophies can be read in his sonnets, *Rimas* (1791–9).

The 19th century

Nationalism, romanticism, and modernism

The 19th century was extremely productive in Portuguese literary terms, and from it emerge some of the most talented, interesting and best-known writers in its history. The Napoleonic invasions of Iberia during the early part of the 19th century gave rise to a feeling of great nationalism within Portugal, which was to manifest itself in the literature of the time. Two writers in particular had spent time in France and England, whence they brought back ideals of liberty and nationalistic feeling: **(João Baptista da) Almeida Garrett** (1799–1854) produced some dramatic works of a historic nature, such as *Frei Luis de Sousa* (1844), with which he hoped to rekindle the Portuguese theatrical tradition. He was more successful as a poet, and perhaps his most best-known work is the romantic satire *Viagens na Minha Terra* (Travels in my Homeland, 1846). **Alexandre Herculano** was a historian of some note, specializing in medieval Portugal, and highly influenced in his writing by Sir Walter Scott, whose novels were in circulation in Portugal at the time. His works include the gripping historical novel *Eurico o Presbítero* (1844), a battle-filled tale set in the time of the Visigoths and Moors, which also introduces the theme of priestly celibacy.

The 'Romantics' in Portugal, (writers who believed in freedom of expression, reproduction of external beauty and nature, and the passionate use of the imagination) produced the delightful novelist **Camilo Castelo Branco** (1825–90). He was orphaned whilst still young, and after a flirtation with the religious life, devoted his time to a writing career which produced a prolific amount of work, which, in 1885, earned him the title of Viscount of Correia-Botelho. Sadly, when his failing health led to blindness, he took his own life. His stories and tales of manners and small-town traditions take the reader on journeys into northern Portugal, such as in the acclaimed *Amor de Perdição* (1862) and *Coração, Cabeça e Estômago* (Heart, Head and Stomach), and his *Contos do Minho*, (Tales from the Minho).

Eça de Queirós (1845–1900)

By the 1860s, a group of young intellectual writers began to take up influences from French and German philosophy, science and socialism, among them the angst-ridden Azorean poet, Antero Tarquínio de Quental and Teófilo Braga, a modern literary historian. However, the writer who stood out more than any other was (José Maria de) Eça de Queirós (spelled Queiroz in its anglicized form), whose fiction underlines the subtleties of his writing and his satirical observation of society, its degenerate activities and sentiments, and its place in the natural environment. Arguably Portugal's finest novelist, Eça spent most of his life in consular service, and from 1888 served in Paris until his death. As an early disciple of the French writer Zola, he was a great advocate of realism, which can be seen from the fine detail in his descriptions of the worlds he created, but he was to become known instead as a truly great satirist. Zola himself declared Eça a better writer than the acclaimed French writer Flaubert! While many of his protagonists are flawed in some way, the reader is always allowed to cast his own judgement on the weakness; Eça's treatment of those flaws is with the understanding of how they originated. This is seen in his attitude to the bitter (*amaro*) priest in *O Crime do Padre Amaro* (The Sin of Father Amaro, 1875) – a story about the deception of women by a series of unscrupulous priests.

His most celebrated work is *Os Maias* (The Maias, 1888), about the progressive degeneration of an aristocratic family over three generations. Written against the background of Portugal's struggles in the early 19th century to settle its constitutional, political and economical situation whilst dependent on Britain and bombarded culturally by France, the novel is said to be one in which the Portuguese can most easily recognize themselves, even so long after it was conceived. So, when the disillusioned Ega states: '*Já não há nada genuíno neste país, nem mesmo o pão que comemos*' (There is nothing original left in this country, not even the bread we eat), Carlos points to the old parts of Lisbon, the religious traditions and '*palacetes decrépitos*', and replies '*Resta aquilo, que é genuíno...*' (That still remains, which is all genuine).

The best of the rest include *A Cidade e as Serras* (The City and the Mountains, 1901), which compares city life in Paris with that in the Portuguese countryside, *O Primo Basílio* (Cousin Basilio, 1878), and collections of short stories.

The 20th century

Social realism, experimentation, and women!

The new century dawned with the innovative cultural movement of Modernism, encompassing a break with all previous rules of writing, experimentation, and deep observation of man's condition and raison d'être in the world. In Portugal the movement was centred around a group of writers responsible for the literary magazine *Orfeu* (Orpheu).

Fernando Pessoa (1888–1935)

A handful of younger poets came to the fore, but none more so than Fernando Pessoa, whose writing career was tragically short-lived. Pessoa is a national icon in Portugal, representative of deep nationalism. In 1915 he wrote to a friend: 'The patriotic idea, always present in my intentions to some extent, is now growing in me, and I can't think of creating anything without aiming to exalt the name of Portugal through whatever I am able to accomplish.'

Pessoa spent some of his formative years in South Africa, and wrote some of his early poetry in English. Once back in Lisbon he worked as a small-time translator, but became part of the group of bohemian intellectuals who would meet at the Brasileira café in the Bairro Alto area of Lisbon. It is here that you will now find a life-size bronze of Pessoa, his distinctive features (small moustache, gold-rimmed spectacles and hat)

clearly visible. Pessoa himself was a strange, melancholy figure, who preferred his own company to that of large groups. He was a prolific drinker, and it was after a lengthy drinking session at the Brasileira that he died of cirrhosis of the liver, aged only 47. During his life he was a staunch anti-Catholic, and his writing portrays something of his ironic, complicated nature. He is a fascinating author, as he wrote under various names (heteronyms), 72 in all, each one having its own personality and style of writing. *Pessoa* means 'person' in Portuguese! The most important of his 'poets' were Álvaro de Campos, (a Glasgow-educated existentialist), Alberto Caeiro (an aesthetic follower of Zen), Ricardo Reis (a neo-classicist), and Bernardo Soares (under whose personality he wrote, but did not finish, *O Livro do Desassosego* – The Book of Disquiet). Later, the novelist José Saramago (see p.68) was to base a story around the chance meeting of Fernando Pessoa and one of his 'alter egos' – Ricardo Reis, in *The Year of the Death of Ricardo Reis*, a book worth reading given its bizarre subject matter. Most of Pessoa's poetry and essays were only published posthumously, and in fact a trunkful of his works was discovered in the late 1980s, and these have been filtering through to an eager readership ever since. His writing, considered by many to be among the greatest creations of the 20th century, also include *Mensagem* (Message), and his walking guide to Lisbon, *Lisboa: o que o turista deve ver* – what the tourist should see.

Miguel Torga (1907–95)

The collapse of the republic in 1926 gave another generation of writers cause for comment on the political and social situation, and a call for reform. One of the most vehement was Miguel Torga, a poet from Trás-os-Montes, who based his *Diário* on current events and the Portuguese nation. Torga was a strong opponent of Salazar's regime, and his feelings towards the oppressive times run through much of his work. He once stated: 'To be a writer in Portugal is like being buried alive and scratching at the lid of one's own coffin'. Not surprisingly, then, his work was banned and he himself imprisoned. He is perhaps remembered best, though, for his tales from his own region – *Contos* and *Novos Contos das Montanhas* (*Tales/ New Tales from the Mountains*). In these short stories he paints a very realistic harsh picture of life in this isolated mountain region, the life-cycles and the seasons, the struggle for survival and the scams resorted to to ensure another Winter is seen through, another mouth filled. One of his stories, *A Son*, begins with the following description:

> To anyone who gazes down from the top of the Mantelinha mountain, the world looks like anything but a vale of tears. During January especially, anyone not blind in his soul who looks down upon pure white snow as far as the eye can see, will be convinced – even if he is a shepherd and his animals are starving in the barn – that the earth was created solely for such whiteness to exist.

These, and the acclaimed *Creation of the World* are available in translation, and give you an insight into a world so far apart from high-rise hotel blocks in the Algarve you would not believe you were in the same country. Torga has won many literary prizes and been nominated three times for the Nobel Prize.

The Three Marias

During the dictatorship, censorship was normal in Portuguese life, and it is not surprising that a ban was put on publication of a work by three writers, all called Maria, which contained erotic passages and a distinctly feminist approach. The work, which was eventually published in America in 1975 under the title of *The Three Marias: New Portuguese Letters*, was based on love letters attributed to a 17th-century nun, Marianna Alcoforado. Originally published in French in 1669, and later in Portuguese in 1819, they were finally translated into English in 1893 under the title *Letters from a Portuguese Nun*. The collection of essays, poetry and stories from the *Three Marias* seemed profane to the devout Salazar, and he had the writers put on trial. However, with their subsequent pardon, the book was published just as the dictatorship was to fall.

After the dictatorship

During the next couple of decades, Portuguese writers used their craft as a means of denouncing the regime the country had had to endure for so long, and the throwing off of the yoke of censorship, which had led to stagnation in Portuguese writing, allowed a freedom of the pen not experienced for many years. Among these recent authors, two in particular have consistently found their way onto awards lists, including the Nobel prize short-list: – the great experimenter **José Cardoso Pires**, and **António Lobo Antunes**. Pires has had success with his novels around the world, including the *Ballada da Praia dos Cães* (Ballad of Dogs Beach), which was subsequently made into a film, and *O Hóspede de Job* (Job's Guest). Antunes was a psychoanalyst by profession, and worked as an army doctor during the wars in Angola, an experience which fuelled his damnation of the thriving middle classes under Salazar. His irreverent works have created polemics of debate in Portugal, but his books continue to hit the best-sellers list. *Act of the Damned* is considered one of his best.

Female writers began to make their mark on the literary stage from the 1960s, with **Agustina Bessa-Luís** leading the way with observations on the psyche of middle-class women. **Helena Marques**, born in 1935 had her first novel, *O Último Cais* (The Last Quay) published when she was 58. It won three literary prizes during its first year. **Alice Vieira** (1943–) had a career as a journalist before establishing herself as a fine writer of children's stories and adaptor of traditional Portuguese and Macanese (from Macau) tales. She has won numerous awards for her stories, many of which revolve around the daily lives of lower and middle-class people in post-revolution Lisbon. **Sophia de Mello Breyner** is rated one of the best contemporary poets. Her earlier works underlined her opposition to the Salazar regime, but with the freedom of 25 April 1974 came a new era for her writing, as seen in her poem with the title of that momentous date:

> This is the dawn I waited for
> The new day clean and whole
> When we emerge from night and silence
> To freely inhabit the substance of time

Lídia Jorge (1946–) is considered by many to be Portugal's leading female writer. Although much of her work portrays recent Portuguese history seen through the eyes of the women who have endured the changes, her novels also reflect universal observations on society, and have earned her fans in many European countries, where translations are now plentiful. Unfortunately, not many of her books are as yet available in English. When they do come on to the market, a much wider audience will be able to appreciate works such as her first novel *O Dia dos Prodígios* (The Day of the Prodigies), set in rural Algarve, and contrasting the old life with the hopes and aspirations made real with the impending revolution.

José Saramago (1922–), whose imaginative works have found international acclaim (many of them translated by the famed Giovanni Pontiero), finally won the Nobel prize in 1998. On award of the prize, it was claimed that here was an author 'who with parables sustained by imagination, compassion, and irony continually enables us once again to apprehend an illusory reality'. It was only in 1987 that Saramago began writing full-time, and won immediate success in 1988 with the novel *O Memorial do Convento* (translated into English as *Baltasar and Blimunda*), a book set against the building of the convent at Mafra, and also incorporating a priest's construction of a flying machine, and a young girl with mystical powers. In 1993 he won the Foreign Fiction Award from the British newspaper, the *Independent*, for the novel *The Year of the Death of Ricardo Reis* (mentioned earlier). An outspoken opponent of all that Salazar stood for (Saramago has made no secret of his Communist leanings), one of his brilliant short stories is based on the deck-chair from which the dictator fell when he suffered a stroke: *The Chair*. Fortunately, there are many translations (in English and other languages) of his works (including some of his travelogues), and including the novel which was to lead to his Nobel prize – *All the Names* – about which he said: '… I set out to write the simplest of stories … about a person who goes in search of another person merely because he realises that life has nothing more important to ask of a human being.'

Literature of other Portuguese-speaking countries

Brazil and the Portuguese African countries have also produced some excellent writers who have received deserved success and recognition, and not just in Portugal. Many of the works have been translated and have been lapped up by keen readers around the globe, interested in the authors' observations on social and political situations in many of these areas. A good number of these books now form integral parts of school and college studies and degree courses, testament to the way the themes have travelled. Although there are far too many to mention in detail, here are some ideas of writers you may wish to explore.

One eminent writer of the 19th century you can find in translation is (Joaquim Maria) **Machado de Assis** (1839–1908), whose reputation as an insightful penetrator of the human pysche continues to grow even today. Novels such as *Memórias Póstumas de Brás Cubas*, *Quincas Borba* and *Dom Casmurro* show an irony tinged with a sad melancholy towards his main protagonists. **José de Alencar** is one of the best examples of writers portraying life in the jungle; with their mix of romantic idealism and vivid description, his works *O Guaraní* (1857) and *Iracema* are colourful portraits of the native people. More recent writers include **José Lins do Rêgo**, whose novel about life on a plantation, *O Menino do Engenho* (1932), translated as *Plantation Boy*, is a typical exploration of Brazilian country ways; and **Jorge Amado**, who achieved particular success in America, with novels such as *Dona Flor e seus dois Maridos*, (Dona Flor and her two Husbands, 1966). He also wrote extensively about the black traditions of the Nordeste – the north-east of Brazil. **Clarice Lispector** is well-known for her strange novels involving allegorical images, such as in *A Paixão segundo GH* (Passion according to GH, 1964), *A Hora da Estrela* (The Hour of the Star), and *Laços de Família* (Family Ties).

From the African countries a number of quality writers have emerged, who have painted scenes of life in the harsh reality of poor, war-torn African colonies, carefully observing the actions and personalities of the natives living in those conditions, their white (Portuguese) colonizers, and those who did deals with them in order to maintain a certain standard of living. Of the many you could choose from, **Luís Honwana** is one of the best. His book of short stories set in Mozambique, *Nós matamos o Cão-Tinhoso* (We killed Mangy Dog and other stories) is a perspicacious exploration of local country life. **Lina Magaia** writes about the brutality of everyday life with the directness of a field reporter. Others, whose writing is available in English, include **Mayombe Pepetela**, **José Luandino Vieira**, and **Mia Couto**.

What are the Portuguese reading now?

Reading books is not a strength of the Portuguese in comparison with the rest of the world. Decades of fighting against illiteracy have led to low numbers of books being read. In 1999, approximately 25% of the population said they read books as part of their leisure time. However, of these, three-quarters had only read between one and five books over the previous twelve-month period. It seems that the TV is still winning in the entertainment stakes (see Chapter 11). Despite this, apart from the more recent writers listed above, crime novels (*ficção policial*) are very popular (both home-grown and translated) in addition to a new wave of modern writers and poets experimenting in style and content, including the journalist and traveller Manuela Gonzaga, Ana Gusmão, the agronomist José Riço Direitinho, and the philosophy teacher Pedro Paixão.

The top ten books sold in 2000 were:

1 *Harry Potter e a Pedra Filosofal*, J.K. Rowling

2 *Dom Afonso Henriques*, Diogo Freitas do Amaral (biography)

3 *Harry Potter e a Câmara de Segredos*, J.K. Rowling

4 *Não há coincidências*, Margarida Rebelo Pinto (novel)

5 *Harry Potter e o Cálice de Fogo*, J.K. Rowling

6 *Socialmente Correcto*, Paula Bobone (novel)

7 *O Demónio e a Senhorita Prym*, Paulo Coelho (mystical novel)

8 *O Sentimento de Si*, António Damásio

9 *Sei Lá*, Margarida Rebelo Pinto (novel)

10 *Harry Potter e o Prisioneiro de Ascaban*, J.K. Rowling

Source: Livrarias Bertrand

It seems there is no escaping the global phenomenon of Harry Potter!

Some starter ideas for Portuguese books – in Portuguese or translation:

Os Lusíadas (The Lusiads), Camões – various translations available
A Peregrinação (The Peregrination), Fernão Mendes Pinto
Amor de Perdição, Camilo Castelo Branco
Anything by Eça de Queirós (many in translation)
Contos das Montanhas (Tales from the Mountains), Miguel Torga
Ballada da Praia dos Cães (Ballad of Dogs Beach), José Cardoso Pires
Anything in translation by José Saramago
Portuguese African writers in the Heinemann African Writers series
The Alchemist and *The 5th Mountain*, Paulo Coelho (Brazilian)

See also next page.

GLOSSARY

a literatura *literature*
escrever *to write*
o livro *book*
ler *to read*
estudar *to study*
o poema *poem*
a poesia *poetry*
o autor/a autora *author*
o escritor/a escritora *writer*
o romance *novel*
as personagens *characters*
a acção *action*
a editora *publisher*
gosto/ não gosto (de) *I like/don't like*
os estudos literários *literary studies*

o teatro *theatre*
o actor/ a actriz *actor/actress*
a peça/obra *play, work*
o/a novelista *novelist*
o conto *short story*
a ficção *fiction*
a tradução *translation*
evocar *to evoke*
citar *to quote*
a novela *short novel*
a ideia *idea*
publicar *to publish*
o prémio *prize*
prefiro *I prefer*
a feira do livro *book fair*

Taking it further

Suggested reading

Babel Guide – Portugal, Brazil, Africa fiction in translation. Reviews and translated snippets, Boulevard Books, 1995

Passport to Portugal – stories and extracts in English from Portuguese and African writers, Passport/ Serpent's tail books, 1994

'Aspects of Portugal' and **'From the Portuguese'** – two series from the publishers Carcanet Press, including literary background, and works in translation. Include:

– Luís de Camões, *Epic and Lyric*, Ed. L.C.Taylor
– *113 Galician-Portuguese Troubadour Poems*, Richard Zenith
– *Fernando Pessoa, A Centenary Pessoa*, Ed. Eugénio Lisboa
– Translations of Eça de Queirós, Miguel Torga and Clarice Lispector

Carcanet Press Ltd, 402–406 Corn Exchange, Manchester M4 3BY. Tel: 0161-834 8730

Portuguese Studies, English-language journal devoted to the literature, culture and history of Portugal, Brazil and Africa. Ed. Helder Macedo. MHRA, King's College London, Strand, London WC2R 2LS

História da Literatura Portuguesa, Ed. A.J. Saraiva/ Oscar Lopes, Porto editora, 1996, and *Iniciação na literatura Portuguesa* (Beginner's guide)

CD-ROMs of Gil Vicente's *Auto da Barca do Inferno* and *Auto da India* – contact: Grant & Cutler booksellers, 55–57 Great Marlborough Street, London W1V 2AY. Tel: 020 7734 2012/8766 and see website below

The Last Kabbalist of Lisbon, Richard Zimler, Arcadia Books, 1998 – murder mystery and highlights a tragic part of Jewish history

Portuguese Literature, A.F.G. Bell, Oxford, 1992

A Small Death in Lisbon, Robert Wilson, HarperCollins, 2000

JL – Jornal de Letras, Artes e Ideais – newspaper on books and the arts, on sale in Portugal

Places to visit

Casa Fernando Pessoa (Pessoa's house, now a museum to his life and work), Rua Coelha da Rocha 16-18, Lisbon 1250
A Brasileira café – Chiado district of the Bairro Alto in Lisbon
Municipal Library – Palácio Galveias, Biblioteca Municipal Central, Campo Pequeno, 1000 Lisboa

Websites

Grant & Cutler – stockists of Portuguese books in the UK: **www.grant-c.demon.co.uk**
For information on writers: **www.portugal-info.net**
Portuguese National Library: **www.biblioteca-nacional.pt**
Publishers Lidel – Edições Técnicas Lda: **www.lidel.pt**
Publishers Porto Editora: **www.portoeditora.pt**
Literature, language and writers:
www.portugalnet.pt/cultura/letras/letras/html
Portuguese pages linked to Amazon site: **www.mediabooks.com**

4 ART AND ARCHITECTURE

Há uma tendência portuguesa para o lírico, enquanto a espanhola é para o dramático. (There is a Portuguese leaning towards the poetic (sentimental), while the Spanish is towards the dramatic) – João Cutileiro, sculptor

As with its great literary heritage, Portugal can also boast a wealth of artistic, architectural, and creative treasures, despite so few of its artists having had recognition on the global art scene through the ages. However, like many of its European neighbours, it can trace its earliest works back to prehistory, can thank its early invaders for initially influencing architecture in particular, and has a long line of painters and sculptors who have produced works in the styles of the times to match some of the most well-known names from France, Spain, Italy and Holland. In addition, there are many features uncommon in the rest of Europe, such as the distinctive Manueline style of the navigational era, and the cultural heritage of *azulejos*, which it shares with Spain, but whose range is far wider. It can also boast excellent contemporary 'plastic artists' – a whole host of them working in various media – painting, sculpture and photography, as well as modern designers working with the latest IT gadgetry, and avant-garde and sometimes controversial architects. So, Portugal's artistic heritage has a longevity not surpassed by other European 'giants' of artistic tradition, a legacy of artistic treasures upheld and promoted by various organizations.

Historical background

Prehistoric influences

The oldest monuments date back to 2300–1500 BC, and you can still find collections of these dolmens, or *antas* – funeral constructions, made from stone, with vertical elements and a horizontal 'lid' – all around Portugal, although many through the ages were broken up. Menhirs and cromelechs also abound– these are not architectural constructions, but mainly stone circles.

In the 6th century BC there was an appearance in architecture of *castros/crastos*, and *citânias* – fortified outcrops, with houses, streets, and walls of stone. Most are found north of the Douro and into Galicia, or in the south, such as Castro Marim in the Algarve. One example which has been well-preserved as a visitor and research centre is Citânia de Briteiros in the Minho. Houses were circular or rectangular, and sometimes near the house were two round claw-like sections. These dwellings were known as 'crab' houses – *casas de caranguejo*. It is likely their shape was to form protection from the elements, but their mystery still remains to be truly uncovered. Some walls measured 3–5 metres thick.

In the caves at Gruta do Escoural, near Évora, paintings have been discovered, mainly of Palaeolithic horses, with the same also scattered around on ruins, e.g. on lintels. Not all pictures show just animal or human forms, some are quite abstract. In the north around the river Douro, there is an abundance of engravings and sculptures at the now-protected Foz Côa site (see Chapter 12), and especially up in Trás-os-Montes. Sculpture, especially by the time of the castros, included figureheads of soldiers and animals – boar and pigs especially.

Roman connections

After the Romans had occupied the territory, they left behind many examples of architecture, sadly mostly in ruins now. Most still standing are bridges, castles and aqueducts, some still functioning such as the one at Chaves. Conímbriga, in the north was a great and beautiful city, as seen today in its remains. You can wander round the preserved site and marvel at the mosaics, one of the Romans' most important legacies in Portugal, and get a feel for life in Roman times. Wonderful mosaics can also be found at Milreu in the Algarve. In Évora, *o templo da Diana* (Diana's Temple) is a perfect example of Corinthian columns, and although it later fell into ignominious use as a slaughterhouse, it is now protected under a UNESCO order, along with the rest of the city.

The Visigoths – time of the barbarian invasions

A great many buildings were wiped out and destroyed in wars, so there is not much evidence remaining from this time. However, the Basilicas of Idanha-a-Velha and Balsemão, and the Church of Santo Amaro in Beja are good examples of early architecture. Although the Arabs had occupied the south, there is little evidence left of their architecture, apart from in the style of household dwellings (see p.97), but the old mosque – *antiga mesquita*, which is now the Christian Church of Mértola, is a testament to their influence. There are no known examples of Visigoth or *Muçulmano* (Arab) paintings, but Mozarabic (Christians who lived under Arab rule) influence in miniatures or book illustrations is seen in a beautiful book of birds, *Livro das Aves*, dating from the 12th century, kept on show in the National Archives, the Torre do Tombo in Lisbon.

The later appearance of Romanesque-style architecture, towards the end of the 11th century, encouraged a spate of cathedral building, such as at Braga, Porto, Coimbra, Lamego, Lisbon, and Évora, as well as other smaller churches, mostly monastic, in the north of the country. The oldest Romanesque church is the Sé of Braga, constructed during 1096–1109, but the old Sé of Lisbon (*c*1160) is the best conserved. In the north the development of religious Orders increased the construction of many convent-style buildings. Churches were very simple, with décor mainly on doorways, windows, and roof supports. Columns were decorated with vegetables or geometrical designs. In terms of civil architecture, one brilliant example stands out – the Domus Municipalis in Bragança. Its main room has a pentagonal lay-out, and windows with round arches. Under the military much was constructed – castles, watch towers etc., although many were modified later, especially from the time of Dom Dinis. You will find interesting castles in Melgaço, Guimarães, and Tomar.

Great Portuguese artists

The 12th to the 14th centuries

The paintings which survive from the 12th century are mainly frescoes in churches. During the following century, though, the most brilliant contribution to the art world were painted panels or altarpieces, known as *retábulos*, with Flemish influence and contribution. The most outstanding is the polyptych (multi-scene) of St Vincent in the Museu Nacional de Arte Antiga in Lisbon. There have been many debates over the years as to the real painter, the panels were even lost for a couple of centuries, and one eminent scholar committed suicide over the debate. However, it is generally considered to be the work of a favourite royal painter, **Nuno Gonçalves**. Many characters of the time feature in the panels – royalty, cavalry, clergy, fishermen, in a series of images across a number of panels. There are echoes of tapestry design, with attention to minute detail. It is considered a monumental work which reads like an epic poem of King Afonso's dreams of conquest and of the magical world of Henrique's navigations.

The sculpture of the time was very decorative, worked in wood and stone, with many images of the Virgin, and fitting in with the decorative Gothic style of architecture, newly arrived from France (see p.85). What had been stern in Romanesque statues became more humanized, with images of the Infant Christ, and clothing following the shape of the bodies. However, the most important feature of 14th- and 15th-century sculpture were tombs, often carved with representations of their inhabitants. Aragon, in Spain, was then the most important centre for sculpture on the peninsula, and Portugal took much inspiration from there. The two tombs of crowning glory of 14th-century Portuguese style are those of Pedro I and Inês de Castro in Alcobaça. Created by an unknown sculptor, the tombs are full of symbols, and facing each other, as Pedro had wished, so that even in death they could look upon each other. In around 1433 the double tomb at Batalha of João I and Philippa of Lancaster was produced. The crowned couple lie open-eyed and hand in hand. These were possibly worked on by English sculptors as the double tomb was rare in Iberia, but more common in England.

From the 15th to the 16th century

By the end of the 15th century Portugal had become a major importer of Flemish painting, with panels or *tábuas*, of famous artists from Bruges and Antwerp finding their way into many churches. Unfortunately, many were later lost in the earthquake of 1755, but Dutch artists who came to Portugal influenced the native painters, and the creation of a 'Luso-Flemish' style came about. This embraced portraits as much as landscape and maritime scenes, with a real love of colour and a sense of monumentality and romanticism.

Francisco Henriques (Frans Hendricks), artist of this mixed culture	He painted the panels in the Cathedral in Évora. Whilst the earlier worked sections are Flemish instyle, those completed later (around 1510)show a more monumental scale in the figures, denser material and brighter colour

During this era painters tended to work in groups, or teams, all contributing to the work in question, so that often it is difficult to determine the true author of works from this time. The two main groups operating at this time were based in Lisbon and Viseu, where specialized painters would be employed on different bits of a picture, such as hands, faces, buildings, etc. The person who handed over the finished product was not necessarily the sole author of it, though he probably put the finishing touches to it.

Vasco Fernandes (c1475–1540)	From the Viseu school. Known as *Grão Vasco* (Great Vasco). Superb examples include: *St Peter* and *The Adoration of the Magi*

Renaissance and Mannerism

The Renaissance period (generally the 14th to 16th centuries) was a time of the revival of classical (Latin and Greek) features, not only in art and architecture, but in literature too, and led by Italy. It was the Italians, also, who created Mannerist art – a portrayal of contorted figures. The art of the 16th century was based almost exclusively on portrait painting, and features many likenesses of royalty and aristocrats. Colour schemes were very much akin to the great Venetian painters of the time – a superb example of which is the portrait of a young gentleman, *O Jovem Cavalheiro*, in the Museu de Arte Antiga in Lisbon.

Unknown artist	One of the most notable works is a portrait of an old lady, often incorrectly designated as that of a nun, wearing a coral rosary. It remains one of the best examples of this genre of art
Cristovão de Morais	Attributed with the magnificent portrait of *Dom Sebastião* – probably one of the most outstanding of all Portuguese Mannerism paintings

Sculpture, which had manifested itself mostly in the magnificent tomb carvings, began to show signs of change during the 16th century. Woodwork started to make an appearance in church décor, but stonework began to move away from the carvings based on maritime themes, so prevalent during the Manueline period (see p.86). The best example is the main entrance to the Jerónimos Monastery in Belém, by the French sculptor Nicolau de Chanterenne. In the 1530s, sculptors from the Alentejo region around Évora came to the fore, working with the perfectly clear marble of the area.

Baroque and Rococo

The Baroque style was exemplified by a tendency towards exuberance and extravagance. Rococo, seen more in architecture and furniture design, was very ornamental, with lots of scrollwork and shell motifs. In contrast with the architecture and sculpture of the 17th and 18th centuries, Portuguese painting was not really that rich or brilliant in quality. However, in the second quarter of the 17th century emerged an artist whose work remained unrivalled right up to the end of the following century.

Domingos Vieira, known as **O Escuro** (the dark one) so as not to confuse him with a contemporary of the same name, lived from 1600–78	He earned his nickname from the darkness of the costumes worn in the Portuguese court at that time, which were translated onto canvas in the magnificent portraits he executed. In his pictures he contrasts this darkness with small touches of light, such as the whites of the eyes or the shine on a weapon, and some of his best work depicts the nobles Dom Miguel de Almeida and Dona Maria Antónia de Melo

Josefa de Ayala (1630–84), one of the most famous women artists in Portuguese history. Originally from Seville, she made her life in the picturesque town of Óbidos, and became known as **Josefa de Óbidos**	Her pictures breathe a feminine softness, with tones of rose and lightness. They include altarpieces, religious pictures for convents and still life paintings. Her pictures depict feast days, religious devotion, presentation of fruit and food, and displays of flowers,but also of the Holy Family. Examples of her work include: *Flagellated Christ wearing a Red Mantle, Still Life: Sweets and Earthenware, Agnus Dei*

Sculpture still flourished during this era, although the penchant now tended towards work in wood and clay. Wood (*madeira*) in particular was sought after as decoration for the elaborate Baroque church altars. The Monastery of Alcobaça is home to some excellent clay sculpting, including the statues in the Sanctuary, the monumental figures of angels and saints at the high altar, and the panel depicting the death of Saint Bernard, although this has almost disintegrated due to the humidity and effects of fungi. Joaquim Machado de Castro (1731–1822) is considered the most talented sculptor of the period. His masterpiece is his statue of Dom José I in 'Black Horse Square' (*Terreiro do Paço*) in Lisbon. Fountains, staircases and steps were all highly decorated at this time, and the art of clay figures (*figuras de barro*) spread, emanating from a lively centre in Aveiro.

Romanticism and Naturalism

The Romantic painters preferred grandeur and passion, irregular beauty to finish and proportion.

Francisco Vieira, '**O Portuense'** (1765–1805)	Travelled considerably around Europe, and in particular picked up the English style of portrait painting, which was less dark and brooding than elsewhere. His best works are probably his landscapes, e.g. *A Fuga de Margarida de Anjou.*
Domingos António de Sequeira (1768–1837)	He also spent time abroad, mostly in Rome to where he returned as a voluntary exile after an agitated lifestyle often on the wrong side of the police! The Italian influence is seen in his works, such as *Alegoria da Casa Pia*, and his later work reflected an elegance and play with light and colour reminiscent of Goya
The Swiss painter, **Roquemont**	Introduced the painting of customs to Portugal

With the European movement towards Naturalism, liberty of expression and the total upholding of nature, so in Portugal there emerged artists who enthusiastically embraced the change. António Carvalho da Silva Porto, and João Marques da Silva Oliveira both became Academy teachers and encouraged artistic activities and meetings. They were both instrumental in the launch of public magazines such as *Arte Portuguesa* and *Crónica Ilustrada*, and organized numerous exhibitions. The effects were long-lasting, and the press was opened up to new artistic ideas.

The 20th century

Early in the century a number of artists went to Paris, some of them staying there indefinitely, but others returned in 1910 when the government stopped paying out grants to Portuguese painters there. World War I persuaded others to go home too, and all of them brought back the seeds for artistic revolution which would bear fruit in the coming decades. With the creation in Lisbon of the

National Museum of Contemporary Art, new ideas were sparked by an exhibition of painters who had resided in France, and in 1915, the setting up of the bohemian Lisbon group '*Orfeu*', offered an ideal forum for the spread of fantastic innovations – in art, literature and philosophy – and also for the spread of wild activities, mainly centred around the Brasileira café-bar in the Chiado district of Lisbon. In true bohemian style, a number of these innovative young artists were to die before their time, including the painter Amadeo de Souza-Cardoso, whose works represented a move towards Cubism. Although he died in 1918, his works were not shown in public until 1959.

José Malhôa (1855–1933)	He created paintings of huge social expression, vivid scenes of ordinary people, such as the *Drunkards*
Almada Negreiros (1893–1970), daring artist whose written work, as well as his art and criticism of society set him apart as a real agitator of Portuguese intellectual activity for 50 years	A great designer – you can see his frescoes on the maritime stations in Lisbon, and later in life he appeared frequently on TV
Abel Manta	His portraits (based on Impressionism, then influenced by Cezanne) contain a psychological depth rarely found in modern Portuguese painting
Carlos Botelho	His works portray the passion of Lisbon in clear, sharp colours
Maria Helena Vieira da Silva	In 1933 she held her first individual exhibition in Paris
António Pedro (1909–66)	A surrealist from the Azores, and colleague of similar artist, António da Costa

The 1943 group, *Os Independentes do Porto*, was the first to show any real leaning towards abstract art. The most important individual to emerge from the period is **Júlio Resende**. His works show solid use of colour and structure, are thoughtful yet sentimental, sometimes violent, and he is seen as one of the most representative of recent Portuguese painters.

Throughout this same period, sculptors had a similar slow start, but soon, exponents such as Francisco Franco (1885–1955) were to marry the traditional with the new and he offered his contemporaries a regained sense of classical monumentality, as seen for example in his statue of Dom João IV in Vila Viçosa in 1940.

Modern art

Contemporary artists include some who have really achieved international fame:

Paula Rego (1935–) has lived and painted in London since the 1960s. Was married to the artist Victor Willing. First artist in residence at the National Gallery in London	Paints larger-than-life characters, many of them women, in natural, everyday poses, or erotically charged environments, with glimpses of silk and lace undergarments. Great expression of gestures and atmosphere. Her latest works are based on the novel *The Sin of Father Amaro* by Eça de Queirós (see p. 63).
Fernanda Seles	Pays homage to strong women who refuse to stand in the shadow of men. Their strength, sadness and tragedy in their fight for liberty are especially visible in the picture *Frida Kalo*, which is reminiscent of Picasso's blue period; it even has a symbolic bull
António Sem	Interested in theatre and dramatic art, particularly in the picture *A Personagem*. He has also created a series of pictures of dancers based on Orff's *Carmina Burana*. He was invited to produce the *azulejo* panels for the station in Sintra, which became a study on the theme of dance

Helena Almeida	A great breaker of rules and enormous imaginative spirit, who works with a combination of drawing, photography, posing and painting. She puts herself into scenarios but sometimes you can only see bits of her, and her face is frequently hidden. *Dentro de mim* (1998) (Inside me) is an enigmatic example. She has exhibited worldwide, and her work is held in collections in Tokyo and Madrid, among other places
Graça Morais	Drawings, pastels and canvases depict life cycles of the harsh Trás-os-Montes region, despite the fact that she lives and paints in Lisbon. She pays testimony to the people who work the land , but more so to the women, as in *Delmina* (1996), a huge image of a woman standing against a background of work in the fields. The image features on the cover of Miguel Torga's book in translation *The Creation of the World*. Created tile decorations for the metro station in Moscow – the first foreign artist to do so. Her soul, though, is in her mountainous village of Vieiro. 'For me, painting the people of my village is almost a calling'
António Jorge Gonçalves	A modern graphic artist and illustrator, whose recent work *Down the Tube* (1998) showed more than 500 drawings of people on the London Underground

In sculpture, the best by any measure is **João Cutileiro**, whose exquisite marble sculptures feature nude women in languid poses. These are sought after as 'must-haves' by the rich and famous, particularly as statues for gardens and ponds. He uses beautiful light marble from the Alentejo quarries, and has been an artistic household name for many years.

Portuguese architecture

Here is a brief glossary of interesting Portuguese architectural terms you may come across in guide books:

Alfarge	Decoration of Arabic origin, used in Portugal and Spain, especially on wooden roofs
Castreja	Relates to the remains of buildings from the time of the castro settlements
Flamejante/ Chamejante	From the Gothic period, when ornamentation followed an undulating pattern, reminiscent of flames
Janelão	Window of huge proportions, usually above a door or entrance, purely for lighting
Mudejar	Decorative style originating from the Moors, across the whole peninsula
Pelourinho	Pillory – often found in Portuguese town squares
Políptico	Series of painted panels often decorating altars, ordered in a particular sequence
Retábulo	Decorative panels (as above), the best examples being in carved wood, decorated in gold
Serliano	Inspired by the famous architect Sebastião Sérlio (1475–1552)
Tríptico	Series of three decorative panels

The Gothic period

The Gothic style, which originated in France, is exemplified by pointed arches, lighter and taller buildings, flying buttresses, and, in Portugal in particular, the light filtering through windows became a metaphor for Divine Light. The Abbey of Alcobaça is a fine example, as one of the most serene and elegant churches in Portugal. It is very tall, with its interior bathed in light. Construction began in 1178, and it was finally consecrated in 1222. One of the more interesting parts of it is the kitchen used by the monks; you will find a small stream running through the middle of it, from where the cooks would grab fresh fish – not even today's celebrity chefs can boast food quite as fresh as that! Batalha monastery – built after the Aljubarrota battle, from 1388 onwards – is another fine building of this time. Its construction was in three stages, the first up to 1438, led by a figure called Huguet, nationality unknown. There was some influence of English Gothic elegance (similar to York and Canterbury), but the Portuguese Gothic church was characterized by large, airy cloisters (*claustros*). The second stage lasted until 1481, in which a second cloister was built, and finally the third stage corresponded to the Manueline period and style, culminating in the arcade of the incomplete chapels and the Royal Cloister. Batalha was to have an influence on churches such as the Cathedral at Guarda and Church of Carmo in Lisbon (later affected by the earthquake in 1755).

Manueline period

At the end of the Gothic period, and thanks to the maritime discoveries, Portugal suddenly became rich and in closer contact with the outside world. The truly great style to emerge at this time was named Manueline architecture, after the King, Dom Manuel (1495–1521). Apart from the space and light found in many of the buildings at this time, the distinctly Portuguese *Manuelino* constructions were decorated with carvings of maritime themes, such as twisted ropes around windows and doorways, naturalist forms, some of them almost grotesque, and the royal coat of arms. Four main architects worked at this time, one of them French, the others being Mateus Fernandes, and the Arruda brothers, Diogo and Francisco. Ironically, the most

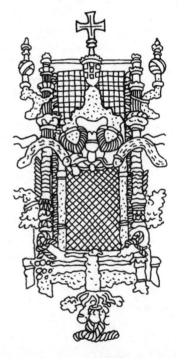

Manuelino window at the Convent of Christ, Tomar

original and notable example in Europe was undertaken by the Frenchman Boitaca; the Mosteiro dos Jerónimos in Belém in Lisbon. The construction was ordered as a pantheon to Dom Manuel's family in 1497, but work only started in 1502. Later Boitaca switched to work on the Batalha construction. The Arruda brothers are known especially for the famous window at the Convent of Christ in Tomar. Other worthy examples of buildings in this style are the Torre de Belém (1515–20) – the jewel of Portuguese military architecture – the aqueduct in Elvas, the Palace in Sintra and the beautiful castle in Évora-Monte.

Renaissance

Renaissance influences came late to Portugal, with Greco-Roman columns and pillars only appearing towards the second quarter of the 16th century, whereas in Italy it had been in full swing as far back as the 15th century. The first real work in this style dates to around 1533, when João de Castilho created the balcony over the entrance of the *Capelas Imperfeitas* (unfinished chapels) in Batalha. Under the patronage of Dom João III, a number of artists were sent to study in Italy, including Francisco de Holanda, who spent the years from 1538 to 1541 there, hob-nobbing with well-known painters such as Michelangelo. Holanda's work on his return to Portugal shows a strong Italian influence, in such buildings as the Church of Conceição in Tomar. In 1571 Holanda was to complain about the lack of great palaces such as those he had seen in Rome and Florence. The Palácio de Bacalhoa in Azeitão was subsequently built in a very Italianate style. The main Portuguese features of this style were balconies overlooking aisles in churches and lateral chapels, and church entrances beneath large windows, surrounded by pillars, often resembling the layout of the altar. Afonso Álvares and the great Manuel Pires constructed the most original church in this style – the Igreja do Espírito Santo in Évora. Built for the Jesuits in 1567–74, its greatest innovation was the incorporation of one single large aisle to enable the maximum number of people to see the high altar and hear the prayers at one time. It was adopted in nearly all Jesuit churches thereafter.

Baroque and Rococo

In some European Catholic countries it was almost impossible to define the strict difference between Baroque and Rococo architecture, which dominated up to the 18th century, and this was the case in Portugal. It was only with the arrival of huge reserves of gold from Brazil during the reign of Dom João V that the highly decorative style took hold. This décor, and a departure from the very regular, circular layout hitherto found in Portuguese churches, to the creation of octagonal and hexagonal designs, gave rise to some interesting constructions. Two of the oldest are the Chapel of Santo Amaro, in Lisbon, which contains magnificent *azulejo* tiles (see p.91), and the hexagonal Chapel of Nossa Senhora das Areias in Aveiro. Probably the most interesting example is the Church of Santa Engrácia, also in the capital. Its lay-out is that of a Greek cross, of huge proportions, and the wealth of marble inside emphasized by the play of light on it, give it a noteworthy monumentality. It took many years to finish, and indeed has only been properly completed in recent times. When the Portuguese wish to convey the feeling that a job will take forever, they refer to the *'Obras de Santa Engrácia'* – the work-in-progress of the church building!

Another mammoth project instigated by João was the monastery-palace at Mafra. Its construction was begun as the result of a vow by João in return for an heir, and he brought in the Italianized German architect Ludovice (Ludwig). The first stone was laid in 1717 and the church blessed in 1730. However, it kept on growing, worked on by a force of some 52,000 men, and in the end it could house 300 monks! The story surrounding its construction forms the backdrop to Saramago's famous novel *Memorial do Convento*. The palace houses a wonderful library of leather-bound, gold-embossed books, including a first edition of the *Lusiads*.

Return to the classics

The Portuguese rather took to the Rococo style, and even when Lisbon was rebuilt after the earthquake in 1755, on a grid basis of modern principles (called *Estilo Pombalino* after its creator Pombal), there was still a connection with previous styles. It was

only from about the late 1780s that a new style emerged, that of
neo-classicism, or a return to classical tendencies, led by the
architect José da Costa e Silva. He was responsible for the beautiful
São Carlos Theatre in Lisbon, modelled on the same one in Naples,
with a façade inspired by the Milan Escala. In 1802 he also started
work on the reconstruction of the Royal Palace in Ajuda, which had
been housing the court within a wooden building since the
earthquake. The work took until 1860, but even then was never
properly finished. Two more great examples in Lisbon are the
National Theatre Dona Maria II (1842–6) and the Paços do
Concelho, which houses many governmental departments
(1867–75). Two English architects also made their mark at this
time: William Elsden, a military engineer, who built the annexes at
Coimbra university, and John Carr, a York designer responsible for
the Saint Anthony Hospital in Oporto. In the north of Portugal
Carlos Amarante (1748–1815), another military engineer, was
most prolific, his work including the beautiful Church of Bom
Jesus do Monte in Braga.

Romanticism

The 19th century gave rise to the Romantic style, one of the
principal representatives being the Palácio da Pena in Sintra. Under
the German military architect Baron de Eschwege, the strange
conglomeration of styles began to take shape in 1839. To some
critics, its mixture of Moorish, Manueline, and medieval styles
results in a piece of bizarre architectural baggage – it is certainly
fascinating to behold. Other buildings treated to Arabic and
oriental-type decoration include the façade to the Rossio station in
Lisbon and the bullring at Campo Pequeno, also in the capital.
Built in 1892, it is a direct copy of the one in Madrid. In Sintra the
British influence of James Knowles was once more felt at the
Quinta de Monserrate, and across the country the novelty of using
iron was indulged in, resulting in numerous elaborate gates and
fancy window decoration on large private residences.

20th-century work

In the first few years of the 20th century there was no really new
artistic movement as there was elsewhere in Europe, and amid the

social and political instability ensuing from the establishment of the Republic, the first decade was simply a continuation of previous work. There was a fleeting influence of Art Nouveau, but really only in floral decorations and worked iron and *azulejos*, and on some façades such as the Galeria de Paris in Oporto. Portugal was evidently lacking a Gaudi or Victor Horta. Raul Lino tentatively tried to re-Lusify the art of construction using modern techniques. A good example is the Casa dos Patudos in Alpiarca, which is decorative and picturesque and set well into its surroundings. Other architects attempted to be more daring and try out forms more in vogue elsewhere. But generally, this was an era of renovation of public buildings and the rapid urban expansion of the capital, something to which we return at the end of the century, with preparations for the Expo in 1998.

Modern architecture

There has been much innovative design in Portugal over the last couple of decades, some of which has been controversial, as is the case with a number of designs by Tomás Tavira. He was responsible for the huge office block and shopping complex *Amoreiras* in Lisbon, in the 1980s, all dark glass and pastel colours. Among other works, one of my favourites is his design for one of the banks, which looks like a guitar from the outside. Portuguese architects can certainly compete with the very best from around the world. You only have to have been familiar with Lisbon over the last few years to see the restorations going on and the exciting new designs – the capital is coping well with a marriage of old and new, although not everyone agrees on the outcome. The Expo site, constructed for the world exhibition in 1998, was breathtaking, with expanded and modernized underground stations, and amazing works including the biggest oceanarium in Europe, which has remained a permanent fixture. In Oporto, the award-winning architect Álvaro Siza has worked on the recently opened Serralves Museum of Contemporary Art, hailed as a rival to Bilbao's Guggenheim.

Azulejos

You cannot get very far in Portugal without noticing the ubiquitous blue and white tiles adorning the fronts of buildings, interiors of churches and railway stations; in fact, everywhere you look you will spot decorative tiles covering either small areas such as surroundings of doors, or as extensive panels depicting scenes from the past. Although decorative tiles can also be seen in Spain, both countries having experienced early Arabic influences (*azulejo* > Arabic *al zulaicha* or *zuleija*, meaning ceramic mosaic), the breadth of range in Portugal is far greater, and it was here that the use of the *azulejo* assumed a particular national tradition.

The earliest decorative tiles date back to around the end of the 15th century, Moorish in origin and imported from Seville, but by the second half of the 16th century, production really took off in Portugal. Influences came initially from Italy and the Flemish ceramists, but with Portugal's voyages of discovery came new ideas from the East (e.g. the colours blue and white from Chinese pottery before the Dutch potteries of Delft adopted them), including exotic themes from India. Tile panels were used to great effect to cover wide areas of the walls of religious buildings, and as such fulfilled a dual purpose of being both part of the architectural design as well as decorative in their own right.

Great tile painters of the 18th century include António Pereira and António and Policarpo Oliveira Bernardes – a father and son team. Baroque complexity and expressive pictorial style were the order of the day, and with wealth flowing in from the gold in Brazil, designs reflected sumptuousness in elaborateness and grandeur. Later, the use of further colours was added, particularly in the figurative panels, although the 'pure' *azulejo* is a monochrome blue and white. The prime colours in the polychromatic designs are cobalt blue, yellow, white and purple. In the 19th century, more homes began to be decorated with panels, and today it is one of the most original features of residential areas in Portugal. Also at this time the 'Everyman' figure of Zé Povinho (Joe Public) was created by the prolific and talented caricaturist and ceramist Rafael Bordalo Pinheiro (1846–1905). During the 20th century, Jorge Colaço decorated the Royal Place at Buçaco, creating a real narrative style of panel – his works can be found in many places, as can that of modern tile artists such as Carlos Botelho, Querubim Lapa and Maria Keil. Lisbon is home to the wonderful Azulejo Museum, in the cloister of the convent of Madre Deus. You can also visit traditional tile factories to see the process first-hand: one of these is the Fábrica de Santa'Ana in Lisbon.

Magnificent examples of azulejos can be found at:

Oporto – São Bento railway station, walls covered with panels

Lisbon – Palácio do Marquês da Fronteira – impressive collection

Almansil (Algarve) – Loulé, St Lawrence church, tiles by Policarpo, 1730

Beja – Convent of the Conception – best collection of Mudejar *azulejos* from the 17th century on

Barcelos – Church of our Lord of the Cross, blue and white tiles from 1730

Aveiro – Church of the Misericórdia – tiles from Lisbon workshops from 1630

Public buildings

There are many examples of interesting and beautiful architecture throughout Portugal, far too many to list here, but here are a few for starters. Guide books such as the wonderfully visual Dorling Kindersley contain more ideas about what to visit whilst you are there.

Pousadas

Pousadas are the equivalent of the Spanish *paradors* – state-run hotels located in sumptuous surroundings. In Portugal, many of these three- and four-star establishments are found in converted castles, convents, manor houses, or in the middle of areas of natural beauty, such as the Pousada da Ria, which overlooks the lagoon in Aveiro. Some have been purpose-built in more modern times and are not as atmospheric. One of the best is the Pousada dos Loios in Évora. A former convent, the nuns' cells form the now far-from-stark guest-rooms. In low season the prices are not beyond many people's reach, and *Enatur* at the Portuguese Tourist Office can provide a guide to the 40 or so pousadas in operation.

Theatres (*teatros*)

The National Theatre (*Teatro Nacional D. Maria II*) is based in the Praça do Rossio in downtown Lisbon. Built in the 1840s, it dominates the square and is a popular spot for evening entertainment. Other grand buildings of note in Lisbon include the City Hall with its 18th-century pillory which used to be a sign of authority; the castle of São Jorge (Moorish/ medieval castle in the old Alfama area); and the National Pantheon housing the tombs of national heroes such as Prince Henry and Pedro Álvares Cabral. Oporto's theatres include the Rivoli Municipal, the Campo Alegre and São João National.

Stadia (*estádios*)

Not renowned for huge sporting events, Portugal can however boast the football grounds of the most popular teams (Benfica at Estádio da Luz, one of Europe's largest, Sporting Lisbon at Estádio José Alvalade in the capital, and Porto FC, who play at Estádio das Antas). World athletics events have been hosted in Lisbon on a number of occasions, including the 2001 World Indoor Championships. Of course, Estoril hosts Grand Prix car racing at its international track, and Portugal has the best range of quality golf courses on the international circuit (see also p.239).

Bullrings (*praças de touros*)

The largest are the 1892 ring Campo Pequeno in Lisbon, built of beautiful red brick in Moorish style, Cascais and Lagos. Many towns and smaller villages have a small-scale arena, often constructed just from wood. There are certainly fewer grand bullrings than in Spain, where bull fighting has a much stronger following (see p.133).

Bridges (*Pontes*)

There are many examples of Roman bridges still in use, such as the small *ponte romana* in Silves, in the Algarve, used as a pedestrian crossing of the river. Additionally, a fair number of Roman aqueducts still stand: impressive is the Amoreiras in Elvas, and the grand Águas Livres in Lisbon. The April 25th bridge in Lisbon, built in 1966, and originally named Ponte Salazar (renamed after the 1974 revolution), was inspired by the Golden Gate in San Francisco. At 2km long it was already the longest suspension bridge in Europe, but since then an even longer one has been built up-river by the Expo site. The Ponte Vasco da Gama measures 13km across a wide stretch of the river. Work is planned to carry across a railway track, like the one which crosses the Douro into Porto, designed by Eiffel. One of the most picturesque bridges, and one which appears in most scenic pictures of Portugal, is that at Amarante, in the Douro valley.

Monuments (*monumentos*)

There are monuments everywhere you glance in Portugal, not surprising for a nation so linked with its past glories. In Lisbon there is an abundance – the monument to the discoveries (Padrão dos Descobrimentos) on the riverfront in Belém; the structure looks like part of a ship jutting out into the river, the sides of which accommodate gigantic stone figures from the past. A short walk from here is also the Torre de Belém, the small 16th-century fortress from where the navigators set sail. In the city centre there are statues of Camões and Pombal among others, and a real favourite is the bronze life-size figure of the writer Fernando Pessoa outside the bohemian café, A Brasileira. People queue up to be photographed with it whilst enjoying a relaxing coffee. Worth mentioning too is the Eiffel-inspired Santa Justa lift, which carries you from the lower to the upper part of the city. Oporto has a fair share of grand monuments too, including the 75m tall Torre dos Clérigos, one of the tallest buildings in Portugal. Elsewhere you might care to visit the modern figure of Dom Sebastião in Lagos town centre, where too you can see the site of the first slave market in Europe, and in the north in Coimbra you can visit Portugal in miniature – *Portugal dos Pequeninos*, and there are many ancient granite statues such as the massive pig at Bragança.

Industrial and commercial architecture

Despite all the innovations in design which are working their way into Portuguese cities, such as those mentioned earlier, there still remain notable examples of older buildings constructed for business. On the southern bank of the Douro in Porto, at Vila Nova de Gaia, are the original port wine lodges, or *caves*, the vast majority open for tours (but you won't manage all of them in one day!). In Mateus, near Vila Real in the Douro you will find the elegant manor house featured on the label of the Mateus Rosé wine bottles. Called *Solar* (manor house), the estate is still part of the wine industry, and you can visit its splendid 18th-century buildings as well as try the produce. In Oporto the stockmarket is housed in the lavish Palácio da Bolsa, built in 1842, and including the beautiful Arabian Room.

Private dwellings

So, where do the Portuguese live? A typical Portuguese town will usually have a busy town centre (*o centro*), with most people living in apartments, many of these in old buildings (modern blocks feature mostly towards the suburbs), and often with shops and cafés on the ground floor, which give a community feel to the area. Some of those in the middle of Lisbon date back 100 years or more, and although austere-looking in many cases, with large, heavy entrance doors, they are fascinating inside, as many have old, wood-panelled lifts (which invariably break down, leaving bags of shopping to be heaved up many flights of stairs). Once inside a Portuguese apartment, you will often find the older generations particularly living in a very traditional environment, with heavy, dark furniture, wooden floors, and dim lighting (in many cases made even darker by the addition of shutters on the windows). Elsewhere in the town, families may live in detached houses, some with gardens, or in smaller, traditional towns and villages, rows of small cottages. But styles of housing differ remarkably from north to south, as a result of building materials and the prevailing climatic conditions.

The north

Granite is the dominant material in the colder, wetter regions of the north. With thick walls, and slate or schist roofs, there is little chance of the rain and wind penetrating them in the Winter. Even the chimneys are small, or in some cases do not exist at all, smoke escaping through tiny vents in the roof. Houses are usually built on two storeys, with a staircase on the outside to the upper floor, to allow extra space inside. Traditionally, animals have been kept downstairs, as well as using the ground floor for storage. Although these villages appear sombre and overbearing, with their shades of grey, this style of housing is born out of practicality and in fact the houses are not unduly uncomfortable to live in. Elsewhere in the north you will come across houses with a distinct northern European feel to them, with verandas and brighter colours. Many of them will have been styled on German and Swiss housing, as that is to where many of the original inhabitants emigrated in

search of work (see also p.248). It is rare nowadays to find traditional thatched houses, but what you might discover are *espigueiros*, or small constructions for storing wheat, built on columns to keep the mice away.

In the coastal towns around Aveiro and the Costa de Prata, long lines of brightly coloured wooden houses adorn the seafronts. Painted in bright tones, with stripes, the houses stand on raised platforms to avoid flooding. Originally, the bright colours helped fishermen identify their own houses during the sea mists, but nowadays people are merely maintaining the colourful tradition as a feature. Other coastal regions, including some down towards the south, still accommodate a few traditional windmills (*moinhos*) – something you will also see in the Azores. In Madeira you can see the quaint triangular houses, made in a basic way from a couple of A-shaped wooden frames, with a thatch covering. The exteriors are painted cheerful colours, and they originally date from the 16th century.

The south

Throughout the country areas of the great plains in Portugal, typical houses are usually made from clay, and painted with whitewash to reflect the sun. They are often decorated with a blue trim, or can be yellow or pink. The blue is reputed to be 'Tunisian blue' and is said to have been a tradition introduced by the Moors when they dominated the region. They certainly look very striking on a bright Summer's day. Of course, Summer brings searing heat to the area, and the low-built houses, with small windows are an attempt to keep the temperature down. It is not uncommon to find the windows shuttered – in Summer it does help against the heat, and Winter (which is equally harsh here) helps to maintain heat inside. It is rare to find central heating (*aquecimento central*) in Portuguese houses, so these external devices are crucial when it comes to heat control.

In the Algarve particularly, the whiteness hits you – a legacy of the Arabs, as too are the flat roofs here, designed for drying fruits on, but more frequently used these days for storage and sunbathing. One feature you can hardly miss in the Algarve (if you look upwards) are the beautifully intricate chimney pots (*chaminés*).

Whitewashed, in a host of delicate designs, they are seen everywhere, even on modern houses without a real need for them. Another thing to strike you about the roofs here, as all over Portugal, are the roofing tiles – typically the terracotta, tubular tile, known as *telha de canudo*. Of course, the other huge architectural phenomenona on the Algarve are the proliferation of high-rise hotels on the coast, and also the growing number of villa parks, mostly the homes of the foreign residents who prefer to live on all-services-included complexes at a price than to opt for the traditional Portuguese home.

GLOSSARY

a arte *art*
as belas artes *fine arts*
pintar *to paint*
o quadro *picture*
o retrato *portrait*
a paisagem *landscape*
a cor *colour*
o estilo *style*
imitar *to imitate*
influenciar *to influence*
o romanticismo *Romanticism*
o realismo *Realism*
a pintura *painting (general)*
a tela *canvas (painting)*
a exposição *exhibition*

o escultor *sculptor*
a escultura *sculpture*
a estátua *statue*
a arquitectura *architecture*
o arquitecto *architect*
desenhar *to design*
romano *Roman*
árabe *Arab*
a Renascença *the Renaissance*
gotico *Gothic*
barroco *Baroque*
moderno *modern*
a cerâmica *ceramics, pottery*
a natureza morta *still life*
o movimento *movement*

Taking it further

Suggested reading

Portugal (with Madeira and the Azores), and Lisbon Eyewitness Travel Guides, Dorling Kindersley, 1997. Beautifully illustrated with detailed information on aspects of art and architecture, and places to visit

The Art of Portugal 1500–1800, Robert C. Smith, Meredith Press, New York, 1968

Portuguese 20th-century Artists: a biographical dictionary, M.Tannock, Phillimore, 1978

Places to visit/ information

There are many, many places all over Portugal, listed in good guide books.

Most museums, galleries, monuments, palaces, etc., charge a small entrance fee (some are free), but the majority close on Mondays. Check at the local tourist office before you set out.

Observatório das Actividades Culturais – a new institute overseeing the arts and culture in Portugal, with reports available on different art sectors. Rua Garrett, 80-1 C, 1200 Lisbon. Tel: 321-98 79

Portuguese Art of the 20th century on CD-ROM: published by the Contemporary Art Institute at the Ministry of Culture in Lisbon. Contact Porto Editora on Tel: 2-608 83 / **www.portoeditora.pt**

Museu de Grão Vasco, Largo da Sé, Viseu. Tel: 032-422 049

Museu do Chiado (new home of the National Museum of Contemporary Art), Rua Serpa Pinto 4–6, Lisbon

Gulbenkian Foundation – private collection and modern art collection, Avenida de Berna, Lisbon

Museu Rafael Bordalo Pinheiro, Campo Grande 382, 1700 Lisbon

Websites

Portuguese Tourist Office, **www.portugalinsite.pt**
Ministry of Culture, **www.min-cultura.pt**
Pousadas, **www.pousadas.pt**
Art /architecture, **www.citi.pt/cultura/index**
　www.portugal-info.net
Portuguese museums, **www.ipmuseus.pt**

5 | MUSIC AND DANCE

Pergunto ao vento que passa, notícias do meu país
E o vento cala a desgraça, O vento nada me diz.
(I ask the wind that is passing, for news of my country
And the wind quietens the misfortune, the wind tells me nothing)
'Trova do vento que passa' – Manuel Alegre, protest song

The Portuguese are enthusiasts when it comes to music – be it classical concerts at lavish halls in Lisbon and Oporto, regional folkloric groups, the sombre (and not-so sombre) *fado*, or indeed music of any of the modern groups singing out from radios on the beaches and in cafés. It seems that, wherever you go in the country, you will find music of some form or other, either participated in or simply listened to, which captures a range of moods and fulfils different functions: enjoyment of a village event; quiet contemplation and reflection; music to inspire revolutionaries; mass of frenzied dance – and many more besides. What is certain is that there has been music in Portugal since the very earliest times, and that over time various musical artists have achieved international acclaim across a range of styles. Yet when asked to name any well-known Portuguese singers or musicians, despite the fact that a good number of singers and groups now give concerts overseas, it appears that Portuguese music is still largely unknown – possibly in part because the concerts rarely emanate beyond the metropolis centres of the world, where the artists are more often than not singing to the already converted. Nevertheless, Portuguese music is widely obtainable from music stores (specialist ones more so), and there are some good ideas in this chapter to get you started. So, let's get wired for sound!

Early music

The discovery in the last decade of the oldest documented secular music proves that music was a solid part of Portuguese culture from the times of Dom Dinis (13th century). As we saw on p.54, Dinis the poet king was very much involved in the troubadour tradition which in Portugal manifested itself through the various *cantigas*. It is also known that the travelling minstrels entertained at court not only with drama and verse, but carried with them medieval instruments such as the lyre, lute and later the zither, of which the modern Portuguese guitar is a descendant. Up until this recent discovery in the Portuguese national archives, only one other manuscript with musical notation had been known of – with fragments of poetry by another troubadour, Martin Codax. After this tremendous find in the Torre do Tombo, in 1994, a CD was recorded of the *cantigas*, by medieval musicologist Paul Hillier, with collaborators, so that modern audiences (both native and non-native Portuguese) can appreciate the fine lyrics and historical sound of medieval poetry. Two later composers of Portuguese Renaissance music have also recently found their way onto CD: **Estêvão Lopes Morago** (*c*1575–after 1630), and **Diogo Dias Melgás** (1638–1700), whose music reflects the sacred choral style of Europe at this time.

Classical and opera

Whilst Portugal cannot boast a Beethoven, Mozart or Tchaikovsky it seems, nonetheless, that its composers of the 18th and 19th centuries worked at the very highest levels, composing and performing for some of the world's aristocracy.

João Sousa de Carvalho (1745–98)

It also appears, almost mythically, that a recent chance discovery has unearthed a real classical heavyweight in the composer João Sousa de Carvalho. Recent findings of his opera scores have led London-based conductor and composer David Chernaik to set about publishing, performing and recording one of his operas – the magnificent *L'amore industrioso*, written in Naples in 1769, at the end of a stay there by Carvalho.

For Mozart aficionados, this may well be a new source of interest, as there is a great similarity in style and story line with *The Marriage of Figaro*. David Chernaik wonders about the possibility that the then 12-year-old Mozart may well have met Carvalho (then 23) in Naples, while the Portuguese was working on his opera. Undoubtedly, Mozart's subsequent work bears some semblance to the earlier style. The story of *l'amore industrioso* is a familiar theme in operas of the time – aristocratic decline paralleled by the rise of the bourgeoisie. With servants who outwit their masters, a love story akin to many of Shakespearean quality, and a series of sub-plots and misunderstandings, the opera is truly a classic. The first modern non-Portuguese production of it took place in Holland Park in London in July 2000, and it has subsequently been recorded for the first time. For opera lovers the world over, this has to be a wonderful opportunity to discover another talented and entertaining composer.

Other classical composers and performers of note include the following:

Domingos Bontempo (1771–1842)

He studied in Lisbon and Paris, but when the French invaded Portugal he fled to London where he achieved enormous success. He returned to Portugal, to the court of Dom João VI, and in 1822 founded the first Royal Philharmonic Society. He died leaving a vast collection of compositions for piano, cantatas, orchestra and a Mass named *Missa de Requiem*, considered to be his best work.

Luísa Todi (1753–1833)

A very popular opera singer who married the Italian violinist Francisco Todi. She had a rich voice and performed mostly in royal courts although she made many public performances. She was invited to perform before Frederick II of Prussia and Catherine II of Russia. After many years touring Europe she eventually settled in Lisbon in 1811. The invasion of Napoleon's troops into her beloved country affected her to such an extent that her health deteriorated and she died shortly afterwards.

José Vianna da Mota (1868–1946)

Born in the Cape Verde Islands, he studied piano in the Royal Conservatory in Lisbon, later moving to Berlin to study at the famous Schawenka School. A public performance there in 1887 brought him instant fame. He soon began a tour of the European centres of culture giving performances in Denmark, Finland, Russia and England. He performed in New York in 1886. He kept his home in Berlin until the start of World War I, when he moved to Geneva, giving lessons at the Geneva Conservatory. In 1917 he returned to Portugal and joined with his protégé, the composer Luís de Freitas Branco, to present concerts and recitals until his death.

Luís de Freitas Branco (1890–1955)

Coming from a renowned musical family, he quickly rose to fame with recognition from the respected Vianna da Mota. His compositions were initially classical. Later he went on to write musical scores that educated and encouraged his audience to enjoy romantic music. He is remembered as the instrumental influence in the creation and development of modern music in Portugal. He left behind a large collection of compositions and many appreciated musical public performances in the memories of his audience.

Today's performers

Portugal is represented on the world stage by artists such as the pianist Maria João Pires, and the highly talented and respected Artur Pizarro, pianist and currently Professor of Piano at the Guildhall School of Music and Drama in London. Since his career started at the age of 13, he has taken the world by storm and performed with some of the great conductors and orchestras. Recordings of his work are available on the Collins Classic label. The Portuguese composer Emmanuel Nunes (1941–) was awarded the International Music Council/UNESCO prize in 2000 for his contribution to the enrichment of music and furthering of world peace. He follows an illustrious line of winners, including Shostakovitch, Bernstein, and the Cape Verdean singer Cesária Évora (see later). The Portuguese Orchestra and Choir, based at the

National Theatre, and the Northern Orchestra (Orquestra do Norte) in Oporto, regularly perform both inside and outside the country.

Often performers collaborate on interesting projects which also gain international recognition, such as the sensational 'Rhythm of Tides'(*Por mares do Imaginário*) which premiered in 1996 in London. Based on the lyrics of Camões and contemporary poet-politician Manuel Alegre, the resulting music is a superb performance by its collaborators – among others, popular singers Paulo de Carvalho and Maria João Silveira, and the kora player Sadjo Djolô from Guinea-Bissau, with backing by an Anglo-Portuguese orchestra.

We cannot finish this first section without reference to the National Anthem, *A Portuguesa*. The anthem was originally composed in 1891 by Alfredo Keil, with words by Henrique Lopes de Mendonça, and adopted as the *Hino Nacional* (National Anthem) in 1910, after the establishment of the republic. It recalls the past glorious deeds of the Portuguese people and urges the people of today to continue the work of making their country glorious.

Heróis do mar, nobre Povo,	Heroes of the sea, noble People
Nação valente, imortal	Brave, immortal Nation
Levantai hoje de novo	Lift again today
O esplendor de Portugal!	The splendour of Portugal!
Entre as brumas da memória	Amid the mists of memory
Ó Pátria, sente-se a voz	O Homeland, the voice is felt
Dos teus egrégios avós	of your illustrious forbears
Que há-de guiar-te à vitória!	Which will guide you to victory!
Às armas! Às armas!	To arms! To arms!
Sobre a terra, sobre o mar!	On land, on sea!
Às armas! Às armas! Pela Pátria lutar!	To arms! To arms! Fight for the homeland!
Contra os canhões marchar, marchar!	March, march against the cannons!

Venues

Lisbon has concert venues of the very highest calibre. The Teatro Nacional de São Carlos was built in 1792–5 to replace an earlier opera house destroyed in the earthquake of 1755. It plays to packed houses, the opera season running roughly from September to June with other performances, in particular ballet, showing at other times. The Fundação Calouste Gulbenkian also provides an arena for concerts and dance and the annual Lisbon Jazz Festival as does the modern (controversial) venue the Centro Cultural de Belém. Large concerts of modern bands are usually played at the Coliseu dos Recreios in the city centre.

In Oporto concerts are held at the Palácio de Cristal, which was built in 1861 based on London's Crystal Palace. In the 1950s the original structure was replaced by a sports pavilion (Pavilhão Rosa Mota), which now hosts the musical events. Open-air concerts can be heard in the surrounding gardens. A Casa da Música opened as a venue during the 2001 European Capital of Culture activities.

Most towns throughout Portugal have cultural centres of some description for live events.

O fado

Fado is to the Portuguese what flamenco is to the Spanish – an emotional searching of the depths of the soul (*a alma*), for feelings that tear at the very strings of one's existence, and it is of no surprise that the two forms of music may share some of their origins. The word *fado* in Portuguese means 'fate' (from the Latin *fatum*), and it is the lament for what fate has bestowed on people that runs through many of the songs; most fado songs speak of nostalgia for times or people past, or lost loves. However, fado also encompasses happier emotions and throughout its history has offered an outlet for writers and musicians to channel any number of feelings. But it is, perhaps, the deeply felt *saudade*, that typically Portuguese of emotions, the yearning for the past, that is portrayed predominantly in the fado of Lisbon.

The haunting sound of fado, heard in small *casas de fado* (fado houses) and *retiros* across Lisbon (see p.110), is sung by one *fadista*, who can be male or female, though more often than not it is the women who have made their mark in this genre. Often dressed in black, or muted colours, with a shawl, the *fadista* is accompanied by the Portuguese guitar – *a guitarra* (see p.110) and an acoustic guitar (*uma viola*), two distinct sounds, which, when combined, lend the song the gravity (or indeed jollity) it demands.

Origins

So, where did fado originate? Unfortunately, no one seems to have a definitive answer, and it looks as if the historical debate on this will continue unresolved. The main theories suggest a few possibilities, all of which seem perfectly plausible. Some people believe that the glancing similarity with Spanish flamenco suggests an Arabic connection, giving fado a history back to the 12th century; certainly traces of it have been found from this era. Although flamenco has a much wilder feel to it, both contain that emotion from the depths, which may have its roots in the nostalgic fatalism present in the culture of the Moors, who occupied Iberia for so long. Even the great singer Amália called it *uma queixa* (a lament or complaint).

Others think the music may have been a channel for the feelings of the explorers during the great discoveries. On long voyages into unknown worlds and so far from home, the navigators may well have expressed the sorrow of their situation, homesickness, through songs of nostalgia. A third camp believe there are links with Brazil, and the African slaves with the heavy beat of their own music, *lundum*. In the 19th century, many nobles fled Portugal to Brazil as a haven during the Napoleonic invasions. Whilst there they would have encountered the sounds of the slaves, whose grief and nostalgia were expressed in soul-searching music. These songs may well have travelled back to the capital later on.

So, take your pick and join the debate! All sides have an air of romantic nostalgia in keeping with the style of music, so any one of them will do. As Amália herself once said – 'each of you choose as you wish'. Whatever the true origin, what is very clear is that it was from the poor, depressed areas of 19th-century Lisbon that fado emerged as the voice of the common people. Initially sung in working-class bars and cafés, particularly around the dreary docklands (which incidentally, and somewhat ironically, have now been transformed into the trendiest nightspots in the capital), fado was the unifying lament of the *povo* (the people). However, a chance encounter between one of its singers, Maria Severa, and an aristocrat who fell in love with her and introduced her to Lisbon's more elegant salons, set fado on the road to wider acclaim, and ultimately to international recognition. Severa (1810–38) achieved notoriety in her short life through a series of scandals, was the subject of the first sound film made in Portugal in 1931 (*A Severa*), and was truly the first great diva of fado. Others who followed in her footsteps included greats such as Cesária and Maria Victória, and through them, and at the time through the touching lyrics of Alfredo Duarte (1891–1982), fado became the true sound of Lisbon.

Amália

However, it was through the voice of Amália da Piedade Rebordão Rodrigues, or simply Amália as she became known, that fado finally found a worldwide audience. Born in 1920, of a poor family in the docklands of Lisbon, the young Amália would listen to the sad songs as she sold fruit on the quayside. A melancholy girl, her fascination for the mystical sounds led her to sing at local celebrations and in the nearby taverns, against her family's wishes, who despite their own lowly background did not consider fado the domain of decent people. But her mournful voice and striking dark looks quickly led to appearances in travelling shows and a career began which was to last 60 years, and earn her the accolades 'Queen of Fado' and 'Voice of Portugal'. During the 1950s and 1960s she electrified audiences worldwide, and her show at the Olympia in Paris catapulted fado into the souls of thousands around the world. She thrived under the dictator Salazar, and so too did the

genre, leading many of the revolutionaries to reject it. Amália continued performing and recording right up to her last days, and upon her death in 1999 three days of official mourning were announced. The woman who had once said 'I am naturally sad', became an icon for the Portuguese soul – a Portuguese Edith Piaf, and luckily she lived long enough to witness a revival in the popularity of fado, with a new generation of fadistas emerging in recent years. Portugal mourned her parting, but the voice of Portugal survives in her music – much of which has been rerecorded and released on CD, in her many imitators, and in the inspiration she gave to those who have embraced fado with the same respect and enthusiasm.

Many singers of fado have provided solid renditions of the music. One of the most traditional female singers of recent years has been Argentina Santos, who also owns one of the most famous fado houses in Lisbon – A Parreirinha de Alfama. Santos (now in her seventies) still gives concerts around the world.

Of the more well-known male singers of the last couple of decades, the beautiful tones of Carlos do Carmo stand out.

One beautifully haunting song tells of a flower-selling fadista, Júlia Florista, wandering the streets of bohemian Lisbon with an air of the common people about her:

A Júlia Florista	Julia the flower-seller
Boémia fadista	bohemian fadista
Diz a tradição	so says tradition
Foi nesta Lisboa	it was in this Lisbon
Figura de proa	figurehead
Da nossa canção	of our songs
Figura bizarra	this strange figure
Que ao som da guitarra	who through the sound of the guitar
O fado viveu	lived the fado
Vendia flores	she used to sell flowers
Mas os seus amores	but her loved ones
Jamais os vendeu.	she never sold.

Younger pretenders to the throne include the talented Ana Sofia Varela, at 24 already a rising star; the handsome Camané, who delighted audiences at the Expo 98 concerts in Lisbon; Dulce

Pontes, already acclaimed a new Amália and the performer Mísia (Susana Maria Alfonso de Aguiar), whose experimental style, combining the old tradition with new instrumentals and the poems of writers such as Pessoa, has led to huge worldwide sales of her latest CD – *Garras dos Sentidos* (Claws of the Heart). But perhaps one of the leading bands of younger exponents of the genre is the multi-talented group Madredeus. Whilst some critics believe the appeal of fado rarely travels outside the realms of the Portuguese-speaking world, this band is proving a huge hit around the world. The group has been performing since the late 1980s, and their beautiful blend of classical music, fado and atmosphere led to their music featuring as the backdrop to the 1994 film *Lisbon Story*, in which they also played a part. Hailed by those who know of them as 'Europe's best-kept musical secret', Madredeus are well-worth listening to.

The fado of Coimbra

Whilst the fado of Lisbon can be both melancholy or more upbeat, in Coimbra there is a very different version, traditionally sung by the male undergraduates of the old university. The Coimbra fado is a serenade, and often tells of unrequited love, or is filled with sad nostalgia. Originally sung under the balconies of the girls who were the objects of their attention, nowadays Coimbra students, dressed in their traditional black capes, will serenade diners in local restaurants to earn money for their studies. The music and sound of the instruments are very different from their Lisbon counterpart.

Fado etiquette

If you want to listen to traditional fado, there are a number of casas de fado in Lisbon, particularly in the old districts of Bairro Alto and Alfama (the former Moorish quarters skirting the castle). Some places are listed in tour guides, as most of them are also eating establishments. Some seem more glitzy than others, drawing in the tourists with a 'show', but many are authentic and give a good taste of the tradition. Some of the most genuine places are hidden down dark cobbled alleys, or *becos* and you may only be aware of them on recommendation, or by chance stumbling upon them. This is particularly so in the labyrinthine Alfama district.

Some of the small bars, or *retiros*, appear to be simply someone's front room transformed into an atmospheric location with a couple of tables and chairs, and the locals dropping in for a glass of wine and a trip into melancholia. At some places, members of the 'audience' can step up and sing themselves if the muse descends. This is the real *povo* in voice – although the quality can plummet sometimes, but when you're that steeped in nostalgia (and alcohol) what do a few flat notes matter?

Wherever you do find your fado (and some areas outside Lisbon also have performers), it is vitally important to adhere to 'house rules':

As soon as the lights go dim and the performers are ready to commence, you must put down your cutlery, even if your meal is in front of you; it is considered extremely bad form to carry on eating, to talk or make any noise whilst the song is being performed. When a singer is considered particularly good (and often you can tell by how well they hold the quiver of notes in the penultimate line of the song) you will hear people shout '*Ó Fadista*', as a sign of respect. The set of songs will not last too long, so you can resume eating once the lights come back on.

Visitors to Portugal who have heard fado often say they either love it or loathe it. I suspect those who hate it haven't heard it in the right ambience, or perhaps haven't understood its importance to the Portuguese soul. As it is so widely available these days, I recommend you have a listen to some and see if it makes your senses tingle as mine do when I hear it.

Portuguese guitar

The *guitarra portuguesa*, as opposed to the *viola* or Spanish (acoustic) guitar, has striking characteristics. It is pear-shaped and has double, metal strings, and there is a distinctive technique for playing it – plucking, or *dedilho*. It is distantly related to the zither of Renaissance Europe, but combines the simplicity of a basic stringed instrument with a refined tuning system allegedly invented by an 18th-century watchmaker. The metallic-like resonation from the plucking gives it a unique sound, one that is so distinctive in fado music.

But it is not just in fado that you will hear it. The *guitarra* is an instrument that has been present in rural communities, as well as making its way into concert halls. Leading exponents of it, like Pedro Cabral, who not only plays it but also makes guitars, believe it forms a 'bridge between the popular and classical'. It is present in many of the protest songs of the 1970s (see p.114), as well as providing enjoyment as an instrument in its own right. Portugal's leading *guitarrista* is Carlos Paredes, who has taken the opportunity on many occasions to publicize the sound abroad.

Another stringed instrument you will hear and see a lot is the *cavaquinho*, which is a baby guitar rather like a ukelele. Its main exponent is Júlio Pereira.

Traditional folk music

Wherever you go in Portugal you will always find a local town or village wind band. Whether a small band, or on a grander scale, these local enthusiasts often play in the parks on summer Sunday afternoons, and always offer entertainment at local festivals and events such as saints' days or village dances. And at these village dos, it is lovely to see a real age range of locals coming out to dance – their enjoyment crossing generations and gender gaps. These are vital human events in Portugal, and it is wonderful to be part of something that has sadly long since passed in many of our own communities. However, the real traditional music of the regions comes in the form of *música folclórica* and is performed in competitions by groups known as *ranchos folclóricos*. The music – most often sung, but also played with a range of instruments – accompanies the folk dances of the regions, performed in the open air in towns and villages, at festivals, and in annual competitions such as the one held in the Algarve. The Azorean group Brigada Vitor Jara is a popular and well-known folk-music band.

PORTUGUESE LANGUAGE, LIFE & CULTURE

Typical instruments

Bagpipes (*a gaita*) – particularly in the North, demonstrating the Celtic links in that part of Portugal

Small pipe, or flageolet, (*a flauta doce*) played like the recorder

Home-made pipes (*a flauta de Pã*) pan-pipes – often played by shepherds, made from boxwood

Drums – the largest called *a zé pereira* (= pear-tree, possibly what it was originally made from)

Large goat-skin drum (*bombo*) – with a deep sound

Adufe – square hand drum or tambourine

Voice – often high-pitched

Folk dances vary from one region to another – some have links with fishing rituals, others with the land. Many are danced in a circle, others with pairs in lines. None are designed for a mere individual (as Spanish flamenco), but some are danced by two people, as in the challenging fandango. As with so many dances across Europe with a folk influence, a great number have been engendered via pagan customs, and are danced on certain festival dates. Although it is predominantly the older generations who remember all the steps, increasingly youngsters are carrying on these old traditions, and actively participate in the *ranchos*. If you happen to be present at a dance, you'll be dragged up to join in too!

A selection of regional dances

Coastal dances – one typical dance is that of the *cantarinhas* – glass jars filled with sand and decorated with flowers. Weighing about 8 pounds when full, the jars are balanced carefully on the heads of the girls, who weave intricate steps during a dance in the round.

The *Beiras* – many similar dances here are based in the round, and are performed by villagers in the streets. Most of them are done with the arms in the air, and clicking fingers. There are some ritual maypole dances too, mainly in villages near the Spanish border.

Lisbon area – the coastal towns have fisherfolk dances in the round, whereas up the Tagus valley towards the Ribatejo, dances feature the traditions of the cowboys (*campinos*). It is a sign of great skill to dance the fandango with a glass half full of wine balanced on the head – the best dancers will not spill a drop! Women traditionally wear wooden clogs to stamp out rhythms, or dance barefoot.

Alentejo – less renowned for dances than other regions, nevertheless Alentejanos participate in simple round dances, but tend not to move about so exuberantly.

Algarve – the regional dance is the *Corridinho* – a fast polka-like dance with pairs in the round. Other dances have their origins in Moorish traditional battle-dances, such as the *Dança dos Mouros*, performed in Pechão in September.

In many regions of Portugal ritual dances take place to celebrate traditions such as Midsummer, as in many other countries. Many of these have roots in pagan or Moorish celebrations, and all are lively and colourful. In the north you are likely to see familiar

Typical folk dress from the Minho, Northern Portugal

accessories such as wooden sticks, colourful scarves and ribbons, with dancing around maypoles. In Lisbon there is a spectacular sword dance, with the men piling on each other's shoulders, and in many regions the traditional giants, dwarfs, dragons and mummers of early pagan rituals are a feature.

Music of the revolution

During the 1970s, songs based on the *fado* of Coimbra, with its doleful laments and regrets, developed into ballads dealing with the current issues in a Portugal restricted under the prolonged dictatorship. Songs of social and political unease (*música de protesto e intervenção social*) were banned under the Caetano regime, but the protagonists of this new musical expression (and an expression of coveted liberation) were merely biding their time. Writers such as José Calvário, José Mário Branco and Sérgio Godinho expressed the hardships of living under the regime, especially for the people on the land, and the occupation of that land in the Alentejo in the months following the revolution. The most famous song of the time is one which was broadcast as a signal on Rádio Renascença at 12.25 a.m. on 25 April 1974, telling the armed forces to begin the revolution. They had previously heard a song called '*E depois do adeus*' (And after goodbye), performed by the popular singer Paulo de Carvalho, to warn them to take up their positions. '*Grândola, Vila Morena*', on the face of it, was just a song about an Alentejan village. Significantly, though, the Alentejo being the heartland of Communism in Portugal, gave the choice of this song a double-edged meaning. José Afonso's famous song is still a reminder of the day that was to bring freedom to the people:

Grândola vila morena	Grândola dark town
Terra da fraternidade	land of fraternity
O povo é quem mais ordena	it's the ordinary folk who make the decisions
Dentro de ti ó cidade.	within you, the city of Grândola.

After the revolution, many of these same performers carried forward their ideals into the emerging pop music of the time, and artists such as Paulo de Carvalho, Fausto and the Alentejo folk-ballad singer Vitorino are still drawing crowds at the Coliseu in Lisbon.

Modern music

Portuguese music today is an eclectic mix of the traditional, national sounds, with that influenced by American and British groups, and there is something for every taste. Fado-based songs are still very popular, from the remaining older stars, to the newcomers taking the genre forwards. Ballad singers have always been popular, and not just with the older generations. Paulo Gonzo is a modern lyrical singer, but there are many others. Interestingly enough, at the time of writing the best-selling CD in Portugal is a compilation of the best hits over the last 20 years of the singer Rui Veloso, whose music spanned from rock and roll, through ballads, and pop, to modern hits still making their mark with the younger aficionados. In the late 1990s a couple of his hits were top sellers in Portugal, and everywhere you went you could hear them on radio and in discos, with all the youngsters screaming out the accompanying words. Modern pop bands include Xutos e Pontapés, GNR, Rádio Macau and Delfins, who all produce rock-pop similar to that in the English-speaking world, and the pop group Santamaria representing what has become known as *música pimba*.

Heavy metal continues to thrive, encouraged by the enduring success of bands such as Nirvana and Bon Jovi. Portugal's own bands, the likes of Sirius and In Velvet Clouds produce pretty grim doom music. In 2001 UK and US music charts were playing tracks by the young Portuguese–Canadian singer Nelly Furtado, whose Latin-tinged hip-hop pop has become a real hit on both sides of the Atlantic. Portugal now has its own 'boy bands' playing to crowds of adoring girls. *Os Rapazes* (The Boys), Miguel and André, are one such duo flexing their Latin sex appeal. Music from Brazil and Africa is also extremely popular, with a number of good venues in the capital devoted to these rhythmic styles (see next section).

The top ten albums by Portuguese artists sold in 2000
Alma Mater by Rodrigo Leão
Onde o Tempo Faz a Curva by Rádio Macau
Post-Scriptum by Cristina Branco (modern fadista)
La Toilette des Etoiles by Belle Chase Hotel
Phados by Lula Pena
Música Exótica para Filmes, Rádio e TV by Cool Hipnoise
Canção para Titi by Carlos Paredes (Portuguese *guitarrista*)
Esta Coisa da Alma by Camané (modern fado singer)
Chorinho Feliz by Maria João/ Mário Laginha
Lupa by Sérgio Godinho

It is interesting to see that, despite the popularity of contemporary bands, the Portuguese music-buying public are still drawn to the likes of Carlos Paredes and Sérgio Godinho (of protest-song fame), as well as the two new fado stars. In the top ten chart for pop/rock, the most albums sold were by international artists, but in the general charts for compilations, or re-releases, Amália features three times, so even after her death, her music is still as popular as ever. Just over 38 per cent of the population say they regularly buy CDs, an increase of 12 per cent since 1996. In 1999 a total of 12 and a half million CDs were sold in Portugal.

Portuguese world music

Brazilian music in particular has recently been enjoying wider success around the world, as the craze of salsa, merengue and general Latin dance classes have caught the world by storm. Samba and lambada are the big rhythms from Brazil, along with the traditional bossa nova – nothing better for the hip-swinging, feet-shuffling devotees letting it all hang loose. Whatever you listen to which has come out of Brazil, you cannot fail to enjoy: from the early exponents of Bossa Nova such as António Carlos Jobim, Hector Villa Lobos, Astrud Gilberto and Vinicius de Moraes, to those who led the psychedelic counterculture of the 1960s, like

Caetano Veloso and Chico Buarque (still wowing audiences today), right up to the popular bands of today playing a mixture of pop and Latin sounds, including the wonderfully seductive rhythms of the black north-east of Brazil, in and around Bahia (Grupo Raça is a good example). Names to go for in a big way include: João Gilberto, Carlinhos Brown, Gilberto Gil, Milton Nascimento, João Bosco, Fagner, Ivan Lins (well-known in the States for his jazz compositions), and the romantic crooners Amado Batista and Roberto Carlos. Among female artists: Maria Bethania, whose current recording of her concert in São Paulo is being hailed as brilliant by the Portuguese music-buying public, Fafá de Belém, Simone, Gal Costa, and new singers making their mark in the past couple of years: Virgínia Rodrigues, Marisa Monte, Ana Carolina and Max de Castro.

From Africa you have catchy sounds with their origins in tribal and slave music – drums which thump out rhythms that tap into your feet so you just have to get up and dance. The music of the Angolan musician Bonga is popular and probably one of the best-loved musicians is the Cape Verdean Cesária Évora, whose concerts are a sell-out throughout the world. Her mixture of African and Cuban rhythms are electric.

GLOSSARY

a música *music*
o concerto *concert*
dançar *to dance*
o baile *dance, ball*
tocar um instrumento, música
  to play an instrument, music
a canção *song*
cantar *to sing*
interpretar *to perform, interpret*
a sala de concertos *concert hall*
escutar *to listen to*
a ópera *opera*
a melodia *melody*
o piano *piano*
adoro/ detesto *I adore/ hate*
o guitarrista *guitarist*

a sinfonia *symphony*
o movimento *movement*
o ritmo *rhythm, tempo*
a música de câmara *chamber music*
o/a músico/a *musician*
o/a cantor/a *singer*
o/a compositor/a *composer*
a orquestra *orchestra*
a música clássica *classical music*
inspirar *to inspire*
influenciar *to influence*
o estilo *style*
a voz *voice*
a guitarra *Portuguese guitar*
sou fã de... *I'm a fan of...*
a música pop/jazz *pop/jazz music*

Taking it further

Suggested reading

The New Oxford Companion to Music, OUP, Oxford, 1983

A History of the Portuguese Fado (book and CD), Paul Vernon, Ashgate Publishing Ltd, 1999

O que o povo canta em Portugal (What the People sing in Portugal), Jaime Cortesão, in Portuguese, Livros Horizonte, Lisbon, 1980

Danças Populares Portuguesas (in Portuguese), Tomaz Ribas, Instituto de Cultura e Língua Portuguesa, Lisbon, Biblioteca Breve No. 69, 1982

10 Dances from Portugal, N. and M. Allenby Jaffe, Folk Dance Enterprise, 1988

Opera in Portugal in the Eighteenth Century, M.C. de Brito, Cambridge, 1989

Information/places to visit

For information on all the main national and regional music festivals, contact the ICEP Portuguese Trade and Tourism Offices.
Annual International Music Festival, Algarve – April–June
Super Bock, Super Rock rock and pop festival, Lisbon and Oporto – February–March
Estoril Jazz Festival – July
In Portugal, musical events take place at various venues, including *Centros Culturais* – Cultural Centres. Local tourist offices have details.
Fado Archives recordings (Heritage label): Interstate Music, 20 Endwell Rd, Bexhill-on-Sea, East Sussex TN40 1EA, UK.
Fonoteca Municipal (music centre), Praça Duque de Saldanha, Edifício Monumental, Loja 17, 1050 Lisboa and
www.Eunet.pt/Fonoteca

Websites

Contemporary Portuguese Politics and History Research Centre (Dundee University), 25 April site has music of the revolution,

with snippets to listen to,
www.dundee.ac.uk/politics/cphrc/sections/anniversary/music menu.htm
Fado, **www.fe.up.pt/~fado/por/index-port.html**
www.amalia.com
Type in 'Portuguese music'or 'Música Portuguesa'to search for many more interesting sites.

Some suggestions to listen to

Any of the artists mentioned in the chapter – much of their music is now available outside Portugal, otherwise explore the music shops in Portugal.

The Rough Guide to Music: Brazil, CD compilation

The Rough Guide to Music: Portugal, CD

Por mares do Imaginário, CD, mentioned in this chapter. Grand Union Music Theatre Ltd, Freepost KE8735, London EC1B 1PE

Cantigas from the Court of Dom Dinis. Devotional, satirical, courtly medieval love songs, interpreted by Theatre of Voices. (Director Paul Hillier, recorded by Harmonia Mundi)

The CD, *Pro Cantione Antiqua* (from Hyperion Records Ltd.) features a selection of pieces by Lopes Morago and Dias Melgás in Latin, and featuring an organ, harp and dulcian. The piece entitled 'Lamentationes'by Melgás, is considered revolutionary

Holy Week at the Chapel of the Dukes of Bragança – A Capella Portuguesa, CD on Hyperion label

Antologia – latest album form Madredeus, on EMI

6 | TRADITIONS, FESTIVALS, CUSTOMS

Não deites foguetes antes da festa (Don't let off your fireworks before the party) – *Proverb*

The Portuguese have occasionally been accused of being dour in comparison with their often fiery neighbours but anyone who has attended one of the myriad festivals there would beg to differ: the Portuguese definitely know how to enjoy themselves, as they prove on numerous occasions throughout the year.

As befits a predominantly Catholic country, many of their celebrations are connected with the Church calendar year, but as a people so tied to the rural and coastal way of life, they also celebrate festivals of the land and sea. Religion and lifestyle sometimes come together, as in the blessing of fishing boats, but at other times festivals are more firmly steeped in Celtic and pagan customs. There are 13 official public holidays in Portugal, when the whole nation joins in both religious and secular celebrations of Holy Days and commemorations of important historical dates. Additionally, though, every region has its own calendar of local festivals and events, translating into a national list of hundreds, if not thousands of local festivities. Some are on a grander scale than others, such as the saints'celebrations of Lisbon and Oporto – St Anthony and St John respectively – and draw participants from far and near. Others, much smaller, such as the Festa de São Mateus in Elvas, may be celebrated by just local inhabitants.

Public holidays in Portugal

New Year	*Ano Novo*	1 January
Carnival	*Carnaval*	February/March
Easter	*Páscoa*	April
Liberty Day	*Dia da Liberdade*	25 April
Labour Day	*Dia do Trabalhador*	1 May
Corpus Christi	*Corpo de Deus*	June
Portugal Day	*O Dia de Portugal*	10 June
St Anthony's Day	*Santo António*	13 June (Lisbon)
St John's Day	*São João*	24 June (Oporto)
Assumption Day	*Assunção de Nossa Senhora*	15 August
Republic Day	*Implantação da República*	5 October
All Saints Day	*Dia de Todos os Santos*	1 November
Restoration of Independence Day	*Restauração da Independência*	1 December
Immaculate Conception	*Imaculada Conceição*	8 December
Christmas	*Natal*	25 December

Festivals

January/*Janeiro*

Janeiro faz o palheiro (Make your haystack in January)

Let's start with the festivities on 31 December. The Portuguese like to celebrate *a Passagem do Ano* – New Year's Eve, whether in small gatherings of family and friends, or at the lavish events in the trendy nightclubs of Lisbon, Oporto, the Algarve and Madeira. In the ex-patriot enclaves of tourist Algarve, New Year is celebrated in the bars in Northern European style, but in small villages around the country people often go to organized parties and dances at their local 'club'or community hall. Here you are likely to have the town band playing, or, more often now, a disco. But wherever the Portuguese may be, on the first stroke of *o Ano Novo* – New Year, everyone eats 12 raisins/sultanas (*passas*) and makes 12 wishes, to the accompaniment of champagne and lots of hugging – and fireworks too in many places. The celebrations continue until the early hours. *Feliz Ano Novo!*

On 6 January the Epiphany (*O Dia dos Reis Magos*) is welcomed with the baking (and eating) of the traditional *Bolo-Rei* (king's cake). This is a cake baked in the shape of a crown, with a hole in the middle, liberally topped with dried, glazed fruits. Custom has it that each cake should contain a lucky charm and a dried bean – with the recipient of the bean buying or making the cake the following year. The *Bolo-Rei* appears in bakeries and *pastelarias* at Christmas, as many eat it at the festive time too.

Bolo-Rei

February/*Fevereiro*

> *Fevereiro quente traz o diabo no ventre* (A hot February brings the devil in its belly)

Depending on the movements of the religious calendar, *Carnaval* (Carnival) may swing between February and March, but more often has fallen in February. Traditionally Carnival has been the few days (usually five) leading up to Shrove Tuesday (*Terça-feira Gorda*) and Ash Wednesday (*Quarta-feira de Cinzas*), during which everyone lets their hair down, and has a final merry fling before the serious and sombre time of Lent (*Quaresma*) and Easter. It was also the time to use up any excess food in the house before Lenten fasting began in earnest, hence the custom in many households of using up their eggs on Shrove Tuesday by making pancakes, or similar. The Portuguese will often make lavish meals for friends and family, and the typical sweet thing to eat are *sonhos* (dreams) – small doughnuts.

Carnival in Portugal cannot match the grand scale of its Brazilian cousins, whose competitions between the samba schools in Rio and São Paulo, reach loftier heights each year. However, the Portuguese come out to celebrate on the streets, with carnival parades in many towns – everyone joining in the fun in fantastic costumes, and on floats. Particularly exuberant festivities can be seen in Ovar, Funchal (Madeira) and Loulé (Algarve), where big statues of well-known personalities are paraded. Today's carnivals reflect much more of the Brazilian influence than previously.

São Valentim – 14 February although not a 'native'celebration, outside influences have brought hearts (*corações*), cards (*cartões*), and presents (*prendas*) to the Portuguese shops, and many young people follow the paths trodden before them around the world, and send cards to their loved ones (*namorados*).

March/*Março*

Março, três e quatro (March, three and four (the partridge nest should have three or four eggs in it by now))

Generally a quiet month, unless you participate in the Festival Intercéltico in Oporto. This is an annual music festival featuring sounds from all over the Iberian peninsula. Usually held at the end of March (sometimes the beginning of April).

Dia do Pai (Father's Day) is celebrated on the Feast of St Joseph, in the third week of the month, with cards and time spent within the family.

April/*Abril*

Abril, águas mil (In April, a thousand waters, i.e. April showers)

Easter (*a Páscoa*) is celebrated in religious ceremonies and processions all over Portugal, but the grandest parades are probably in the north, which is still the stronghold of the Catholic Church.

Braga, as the religious capital of Portugal, holds a solemn, yet lavish, torchlight procession, presided over by the leading authorities from the diocese. Although the Holy week (*Semana Santa*) processions in Spain (particularly Seville) are more famed for the cloaked and masked paraders, the parades in Portugal are just as serious, and bring a tingle to your spine if you're watching. It's the point in the church calendar when sacred statues are brought out and carried through the streets on floats, or on the shoulders of a number of men. In many towns a cross is carried by the priest from the church to every household, to be kissed by the parishioners.

Good Friday (*Sexta-feira Santa*) is spent in religious contemplation, and Easter Sunday (*Domingo de Páscoa*) usually involves a hearty lunch with the family. Typical food at this time might be:

cabrito assado com arroz no forno – roast kid with rice

ninhos de Páscoa (Easter nests) – a 'nest'of thinly cut chips surrounding a poached egg, on a bed of garlic-soaked mushrooms

bola de enchidos – a large cake filled with sausage and *chouriço*

folar – a kind of sweet cake (bread filled with apple and containing hard-boiled eggs on the top)

Plus many other cakes.

ovos de Páscoa too (Easter eggs)

Easter traditionally marks the start of the bull-fighting season (see p.133).

O 25 de Abril (25 April)

The date of the 1974 revolution is remembered, and celebrated as a public holiday, often with parades and fireworks.

May/*Maio*

Não há Maio sem trovões nem burro macho sem alforjões
(May without thunder is like a donkey without a load)

Dia da Mãe (Mother's Day) is the second Sunday in May, and whilst the Portuguese may not go overboard spending on gifts and lavish cards as in some countries, they do recognize the day, and the importance of the mother in the family by a family get-together or a meal out.

May is a busy month in the Portuguese church calendar, with many festivals celebrating religious occasions. The largest of these is the first of two annual pilgrimages, or *romarias* to Fátima (the other on 13 October) but other festivities take place elsewhere (see p.130). Fátima, in northern Portugal, is the place where the Virgin Mary is reported to have appeared to three shepherd children in 1917. The young Lúcia Santos and her cousins, Francisco and Jacinta Marta, claim to have seen an apparition of the Virgin on a holm-oak tree (*azinheira*) while out in the fields. They were told by her to return to the tree on the same date for the next six months. The villagers at first didn't believe the children, but by the sixth month (13 October), coinciding with an eclipse – taken to be a sign – thousands had gathered by the oak tree. Lúcia is the only one to have 'heard' the 'three secrets of Fátima', and so far (as she is the only survivor of the three children) she has revealed two – one of peace after World War I, one about Russia, and the third was supposed to be too devastating to tell. However, it was revealed in 2000 by the Pope: a pope would be shot (John Paul II). The secret was to have been told in 1960 but the Vatican did not reveal it for another 40 years, when the current Pope beatified Francisco and Jacinta.

The devoted who make the pilgrimage often travel great distances, even from outside Portugal, (as they do to Lourdes), many of them on their knees *de penitência* – in penance. The shrine at Fátima, a chapel and holm-oak, are approached down a slope from an impersonal car park, but even in the gathering heat of mid-May, people walk the pathway *ajoelhado* – on their knees. Thousands of candles burn on a continuous 'furnace'along with macabre waxen limbs – tokens of thanks for miracles (see also p.132).

June/*Junho*

Junho, foice em punho (In June a scythe in the hand)

Corpus Christi is celebrated around the country in various ways – one of the most entertaining is in Monção (Minho), where comic re-enactments of St George fighting the dragon take place.

St George, as in England, is Portugal's patron saint, although in England he is celebrated on 23 April. Adopted around the time the English came to help the Portuguese in their battles against the Moors and the Spanish, the Portuguese soldiers would charge into battle with the war-cry '*São Jorge*', against Spanish cries of '*Santiago*' (St James). São Tiago is also venerated in Portugal, with a religious order named after him – *A Ordem de São Tiago*.

On 10 June, Portuguese living all around the world celebrate their National Day – officially called *O Dia de Portugal*. It is commonly known as *O Dia de Camões e das Comunidades*, named after their most illustrious poet, Luís de Camões, and all Portuguese communities around the world. In the UK, there is a huge annual party in a major London park, an event mirrored in the many countries home to Portuguese emigrants, including Canada, the US and South Africa. In Portugal there are festivities everywhere, public readings of the Lusíadas with pomp and ceremony. And the President may confer *condecorações* on worthy people as the Queen does in Britain at New Year and on her birthday.

However, if you were looking for a reason to be in Portugal during this month, you would find no better than the festivals of the Saints Anthony, John, Peter and (to a lesser extent) Paul, commonly referred to as the '*Santos Populares*'. Although there are festivities all over Portugal, the two largest cities have particular renown. It is Lisbon that really goes to town over its own Saint, Anthony, on 13 June, but as it also enjoys the festival of the Saints Peter and Paul later on, you tend to find festivities overspilling and lasting a couple of weeks. St Anthony was born in Lisbon and made a Doctor of the Church in the 1940s. The Portuguese call him St Anthony of Lisbon, but outside Portugal he is known as St Anthony of Padua, which is where he died. Many of the districts of Lisbon (*bairros*), organize their own activities – street and square parties with trestle-tables laden with food, grilled chicken and sardines, wine, and with *fado* and dancing outside under trees decorated with lights and lanterns. Very typical, and in romantically magical locations, are those around the old Alfama district, near the castle. Anyone can go along – thousands do – and even 'outsiders'are welcomed. Some of the older generations complain that the true significance of the dates has given way to secular fun, and religious authorities try to maintain a certain dignity throughout, but no one can deny that the festivities belong firmly with the people '*o povo*'.

Similarly in Oporto, on 24 June, the feast of St John the Baptist is celebrated in conjunction with mid-Summer festivities. Here (as elsewhere in the country) people leap over small fires (*fogueiras*), making a wish if they land safely (and no doubt wishing they had not bothered if they don't!). One of the strange sights in Oporto is that of people hitting each other over the head with giant leeks (*alho-porro*), an ancient pagan fertility rite – in more recent times these have been replaced by large novelty plastic hammers (*martelos plásticos*). Another modern event introduced at this time is the annual race down the Douro river of the special boats that carry the barrels of wine to the port wine lodges – the *barcos rabelos*.

July/*Julho*

> *Julho, bons pró bandulho* (In July (the partridges) are good for the stomach)

Although not a national celebration, there are two events in July which attract much attention and attendance. One is the 'Festival of the Red Waistcoat' (*Festa do Colete Encarnado*), in Vila Franca de Xira in the Ribatejo. In the heart of the bull country, this festival, named after the traditional costumes of the horsemen, includes bull running and fighting. The other spectacle worth catching (although it only takes place every few years), is the 'Festival of Trays' (*Festa dos Tabuleiros*) in Tomar, also in the Ribatejo. In addition to typical activities of bull runs, music and dancing, the main event is a huge procession of young women carrying trays with decorated loaves on their heads.

August/*Agosto*

> *Em Agosto, sardinhas e mosto* (In August, sardines and wine-must)

The Festival of the Assumption is celebrated on 15 August with processions, including some in the north with giant statues, said to pre-date Christian belief. August also sees many festivals along the northern coastline connected with the blessing of the fishing fleets, or in honour of *Nossa Senhora da Agonia* (Our Lady of Anguish). The largest is in Viana do Castelo, where a religious procession precedes more secular entertainment and a blessing of the boats. In Peniche, *Nossa Senhora da Boa Viagem* (Our Lady of Good Journeys) is celebrated, with everyone carrying lighted candles to the harbour to wait for a statue of the Virgin arriving by boat. In the smaller fishing town of Póvoa de Varzim, near Oporto, the hardy fishermen let off fireworks from their boats, often throwing them into the air by hand! Prayer for the safe-keeping of the (*frotas*) fishing fleets, and a return of good stocks, has always been an important part of life in the fishing villages, and the annual celebrations reinforce the belief in the power of the Virgin's guidance, as well as being a time for everyone to enjoy themselves as a community.

September/*Setembro*

Setembro molhado, figo estragado (Wet September, ruined fig)

The grape harvests (*vindima*) begin up in the Douro valley, the Portuguese Grand Prix is held in Estoril, and the Algarve welcomes the many regional folklore groups to participate in the annual Folklore Festival. Elsewhere the pilgrimages continue, one of the most important being that in Lamego (Beira Alta), the *Romaria de Nossa Senhora dos Remédios* (Our Lady of Cures). The pilgrimage to the huge Baroque shrine in the mountains lasts three days, with torch-lit processions.

October/*Outubro*

Nevoeiro de Outubro queima o candeio (The October fog ruins the torch, i.e. the night-fishing lamp is of no use)

As the year starts to head towards Winter, festivals begin winding down. Vila Franca de Xira has another burst of bull-related activity in its October bull-running event, and in Fátima the devoted make their way to the shrine on 13 October, to mark the last appearance of the Virgin to the children.

November/*Novembro*

Dos Santos ao Natal, vai um salto de pardal (From All Saints to Christmas is just a sparrow's hop)

All Saints' Day (*Dia de Todos os Santos*) on 1 November is celebrated in church, but the following day, *O Dia dos Defuntos / Dia dos Finados* (All Souls'Day) is commemorated by placing flowers and lit candles on graves. Later in the month St Martin (*São Martinho*) is remembered by eating chestnuts and drinking *água-pé*, a lightweight wine. The day also coincides with the Horse Fair in Golegã (Ribatejo), which draws equine enthusiasts from all over Portugal.

December/*Dezembro*

Até ao Natal, bem ou mal: do Natal em diente a barriga o sente (Up to Christmas so-so: after Christmas the belly feels it, i.e. in rural areas times get difficult in January)

Christmas (*O Natal*) has become slightly more commercialized of late in some parts of Portugal, namely in the larger cities and the Algarve, under external influences. However, despite the many TV adverts and lavish displays in the shopping centres, the run-up to Christmas can be a really lovely time in Portugal, with the town squares decorated with fairy lights, music singing out, and crib displays in the churches. In the past families would decorate their own *presépio* (crib) in the house, with figures usually made of clay. Some children still put out a shoe by the hearth, or *sapatinho na chaminé*, which will be filled with small sweets and chocolate by the morning; in the past these were the only presents children would have received. Nowadays, with most people receiving the '13th salary'(see p.232) in December, there is some extra money to spend. For those in a difficult economic situation, many local councils and churches give special help at this time of the year.

The main celebrations take place on Christmas Eve (*a véspera do Natal*), when a special meal is eaten in the family. *A consoada* usually consists of *bacalhau* (salted cod), with trimmings. Presents are opened now, then everyone goes to Midnight Mass (*A Missa do Galo*), and the churches are a lively throng of lights, candles and local people. Some churches burn logs outside right through until Twelfth Night. On Christmas Day (*o dia de Natal*) itself, families spend the day together, often going out for lunch, or a walk followed by afternoon tea (sweet cakes and coffee). Larger towns may have circus spectacles the youngsters love to visit.

Regional festivals

Here is a small sample of other interesting events on offer around the country:

Aveiro	January	*Festa de São Gonçalinho* – loaves of bread are thrown down to the crowds from a chapel, in thanks for a fisherman's safe return from the seas, or in gratitude for finding a husband!
Bragança area	December/ January	*Festa dos Rapazes* – young boys dressed in masks and fringed outfits, run amok through the villages in a pagan rite of passage
Funchal, Madeira	April/May	Beautiful flower festival
Barcelos	May	*Festa das Cruzes* – a festival of crosses in celebration of a day when the shape of a cross was supposed to have appeared on earth in the 15th century
Coimbra	May	*Queima das Fitas* – the traditional burning of the ribbons on the gowns of the university students to mark the end of their studies
Braga	May	Pilgrimage to the shrine at Bom Jesus. People often climb the magnificent Baroque stone staircase on their knees
Azores	May	*Festas do Espírito Santo* – Holy Spirit festivities lasting until Whit Sunday. A child is crowned 'emperor'for the festival, bread and

		soup is distributed, and chapels have a decorated centrepiece known as an *império*, or empire
Amarante	June	A traditional love-festival, where phallus-shaped cakes are exchanged between young men and women hoping to find a partner
Silves	August	International Beer Festival in the castle, with music and dance
Ponte de Lima	September	*Feiras Novas* – massive market and fairground, with band competition

The Portuguese Tourist Office leaflets and general guide books cover the festivals in more detail.

Customs, folklore and legends

In a country where so much of the population has strong ties with both the land and the sea, it is not surprising that many of the traditions are also linked with rural and maritime ways. Northern Portugal in particular is rich with customs and legends based on ancient (often pagan) rituals and practices, especially if you travel into some of the more remote mountain villages. What is surprising, perhaps, is that in this, the most religious part of the country, pagan elements are allowed to sit next to strong Catholic beliefs – and not only tolerated, but seemingly condoned. Perhaps the village priests realize that the influences are so deep-rooted that to condemn and try to prevent them might turn the locals against the undoubted pulling-power of the Catholic church. There is certainly some concern that the people tend towards their secular festivities (or those linked with primeval rituals) and perhaps forget the true meaning of some of the religious festivals. According to one priest:

> *Hoje as festas estão mais pagãs que religiosas. O povo já vai à festa não por devoção mas por obrigação.* (Today the festivities are more pagan than religious. The people go to festivals not through devotion, but through obligation)

This is the land where *santuários* (shrines) are found on roadsides to protect travellers, saints are called on to cure physical illness (St Lawrence for toothache, the Holy Family for family problems), and *promessas*, or payment for prayers answered (miracles) often take the form of the commissioning of waxen limbs or even animals, or the offering of jewellery, photos and tresses of hair. You may be taken aback if you visit small churches or chapels and find rows of wax articles hanging up, or a room full of personal artefacts, such as wedding photos and clothing – all are tokens of thanks. One of the most fascinating scenes I recall is a whole waxen body chained up in a cave shrine.

Beliefs

There are dozens of beliefs based on the natural elements, or surrounding life events:

- The moon and fountains are important influences, with healing powers and the ability to aid conception of healthy children.
- Once you have a newborn baby, you should protect it from the 'evil air', by not taking it out during certain hours, and the father's trousers should be placed over the cot to frighten off malevolent forces.
- In some places Midnight Baptism is still carried out (Ponte da Barca in Minho is one example). For a woman prone to miscarriage, when she is pregnant, she will go down to a bridge dividing two municipalities at midnight. Hence she will be in neither one place nor the other, at neither one day nor the next. Whilst family guard the bridge for straying evil spirits, the first person to appear after the bells chime, is invited to pour river water over the woman's belly. The final 'Amen' of this baptism is not said, though, as the official baptism of a healthy child must be awaited.
- Other practices are based on the dead, such as the Procession of the Dead, a common belief in the north-west of the Iberian peninsula. Some people claim to have the power to hear and see a procession of the ghosts of parishioners who have recently died. The procession is seen leaving the cemetery with a coffin in the centre. On its return, the coffin is carrying the ghost of the

next villager to die. If the person who sees the procession wants to stay alive they must not reveal the name of the next to die!

■ Another belief strongly adhered to is the Cult of the Dead, wherein a buried body which has not undergone a thorough decaying process is considered to be that of a saint, and a shrine is constructed where the corpse is exposed. The Church has always been opposed to the practice, but came to tolerate it because of its popularity. Saints shrines are said to exist in Guimarães (São Torcato), and Oporto (Santinha de Arcozelo), among others.

Far from unusual is the existence of *curandeiras* – spiritualist-type faith healers, especially in the mountains (some of these villages would make perfect sets for atmospheric horror films!). Witches, sorcerers, exorcists, occult leaders – they all practise in the north, and have strong followings from people often desperate for cures or for a miracle on their land. These locals are shaped by a mixture of pagan superstition, Roman Catholicism and peasant folklore – their every move can be related to some belief or other.

Of course, not all rural traditions are free from controversy, and those which involve animal cruelty of any kind are condemned by the outside world, whilst those practising them are left wondering what the fuss is all about. One such practice, which has been widely carried out in many countries over the years, is the annual *matança* (*do porco*), pig-sticking. Perhaps it is the name for it which makes it sound so horrific – after all, in rural areas the village, or family, pig has always been fattened and then killed to provide for the coming year. In Portugal, it is common practice for neighbours to jointly own a pig for this purpose. Perhaps it is the ritualistic nature of it that makes it appear distasteful to those not used to it. Certainly the whole process is organized with military precision, so that once killed, nothing is wasted, and everyone is on hand to help out.

Bull fights (*Touradas*)

Although the Portuguese are not as discernibly fervent over their bull fighting as their Spanish neighbours, they do take it all quite seriously, especially in the Ribatejo region, the heart of the bull-breeding country, and in rural areas all over. No more so than in the Alentejano border town of Barrancos, where their annual August festivities include the public slaughter of bulls and some cows, a practice outlawed by the Government. In 1998 the town, which speaks a strange mixture of Spanish and Portuguese (*Barranquenho*), went to the highest authorities to defend their right to organize the *'toiros de morte'*(death bulls) events, which provoked a huge debate at all levels throughout Portugal. The prevailing argument of these locals, and of bull-fight aficionados in general, seems to be that the animal is going to be killed anyway, at an abattoir, so why not let it have some sport first? For do not be under any illusion, whatever any guide book or tourist information brochure says about the bull not being killed in Portuguese fights (unlike in Spain!), bulls are not simply allowed to have a little romp around the ring to entertain the crowds before being led off to pastures green! Portuguese fights are conducted on horseback, and as such are more a display of the artistry and skill of the rider (*o cavaleiro*) and horse (usually a Lusitanian, the world's oldest saddle-horse) than anything else, the intricate and breathtaking dressage moves being based on those established by the Marquis of Marialva, King's Master of the Horse in the 18th century. The fight itself (*a corrida or tourada*) goes through various stages:

Peões de brega	Fighters on foot distract the bull with capes
Cavaleiro	The main fighter on horse aims to tire and confuse the bull with many changes of direction, before stabbing a number of darts (*farpas*) into the bull's shoulders. The bull's horns have been blunted and wrapped in leather to prevent much damage to the horse. The *toureiro* is judged on his skill and grace
The *pega*	Eight men known as *forcados* then attempt to overcome the bull with their bare hands. The leader challenges the bull to charge him, then launches himself over its head and hangs on. The others try to hold on, with one holding the tail, until the bull is brought to a stop. This stage often lasts a while as the men are tossed off and start again
The end	The bull is finally unceremoniously escorted out of the ring by a group of oxen. It will usually then be slaughtered

One ex-fighter who set up a school of bull fighting in Lisbon (where would-be hopefuls practice with a wheelbarrow for a bull!), called for the only bull-fighting nation in the world not to kill its bulls in the ring to change its ways: 'What bull fighting is about is a delicate balance between life and death. The Portuguese way is artistic and noble but not the real thing,' said Fernando Segarra, campaigning for a more Spanish approach to the tradition. The Animal Protection League in Portugal (*Sociedade Protectora dos Animais*), as in Spain, is a small voice against a long tradition.

The Barcelos cockerel (*O galo de Barcelos*)

This legend involving a creature is definitely more positive! You cannot help but notice the ubiquitous coloured cockerel motif decorating tea-towels, table linen, bags, tin openers, in fact everything! The bright little cockerel, as legend goes, saved the life of a condemned man in Barcelos, near the northern Spanish border. The man, from nearby Galicia, stood accused of stealing silver from the town, and despite his pleas to the local judge, who was about to tuck into a roasted cockerel at dinner, he was taken to be hanged. However, he had said that the cockerel would crow in his innocence, and the miraculous creature did so, prompting the judge to dash to the hanging and the life of the man was saved. The cockerel has come to be Portugal's national symbol of friendship.

The Portuguese life-cycle

Birth and baptism (*nascimento e baptismo*)

The birth rate in Portugal has been declining very slightly over the past few years. It currently stands at about 10.6 births per 1000 of the population, with women having an average of 1.4 children. Most families in fact now have much smaller families than ever before, but the number of births outside marriage has grown considerably over the past decade. The birth of a child is still a great occasion for celebration in Portugal, and is the time to send cards and small gifts to the new mother. The baptism, or christening, within a year of the birth, is still a big family affair, when the Portuguese will dress well and celebrate in a local restaurant.

First communion (*a comunhão*)

Another important rite of passage for the young child in a Catholic family, first communion is taken very seriously, and once more links the family inextricably with the church. The ceremony is again followed by celebrations of food and drink in a local eating house.

Birthday (*o dia de anos*)

Birthdays are celebrated with presents and cards as elsewhere in the world. Shops in Portugal, especially in the larger shopping centres, are geared up with a range of cards and gifts, as they are now too for special days such as Mothers'Day. Special birthdays are celebrated with a big get-together at home, with tables groaning with food and drink. In restaurants it is common for cakes to be brought out as a surprise to a birthday person, whilst the whole place sings 'Happy Birthday'.

Here are the words so that you can join in:

Parabéns a você   *Hoje é dia de festa*
Nesta data querida   *Cantam as nossas almas*
Muitas felicidades   *Vamos dar a* (name)
Muitos anos de vida   *Uma salva de palmas*

Marriage (*o casamento*)

This remains an important institution in Portugal, with the highest rate in Europe apart from the UK, at 6.7 marriages per 1000 of the population. Most people marry between the age of 20–30, the average in 1995 being 26.8 for men and 24.9 for women, significantly older than in 1981, when the averages were 25.5 and 23.3. The divorce rate hovers at around 1.5 per 1000 of the population, in comparison with 4.5 in the United States, 3.3 in the UK, and 2.0 in France. Weddings usually take place on a Saturday afternoon and are not unlike those in other countries – preference is still for a church ceremony, although civil weddings are also available. After the official ceremony, the wedding party often drives around town, with all the horns hooting, livening up what is otherwise a dead time in the Portuguese week. In the countryside, the guests and bridal party may still be ferried about in decorated mule-drawn carts. A reception (*copo d'água*) follows usually at a local restaurant, or at some village hall, where an accordion and other musicians may lead the festivities, and lots of *brindes* (toasts) are drunk. In some rural areas 'arranged marriages' still exist, in the expectation of joining two farms and their land, and to the benefit of the community.

Death (*a morte*)

The annual death rate in Portugal is round about 11 people per 1000, about the norm for Europe, but higher than Australia or the USA. The dead are normally buried within 24 hours in Portugal. Funerals are sombre affairs with music quite rare, and no wake to follow the burial. As the coffin is lowered into the ground it is often opened up again for final prayers and a last goodbye. People kiss or touch the head or face of the deceased, then the coffin is placed into the grave. Relatives and friends send flowers and cards of condolence. There will usually also be a seventh-day Mass for the deceased (*o falecido*). Mourning traditionally lasted a year, but now can be as short as three months. However, some widows still maintain the old way of wearing black for the rest of their life.

GLOSSARY

celebrar, festejar *to celebrate*
comemorar *to commemorate*
a prenda *present, gift*
o desfile *procession, parade*
o baile *dance, ball*
dançar *to dance*
alegre *joyful, happy*
solene *solemn*
cantar *to sing*
a canção de Natal *Christmas carol*
o peregrino, a peregrina *pilgrim*
a romaria *pilgrimage*
andar *to walk*
passear *to stroll, promenade*
o feriado *public holiday*

divertir-se *to enjoy oneself*
a fantasia *fancy dress*
fantasiar-se *to wear fancy dress*
queimar *to burn*
a fogueira *bonfire*
matar *to kill*
morrer *to die*
a morte *death*
nascer *to be born*
baptizar *to baptize*
casar-se (com) *to get married (to)*
o casamento *wedding*
dar os pêsames *to offer condolences*
o enterro *funeral, burial*
a festa *party*

Taking it further

Suggested reading

Tales from the Mountains, Miguel Torga, Carcanet, 1995 (for insight into the lifestyle of the mountains)

Festas e Comeres do Povo Português 1 (Festivals and food of the Portuguese), Maria de Lourdes Modesto, Afonso Praça, Nuno Calvet, Editorial Verbo

Portugal, a Book of Folkways, Rodney Gallop, Folklore, CUP, 1936

A Portuguese Rural Society, José Cutileiro, Clarendon Press, 1971

Events/places to visit

As all towns throughout Portugal have their own festivals, the wisest thing to do in order to participate in any of them is to check with the Portuguese National Tourist Office in your own country, or at any of the local offices within Portugal. Many event listings are also posted on the official website. At times of large festivals it may be more difficult to arrange accommodation, although you may be able to stay outside the locality and travel in to the events.

Bull fights are advertized on huge posters (*cartazes*) around towns, and sometimes via loudspeakers blaring out from passing cars. They usually take place on Saturday afternoons or early evenings. One of the largest rings is in Cascais, near Lisbon.

Museu Antoniano (Cult of St Anthony), Largo de Santo António da Sé, 24, 1100 Lisboa.

Websites

www.portugal-info.net
Tourist Board, **www.portugal.org** and **www.icep.pt**
Tourism, **www.portugalinsite.pt**
Tourism, **www.maisturismo.pt**
Tourism, **www.algarve.com**
Bull fighting, **www.tauromaquia.multibase.pt**

7 | FOOD AND FASHION

Os portugueses têm boa comida, gostam de boa comida e falam muito acerca de comida. (The Portuguese have good food, like good food and speak a lot about food) – Edite Vieira, broadcaster and cookery writer

Food and drink

Portuguese food has always been traditional, hearty and wholesome – the food of farmers and fishermen. Although not entirely a Mediterranean country, Portugal does, nevertheless, enjoy the health benefits of a southern European diet – olive oil (*azeite*), plenty of fish (*peixe*), fresh fruit (*frutas*), and a home-grown stock of good wine (*vinho*). Not renowned for fancy or fussy food, what you are guaranteed here is tasty food in gargantuan portions (the Portuguese love their food) – so much so that you are often advised to select just a *meia-dose* (half portion), which is usually sufficient. If eating in the home of Portuguese people, you will always be regaled with expressions such as: *coma mais* (eat more), or *não quer mais?* (don't you want any more?). To refuse may cast aspersions on the cook – so fast for a few days beforehand!

Over hundreds of years Portuguese cuisine has picked up influences from the people who invaded and settled there, and from the results of the explorations to distant lands. It was the discovery of the spice routes which gave the Portuguese access to coriander, pepper, ginger, curry, saffron and paprika, which they introduced to an unsuspecting Europe. Many of these spices grace Portuguese dishes to this day, but particularly coriander (*coentros*) and black pepper (*pimento*), in addition to the indispensable cinnamon (*canela*) used in many desserts; the Spanish brought back vanilla and chocolate from Mexico to add to their dishes. Further explorations brought back tea and rice from the east, coffee and nuts from Africa, along with the fiery piri-piri chilli, used as a sauce on chicken piri-piri. From Brazil came pineapples, potatoes and tomatoes – and those growing in the Alentejo region are reputed to be the best around. The next time you see a French menu look for the expression '*à la portugaise*'– it means full of lush tomatoes!

Other main ingredients include garlic (*alho*) and onions (*cebolas*), which came with the Romans. The Romans also introduced wheat, intending to make Iberia the 'granary of Rome'– the vast Alentejo region is known within Portugal as the 'bread basket' or 'granary' (*terra de pão/celeiro*), for its huge expanses of wheatfields. The Arabs brought rice (*arroz*) – and the methods of irrigation, in addition to the almond trees (*amendoeiras*) in the Algarve, where marzipan sweets adorn every café counter. One word of warning, the Portuguese tend to use a lot of salt in their cooking, so it's prudent to try first before heading for the *sal*. If you travel through the eastern Algarve you will come across some of the huge salt works, the production process dating back to the times when the Phoenicians set up trading posts around the Mediterranean. On average the Portuguese consume about 12 gms. a day; the recommendation is 5–7.5 gms.

Meals (*as refeições*)

Changes in lifestyle, principally in the larger towns and cities, mean that people are spending less time together around the table – an unthinkable aspect of modern living in the minds of many. Meals have always been at the heart of family life – and indeed still are in the many country areas. But elsewhere, a faster, business-like approach to life, has consigned the sharing of lunch at home to special occasions such as birthdays.

Breakfast (*o pequeno almoço*) is the most neglected of meals in Portugal. Most people will grab a quick coffee at home, then head to their nearest café for a snack (sweet or savoury) and another injection of caffeine on the move. Children, on the other hand, or those who have less need to dash off into the early-morning rush, may have bread (see p.148) and jam, or cheese, or cereals, which have crept into the nation over the past couple of decades, and are as accessible as in most other places.

A note about coffee – *café* (the same word for a café). There are numerous variations on the theme, and although you may simply enjoy a normal white coffee (*café com leite*) yourself, why not branch out and explore some of these delights:

Cafés portugueses (a selection)

> *um café/uma bica* – small espresso
> *um carioca* – weaker, small espresso
> *uma italiana* – black, stronger espresso
> *um café duplo* – double espresso
> *um garoto* – small white
> *um pingado/ um pingo* – small, with just a drop of milk
> *uma meia de leite* – half coffee, half milk in a large cup
> *um galão* – large, milky coffee served in a glass

Coffee is enjoyed throughout the Portuguese working day, at breaks, with lunch, after work, but to counterbalance the strength of the caffeine, you will often see the Portuguese drink a glass of water straight afterwards – a tip well worth following if you wish to avoid problems with blood pressure.

Lunch (*o almoço*) is almost invariably eaten out by working people. If you walk around any reasonably sized town between 1 p.m. and 3 p.m. you'll find most eating establishments a heaving mass of eating, talking, moving people. It is relatively cheap to eat out in Portugal, especially at the places where all the locals go, and as most shops and many working establishments shut down for a couple of hours, the best thing to do is get a hearty meal. Even in the sticky summer months the Portuguese are likely to opt for a hot meal – whatever happens to be the dish of the day, or soup, and omelettes. Business lunches, as everywhere, can be protracted into a marathon afternoon session, including wine and often cognac or similar to sign the deal!

There are also dozens of filling snacks as an alternative to a three-course meal, and many Portuguese will plump for a filled roll (though the choice of fillings is less extensive/imaginative than you may be used to). The popular ones are: ham/cheese/ham and cheese/egg (omelette)/tuna. Hot rolls such as the *prego* (steak Canadien) and *bifana* (pork) and cheese and ham toasties are also popular. The Portuguese will also eat these as snacks at other times of the day – on the move, or at weekends whilst out and about. There are also dozens of savoury nibbles and cakes, often eaten out in cafés as a *'lanche'* – a snack (*not* lunch as the name suggests). This may be taken in the afternoon, or early evening whilst out promenading, and is usually the custom when arranging to meet friends.

For the thousands of agricultural workers, lunch is normally eaten out in the fields – bread, cheese, olives, fruit and wine being the staple. Wholesome country food is eulogized (sometimes with an air of irony) by many characters in the novels of Eça de Queirós, as in:

> *Oh que favas! Que delícia! Deste arroz com fava nem em Paris Melchior amigo!... Pois é cá a comidinha dos moços da quinta!* (Oh what beans! How delicious! You can't even find this rice with beans in Paris, my friend Melchior!... Of course it's here you'll get the farm-lads'food!) from *A Cidade e as Serras*

Dinner (*o jantar*), is still the most important family meal in many households, an opportunity to sit down and talk. However, this too is changing, as longer working days encroach on the time traditionally spent at home. Younger people in particular, are quite happy to get take-away food, or stock up on frozen (*congelado*) TV meals. A glance in the freezers at any supermarket will show how much 'instant' food has invaded Portuguese lifestyles. For those who do manage to adhere to tradition, *o jantar* may typically consist of soup with bread, a cooked meal with fish or meat as the main focus, and fruit or cheese to finish. At more lavish gatherings expect a dessert too. The Portuguese do not eat as late as their Spanish colleagues – around 7–8 p.m. is the norm.

Finally, there is another meal, *a ceia* (supper) usually reserved for special occasions, when a late meal may be enjoyed, such as during festivals. The most typical of this is the Christmas Eve *consoada*, when a cooked meal of *bacalhau* (see p.129) is usually eaten.

Favourite foods

Given the wholesome aspect of Portugal's natural foodstuffs, it is not surprising that many of the most popular dishes are of a hearty variety – with regional differences on a fairly static theme. Most Portuguese grow up with wonderful, thick filling soups – many thickened with potato purée, which, along with some home-made bread, makes a meal in itself. Common soups include seafood, vegetable, watercress and the unique *caldo verde* (shredded kale) which comes with a slice of *chouriço* sausage floating on the top, and is delicious. Not so the *sopa à alentejana*, which is a much more watery affair with bits of bread floating in the garlic-tasting liquid, and an egg poached in the middle of it. A real experience!

As main courses, the most popular meats are *carne de porco* (pork – the earliest reference to which is in a document dating from the year 908), *borrego* (lamb), *cabrito* (goat), *carne de vaca* (beef), *perú* (turkey) and *frango* (chicken). More unusual dishes also include *javalí* (wild boar), *perdiz* (partridge) and *leitão* (suckling pig). Portugal, along with other European countries in recent years, has suffered from infected beef, resulting in an embargo of its exports, but although beef forms part of dishes such as *cozido à portuguesa* (meat and vegetable stew) and is enjoyed as cooked steaks, pig is the supreme animal in Portugal, living mostly on a diet of acorns (*bolotas*) in the shade of cork olives in the Alentejo. For fish see p.149. Most dishes in Portugal are served with rice, chips or potatoes and salad. Strangely enough, vegetables are a rare accompaniment (apart from in the very rural communities where little else may be available).

External influences, mostly from other areas of the Portuguese empire, are also felt in the cuisine. Chicken (*frango piri-piri*) is popular, and has become a real tourist pull in the Algarve. *Feijoada* – a kind of bean and offal stew, popular in the north – is also available in its Brazilian form (*Feijoada à Brasileira*), where black beans are used. In Lisbon, Oporto and the Algarve in particular, cuisine has adopted a wider range to include Chinese restaurants alongside typical African and Brazilian ones, although the vast majority still remain most definitely home-grown.

Regional dishes

Food in Portugal requires a book in itself, and some cookery books have been recommended in the reading list. But to give you some tips on what to expect as you travel the country, here is a summary of what is eaten typically in each region, in addition to food generally available all over the country.

Costa Verde

Duck, octopus, steamed conger-eel, roasted kid, lamprey, a range of smoked hams, tripe (Oporto's famous dish – the people who live there are known as *tripeiros*), dozens of desserts based on the egg-sweets.

Costa de Prata

Many fish dishes, including *caldeirada* stews of eel, clams and cockles, grilled pork kebabs, stewed chicken, and kid. Again, many sweet dishes including the *ovos moles* and the bean cakes from Torres Vedras (*pastéis de feijão*). Dried fruits and preserves.

The mountain areas

Strong-tasting food such as the various sausages, including the *alheiras* (veal and bread) and *morcela* (blood sausage), wholesome stews (*feijoada*), partridge, trout, and *maranhos* (lamb and chicken giblets cooked with rice). Famous cheeses.

Lisbon area

Lots of fish – bass, mussels, red mullet, swordfish, lobster and crab. Goat and sheeps' cheeses, special sponge cake (*pão de ló*), Sintra's cheese cakes (*queijadas*), and gin cakes (*zimbros*) from Sesimbra. And don't forget the delicious custard-cream pastries – *pastéis de Belém* (or *pastéis de nata*).

The plains

Stewed eels, lamprey, sausages, kid stew and pork with clams, hare with red beans and fried rabbit. Tasty bread and cheese, as well as sweet pastries such as the Évora egg and almond paste sweets. Excellent melon, and the famous Elvas sugar plums.

Algarve

Seafood dishes, including seafood rice and *caldeirada* stew, *cataplana* dishes, grilled fish, especially sardines. Sweets made from almond and fig paste, often in the shape of fruits and animals.

Madeira and the Azores

Meat and fish kebabs (*espetadas*), tuna steaks, *peixe-espada* (scabbard fish) a deep-sea fish never seen alive as it dies of decompression before reaching the surface, it is particularly good with banana, octopus stew, yams and pork sausages, honey cake, and tropical fruits and island cheeses.

Desserts popular with the Portuguese are fruit, cheese and sweet puddings. Fruit is often served peeled and decorated – oranges arriving in sweet liqueurs. For the Portuguese, it has to be said, are incredibly sweet-toothed, a fact witnessed not only in the types of desserts on sale (Molotov pudding, chocolate mousse, rice pudding Portuguese-style, crême caramel, to name but a few), but also in the tempting array of cakes and pastries in the *pastelarias* (cake shops and cafés). It's no wonder the Portuguese reputedly have the worst dental record in Europe. Many of these desserts are made from egg-yolks (and sugar!), the *doces de ovos* (egg-sweets – said to have been first introduced by the Moors), which then proliferated in convents in the 17th and 18th centuries. Many of them have bizarre names linked to the nuns who championed their cause: *toucinho do céu* (bacon from heaven), *manjar celeste* (heavenly food) and others such as *ovos moles* (sweet eggs). They are excruciatingly sweet, but here's a recipe if you want to try one out:

Soft eggs – *Ovos moles*

9 oz (250g) granulated sugar	250g de açúcar granulado
8 egg yolks	8 gémeas
¼ pint (150ml) water	150ml água

Bring the water and sugar to the boil on a low flame until you see pearl-like bubbles on the surface. Cool slightly then mix with the beaten yolks, dropping the syrup over them slowly, and beating constantly. Bring to a gentle boil once more, until the mixture thickens. Divide it into small dishes and let cool.

Be warned: extremely sweet! You can add a few nuts to the top, or use the mixture as a filling in another dish, such as a cake or pastry.

It is this enthusiastic intake of sugar, which, coupled with a rise in the consumption of saturated fats, salt and alcohol, has given rise for concern in recent years. The latest findings from the Portuguese National Health Observatory show that more men between the ages of 55–74 are now suffering from diabetes than ever before, and, worryingly, more women over 35. The dietary situation in Portugal, despite all of the fresh foods available, has been deteriorating and heart-related disease is now the principal cause of death there. A study carried out over the 12-year period in the 1980s and early 1990s showed that food consumption had risen from 6.5 to 8 million tonnes per year – an average daily increase of 463 calories per person. The study showed that whilst more nutritious food was being eaten, there was an equally continuous trend to take in detrimental levels of fats and oils. It would appear that with the advent of US-style fast-food chains such as McDonald's and Pizza Hut, the Portuguese are starting to abandon some of their dietary traditions.

The basics

Shopping habits

With the availability of so much fresh produce, the traditional way of shopping has been in the marketplace, and small, specialist shops. Housewives have always bought fresh meat or fish on a daily basis, along with newly baked bread warm from the bakery, and a certain amount of vegetables and fruit. Other grocery products would be purchased as and when stocks got low, but bulk-buying and storage was unusual. It is still common today, especially in smaller towns and rural communities, to see women out in the morning getting the day's provisions. However, times are changing, and whereas previously the local *mercearia* (grocers') and *mini-mercado* (small supermarket) provided a daily supply of produce, a growing number of Portuguese families now head for one of a number of burgeoning *hipermercados*, and do all their shopping under one roof.

Often these visits are a whole family affair, as the locations of the stores also incorporate other shops, or eating (fast-food) places, so the occasion can become a real event. And as most of the large chains, such as Modelo, Pão de Açúcar, Prisunic, and Jumbo, open late into the evening (and very late at the weekend), the places buzz with a seemingly never-ending stream of shoppers. Certainly the range of products is impressive – the largest of them stocking from clothes and books to fresh bread, frozen foods (although only 55 per cent of households as yet possess a freezer) and hundreds of lines. But, as with all stores like this, the service, whilst loud and chirpy, just isn't the same as the personal attention you would get from your local *padeiro* (baker) and *peixeiro* (fishmonger).

A recent development is the diversification into food retailing of some of the large petrol stations. BP, in collaboration with a leading supermarket chain, has been opening up 24-hour Modelo Expresso shops at their garages across the country. It seems that much of Portugal is catching up with life in the fast lane, and modifying their shopping habits accordingly. For the traditionalists among us, though, happily the *mercado* (market), *padaria* (bakery) and *talho* (butcher's) still offer the opportunity to buy fresh produce daily and pass the time of day, and it is improbable that these will be replaced totally by hyper-shopping, especially in the numerous rural villages.

So, what are the basics of daily eating?

O pão (bread)

No self-respecting southern European family would contemplate a meal without bread, and Portugal is no exception. And with the huge expanse of wheat growing in the Alentejo, availability is never a problem. There is nothing to beat the warm smell of freshly baked bread emanating from the door of a local bakery. You have to be careful not to miss the place itself, as many of them do not have a shop-front – simply an open doorway into a dimly lit room with a counter. But the smell wafting onto the street first thing in the morning is unmistakable. Bread is also on sale in the markets, but you have to be quick, as bakers have usually sold out by lunch. The grocers/supermarkets generally have a limited number of fresh loaves, but now also stock packs of sliced bread (*pão de forma*), usually confined to toastie making. Across the length and breadth of the country, fresh bread is delicious, but there are some regional variations. Here are a few examples of bread names:

pão – general word for bread
pãezinhos – bread rolls
papos-secos – smaller, rounder rolls
carcaça – unsliced loaf
pão de milho – corn bread
broa – maize bread with crunchy crust from the north
pão alentejano – 'peasant loaf'
pão de chouriço – bread with spicy sausage cooked inside it
folhada – loaf cooked with meats inside it, popular at Easter
cacete – French-style baguette

O queijo (cheese)

The range of cheeses in Portugal is fairly limited, but goats'cheeses are plentiful and delicious, and compare very favourably with the best French cheeses. The best cheeses come from the mountainous Serra da Estrela region, the Alentejo, the town of Azeitão (near Setúbal) and to some extent the Azores. As cows are rarer than goats and sheep in Portugal, it is not surprising that a good many cheeses come from the latter. Often on menus in restaurants (and often pricey), is the popular Queijo da Serra, from the high Spa resort of Estrela. It is very smooth and creamy – often compared to Brie. The northern region of Trás-os Montes produces an interesting mix of cow/ewe milk cheese called Monte, while another popular mild variety, Rabaçal, comes from Coimbra. Limiano cheese is also worth trying. For a more distinct taste, Azeitão is quite strong, as is Nisa from the Alentejo. Évora cheese is also popular. Most of the goats'cheeses can be bought in small rounds – some of them pretty small so you can have a taste. The Queijo da Ilha variety from the Azores, is a more processed type of cheese, similar to Emmental or Gouda, and has a blander taste. It is more often than not used for grating, or in toasted sandwiches. Also popular is *requeijão*, a sort of smooth cottage cheese for spreading on bread. It is sold is different sizes of round containers, but does not suit everybody as it rather lacks taste. The Portuguese often sprinkle it with cinnamon or sugar and eat it as a dessert.

O peixe (fish)

Where does one start with fish, in a country with such a long coast-line, and a large (though dwindling) fishing industry? The fish stall in the market is a good starting-point, as you will discover types of fish here that may be totally alien to your own cuisine. However, all fish in Portugal is delicious, especially when grilled. One of the most popular (and cheapest) meals is grilled sardines – *sardinhas grelhadas/ assadas*. These are huge sardines – not the tiddlers confined to tins, coated in sea-salt, grilled on outdoor barbecues, (*churrascos*) and served with salad and bread. The Portuguese way to eat them is with your fingers, with a piece of bread to mop up the flavour. In the Algarve particularly, the best places to get them straight from the catch is at one of the restaurants along the quay in

Portimão, or at any beach café, such as the one on the edge of the sand in the old part of Albufeira. No Portuguese festival would be complete without its *sardinhada*, and if you walk around the narrow alleys of Alfama, in Lisbon, you will also find people grilling their lunch on the step outside their house. A good, meatier alternative is the *carapau* – horse mackerel – also excellent for grilling, and not too expensive.

You cannot go anywhere in Portugal, or read any guide book without confronting the ubiquitous *bacalhau* (salted cod), said to have a separate recipe for each day of the year (yet to be discovered!). It is claimed to be the *prato nacional* – national dish – although in this it must compete with pork-based dishes. It has never been found off Portuguese shores – the bravest of fishermen have endured long, cold trawls to Newfoundland to bring it back, salted and dried in huge flat pieces looking like large flat loofahs ready for soaking in water and reconstitution. Various dishes are made from it – the tastiest I have tried is *Bacalhau à Brás*, which is shredded fish with potatoes and egg, like a kedgeree. *Bacalhau* cooked in the oven (*no forno*) tends to be uncomfortably salty, but one of the nicest ways to try it is in the form of tasty nibbles called *pastéis* (*or bolinhos*) *de bacalhau* – deep-fried croquettes with cod/potato and herbs.

Seafood (*mariscos*), is also very popular and tasty, especially in some of the imaginative dishes found on the coast. *Caldeirada* is a fish stew incorporating endless ingredients, although I have always struggled to cope with the straggly bits of prawns and crab. A good alternative is the *arroz de marisco* (seafood rice), but the real epitome of seafood dishes has to be those cooked in the *cataplana*. This round copper cooking vessel with a lid was introduced to the Algarve by the Moors, and cooks its contents by steam – the forerunner of the pressure-cooker. Usually the lid is not opened until the *cataplana* reaches your table, so that you can appreciate its aroma under your nose! Clams (*ameîjoas*) and mussels (*mexilhões*) are often cooked in this way, and the *cataplana* itself can be bought quite reasonably from hardware stores.

Other fish popular in Portugal include sole (*linguado*), red mullet (*salmonete*), swordfish (*espadarte*), scabbard (*peixe espada* – often mistaken for the sword fish), tuna (*atum*), and in northern Portugal freshwater fish such as salmon (*salmão*) and trout (*truta*).

A água e o vinho (water and wine)

Along with bread, water is the other fundamental component of any Portuguese meal – be it at home or in a restaurant. Many visitors to Portugal ask whether it is safe to drink tap water, and generally speaking it is much cleaner and safer than in other southern European countries. A number of Portuguese households have an earthenware water filter in the kitchen, furnishing a steady supply of extra-clean, cool liquid. But if in any doubt, and perhaps more so in the Algarve, where lots of development has caused constant disruptions to water supply, the bottled mineral water (*água mineral*) is cheap enough to keep a good supply – and should be part of your daily diet, especially if travelling around in the warmer parts of the year. Portugal benefits from a high number of spa-towns, such as Caldas de Monchique in the Algarve, Luso and Vidago in the north, among many others. The last two produce some of the most commonly bottled mineral water, but there is an additional drink you can opt for if you have an upset stomach, an effervescent *Água das Pedras*, (water of the stones) or *Pedras Salgadas* (salted stones), which work wonders.

If ever an excuse were needed for buying alcohol, the fact that many bottles of Portuguese wine cost less than a bottle of water could be the argument! Some of these may well be fairly rough, but

Typical wine label

the vast majority are very palatable. The Portuguese are the third largest consumers of wine in Europe, just slightly behind the French (the people of Luxembourg drink the most at an average of 70 litres of wine each a year), but it is not surprising, given its range and accessibility, however remote a village may appear. It is rare to come across a bad red wine (*vinho tinto*), but getting the perfect white (*vinho branco*) needs a bit more expertise – the Portuguese know, so it's worth asking for recommendations. The best wines come from one of the demarcated regions, some of which are the oldest designated wine regions in Europe. In general, you won't have any problems with any of the following:

Douro wines	both white and red
Dão	red and white, the red being particularly velvety and a beautiful deep ruby colour.
Bairrada	excellent reds, often still foot-trodden
Estremadura	wines from Lisbon area
Alentejo wines	particularly Borba, Redondo, and Vidigueira
Wines from Colares	near Lisbon, the only area to survive the devastating phylloxera disease in the 1870s, due to the sandy earth the vines grow in
White Bucelas	the older the drier
Algarve wines	light and fruity

In addition, you should not miss the unique *vinho verde* (green wine) from the northern Minho region. Technically a young, light, slightly bubbly wine, this 'green' wine can actually be white or red. The white is perfect chilled on a hot day, to accompany an outdoor lunch. *Vinho verde* accounts for a quarter of the production of wine in Portugal, but of the 80,000 grape growers in the Minho, half only produce 110 cases a year. What you will rarely see is the Portuguese drinking their rosé wines, although these still remain popular (and palatable) outside the country, especially the well-known Mateus, whose label bears the picture of the palace at the Mateus vineyards, where you can have a guided tour. Pandering to the sweet-toothed natives and non-natives alike are the Madeira wines (equally quaffable as an appetizer or as a dessert wine), and the muscatel-originated dessert wines from Setúbal, south of Lisbon.

The wine industry is an integral part of the Portuguese lifestyle, from the numerous small-scale cooperatives, to the big-business enterprises contributing to the nation's economy. Everyone drinks wine – the labourer in the fields, the old man having a small glass with a basic meal in a bar, families out for meals, or the trendy youngsters in cool wine-bars. Wine is not taboo, and young children have been brought up with it at the dinner table, and have learned to respect it – it is interesting to note how so many of the southern European countries (Portugal included) seem to suffer less from alcohol-related hooliganism than the rest of Europe.

In terms of drinking some new-found delights once you are back home, happily more and more Portuguese wine is starting to make an appearance on the shelves of supermarkets and wine-merchants in many parts of the world, and much of it very reasonably priced. Once you've discovered a source, you'll never consider wine from anywhere else again!

A note on cork: any wine can be ruined by a cork that has gone bad. Although this does not happen too often, some wine bottlers have been turning to plastic corks in recent years. The disadvantage with these is that they do not allow the wine to 'breathe' as cork does – and this is vitally important for Portuguese wine in particular. On p.263 cork production and the plastic debate is examined in more detail.

Reading the label

Here's a guide to understanding what you're getting:

Adega *winery/ wine cellar*	DOC *Denominação de Origem Controlada* (established wine region) – this is the equivalent of the French label Appellation d'origine Contrôlée (AOC)
Casta *variety of grape*	IPR – *Indicação de Proveniência Regulamentada* (newer wine regions)
Colheita *harvest, vintage*	Vinho regional *larger wine regions*

Engarrafado *bottled*	Vinho de Mesa *table wine*
Espumante *sparkling*	
Garrafeira *red wine from a good harvest, aged well*	
Quinta *farm/ estate*	
Reserva *reserve*	
Seco *dry*	
Selo de origem *seal of origin*	
Solar *manor house*	
Vinho maduro *mature, aged wine*	

O vinho do Porto (port (wine))

The British have had links with the Portuguese wine trade since the 17th century, when they first drank it after Charles II imposed a boycott on Claret, during a dispute between England and France. In the absence of this much-supped wine, English merchants were to discover the delights of the fortified wine from Oporto – where many English businessmen were keenly trading and residing. These merchants set up offices in Oporto, and the first links with the trade were firmly established, which resulted in the Methuen Treaty of 1703, which gave lower customs tariffs to the English. The links have gone from strength to strength over the past 300 years, and many traditional British names such as Cockburns, Sandemans and Taylors continue to thrive alongside many other established companies.

The British influence is so strong in Oporto that there is still an exclusive gentleman's club forming the headquarters of the Port-shippers British Association. The 18th-century Feitoria Inglesa is a haven of Englishness, with the English daily papers in its reading-room and the smoke of after-dinner cigars in its bar. It is perhaps ironic, in the midst of such long-standing Anglo–Portuguese trading ties, that by the late 20th century it was in fact the French who were outstripping the English at port drinking – by three to one!

There are a few stories about the exact origin of this fortified wine – (grape spirit or *aguardente* (brandy) is added during fermentation). One is that it came about by monks blending the strong local wine with spirit, another that spirit was added to the barrels of consignments of wine being shipped abroad, to ensure its survival. Whatever the truth, the demarcated region for port wine growing dates back to 1756, and since then the Portuguese and Anglo wine producers have been providing a steady flow of the stuff around the world.

The vineyards of the Douro valley are steeply sloped all the way along the river, with terraces carved out to ease access. Although much of the wine process has been modernized, many tasks are still carried out manually, including the grape picking. Around September the fully ripened grapes are picked into huge baskets which are carried on the head and shoulders along the steep terraces, to the accompaniment of a basic drum beat or similar music. The grapes are placed in large vats or tanks to ferment – some estates choosing to continue the tradition of treading the grapes by foot, as they believe the grape is damaged less this way. The fermenting wines tend to spend up to a year on the estate, or *quinta*, before being transported down river to Vila Nova de Gaia, facing Oporto proper, to the port wine lodges. This was traditionally carried out by the flat-bottomed boats (*barcos rabelos*), which you can see lined up along the quaysides – nowadays they are mostly used in annual festivals. Once in the cool dark cellars of the lodges, the wine is left to mature, and is constantly monitored by specialists who assess when the port has the desired qualities to be bottled. The port wine lodges run tours and tastings, a perfect opportunity to have a tot straight from the barrel's tap! Equally popular now, too, are the cruise trips along the River Douro.

The wine estates or vineyards of the Douro are subject to stringent classifications, imposed by the Port Wine Institute in order to preserve the quality and reputation of port wine. The vineyards are awarded points on a huge scale for aspects such as: productivity, soil type, upkeep of vineyard, gradient of slopes, age of vines, and the nature of the land. The overall score controls how many litres of liquid per 1000 vines can be used in port each year. Anything else has to go into the less profitable table wine. Portuguese families often offer their guests a drop of port wine at meals, or you can sample literally hundreds of different ones at the Solar do Vinho do Porto in Lisbon or at the lodges in Oporto.

Types of port

But what is the difference between the various types of port? You may not have come across *vinho do Porto branco* (white port), but, chilled, this makes a refreshing change and ensures a crisp, clean palate before a meal. Ruby is a blend of ports which have spent about three years maturing in wood. It is dark ruby in colour and has a fruity full taste. A port of 'vintage character' is a blended wine about four years old. High quality, and similar in nature to the true vintage, they are full-bodied. Tawny ports come from a number of different harvests, aged for longer in wood, and are smooth and tawny-coloured. This is a wine the port shippers often drink straight from the fridge on a hot summer day. A tawny from a single harvest is known as a *colheita*, and has aged for at least seven years. The label must state both the harvest and bottling dates. Port from a good harvest which is bottled after five or six years in wood is called an 'LBV' (late bottled vintage). Easier to manage than a full vintage, most can be poured straight from the bottle, although those labelled 'traditional' will benefit from a few years before being decanted before serving. Crusted or crusting ports are blended, quality wines, which throw a 'crust' after ageing in the bottle. Dark and rich, they need decanting before you can drink them. Finally, at the top end of the range are the single quinta vintages – port from one harvest and belonging to a particular estate, and the true vintages – port from a single harvest, considered outstanding, and 'declared' by the Port Wine Institute. It matures for just two or three years in wood, but continues the process once bottled, and many are at their best after 20 years or more. This too should be decanted to remove the sediment.

Other alcoholic drinks

There is a whole variety of drinks in Portugal to suit a wide taste range. Many of these are sweet liqueurs, such as those typical in the

Algarve – *Amarguinha* and *Amêndoa Amarga*, made from almonds, *Medronha* ('fire-water' made from wild strawberry), and the version sweetened with honey (*mel*) – *Medronheira*, or *Brandymel* (brandy with honey). From central Portugal come various other drinks based on brandy (*aguardente*) such as *Licor Beirão*. In the north brandy also features strongly, as does a clearer, distilled fire-water called *Bagaceira* and *Ginginha*. It is not unusual to see brandy (of whatever denomination) being drunk in small bars and cafés along with a cup of coffee. The Portuguese also enjoy a drop of *aguardente* in their coffee, known as a *cheirinho*.

The other popular drink is beer (*cerveja*), drunk on all occasions, but particularly refreshing on a warm day, as this European lager-type beer is served cold. The Portuguese tend to drink it in smaller glasses, called an *imperial*, or in the north a *fino*, which also means it is draught beer of a national brand – Sagres, Superbock and Cristal. A large glass (pint) is a *caneca*, but these tend to feature mostly in the tourist areas. If you just ask for *uma cerveja* you may be given a can of imported beer, which is more expensive, so it pays to specify precisely what you want (and go local!). *Cerveja preta*, literally black beer, is rarely seen, but available. The Portuguese like to nibble while they have a beer, but you won't find them tucking into packets of crisps/potato chips. They eat *tremoços*, chunky yellow lupin seeds soaked in brine – a good excuse for another beer – '*mais uma!*'

Eating out

The Portuguese love eating out – it's part of their social make-up. Quite apart from the lunchtime activity, cafés and restaurants (from the small, family-run establishments with only a couple of tables, to the more lavish gourmet houses) fill with couples and families particularly at the weekends and for Sunday lunch. It is quite usual to see young children out with the family, sometimes until quite late – all are welcome in Portuguese restaurants **and** they behave! Some establishments charge their food according to weight (*peso*), so you help yourself to what you want, and there is a price per kilo. Surprisingly, this works out at a very reasonable deal, as you can fit a lot on a plate before it adds up to very much.

As mentioned earlier, the once alien fast-food chains now drawing custom, particularly at the shopping centres. Youngsters are growing up in the McDonald's era – it now has 100 branches in Portugal. In fact, franchise fast-food outlets, particularly in large shopping centres, are a rapidly expanding area, and not only for foreign names. '*Mestre Camarão*'(Mister Prawn) is a recent innovation in reasonably priced seafood outlets, and other '*restaurantes temáticos*' have been springing up, such as Cantina Mariachi (Mexican), Sumo (Oriental), and Skiros (Greek).

Fashion

It is not difficult to notice that the Portuguese are a well-dressed nation – men and women take care over their appearances, especially for workwear and clothing for going out. Appearance is important to them (see also p.261), and a glance in fashion shops will show you a range of suits for both sexes, often in shades of brown and olive, and wonderful quality shoes (at some reasonable prices). Portuguese men often wear their jackets casually over the shoulders, and in the rural winter wear a long, thick cape-coat, like the ones you see shepherds wearing in the Alentejo or the hills of the north. Young people live in jeans, but dress up for special occasions and to go out at weekends. Generally speaking, clothes follow the same influences and fashions as dictated by the industry around the world.

Shepherd's cape

Portuguese fashion (*a moda*) has been less of an industry than elsewhere in Europe, with few big names to boast of until the last couple of decades. The forerunner of it all was **Ana Maravilhas**, who for a long time was the only real representative of Haute Couture in Portugal. She started life as an ordinary housewife who had a go at making a blouse for someone. Her creation was admired by all, and at the start of World War II she was invited to work at the esteemed fashion house of **Maria Luísa Teixeira**. From here she made her mark, visiting Paris and bringing back to Portugal the ideas and styles prevalent in the large fashion houses there, and then reworking them for the home market.

During the 1970s a number of names began to make an impression including: **António Augusto**, whose label is known simply as *Augustus*, and **Jorge Virgílio** who opened his first shop in 1975, specializing in fashion for men, importing fresh ideas and quality garments from abroad.

Ana Salazar is probably one of the names which has travelled the furthest in recent years. Although she struggled in the early years to gain an acceptance within Portugal for her new ideas, in 1974 the launch of her own brand 'Harlow' put her on the road to fame. By 1978 she had won her first award for best collection in Portugal and in the same year presented her *Pronto-a-vestir* (ready-to-wear) collection in Paris. By the beginning of the 1980s she launched her definitive label *Ana Salazar*, and has since gone on to conquer foreign markets, particularly in Paris.

Fashion is gaining momentum within Portugal, supported and promoted by events such as Portugal Fashion, an annual event in Oporto, and Moda Lisboa, a similar show in the capital.

GLOSSARY

cozinhar *to cook*
comer *to eat*
beber *to drink*
o sabor *flavour*
gostoso *tasty*
a receita *recipe*
o prato *dish (culinary), plate*
a adega *wine cellar*
bebível *drinkable, palatable*
a comida regional *regional food*
a moda *fashion*
estar na moda *to be in fashion*
fora de moda *out of fashion*
a etiqueta *label*
a marca *brand name*

lanchar *to have a snack*
comes e bebes *eats and drinks*
os congelados *frozen foods*
a comida rápida *fast food*
a água mineral *mineral water*
com gás/ sem gás *sparkling/flat*
saber a *to taste of*
provar *to try, taste*
adoro/ não aguento *I love/can't stand*
a safra de 1985 *the 1985 vintage*
um desfile *fashion show, parade*
o/a estilista *fashion designer*
a colecção *collection*
pronto-a-vestir *ready-to-wear*
uma lufada de ar fresco *a breath of fresh air*

Taking it further

Suggested reading

The Portuguese Trade and Tourism Offices (ICEP) round the world have leaflets on wine and food.

Portuguese cookery magazines have wonderful recipes and pictures to drool over: try the weekly *Segredos de Cozinha*.

Algarve Country Cooking, Rainer Horbelt/ Sonja Spindler, VIP Publications, 1996

Portuguese Cooking, Hilaire Walden, Apple Press, 1994

The Taste of Portugal, Edite Vieira – origins, anecdotes and recipes – Robinson, 1989

Portugal's Wines and Winemakers, Richard Mayson, Ebury, 1992

The Wines of Portugal, Jan Read, Faber & Faber, 1987

The Story of Dow's Port, Richard Mason, Segrave Foulkes, 1999

Places/events/information

The Port Wine Institute, Rua Ferreira Borges, 4050 Porto. Tel: 22-200 6522: information about port wine and the trade

Taylors Wine Lodge, Porto, for free tours of the 400-year old lodge on Rua do Choupelo Tel: 22-371 9999

Solar do Vinho do Porto (over 300 ports to try), Jardim do Palácio de Cristal, Porto

Ana Salazar fashion shop: 87 Rua do Carmo, 1200 Lisbon

José Carlos designer fashion : 2 Travessa do Monte do Carmo, 1250 Lisbon

Gardénia Young Fashion, street fashion: 96 Rua Nova do Almada, 1200 Lisbon

Websites

Fashion, **www.citi.pt/cultura/moda**

Type in 'moda portuguesa' to search for fashion sites

Type in 'comida portuguesa' and 'vinho português' for food and wine

Many general sites on Portugal cover eating and drinking

Try, **www.portugal-info.net/**

Food, **www.gastronomias.com**
 www.ip.pt/gourmet

Port wine, **www.ivp.pt**

Wine Institute, **www.ivv.pt**

8 CREATIVITY IN OTHER SPHERES

Valeu a pena? Tudo vale a pena se a alma não é pequena.
(Was it worthwhile? Everything is worthwhile if the spirit is not small) – Fernando Pessoa

The Portuguese enjoy a relatively small, albeit thriving cinema, TV and radio network, and theatre is a well-attended means of entertainment, particularly in Lisbon. Personalities involved in these cultural productions are starting to gain an increased international audience and appreciation through the general release of Portuguese films and by travelling theatrical groups. The press, once suppressed for so long under Salazar, has flourished, and nowadays the Portuguese can enjoy a wide choice of newspapers and magazines, as can be witnessed in the displays in the *quiosques* (news stands) and *tabacarias* (tobacconist–paper shops). Although lagging behind in some technological advances, Portugal is beginning to realize the potential of IT (information technology), and investment is being poured into the development of computer systems and programmes, along with the rapidly expanding mobile phone market. The Portuguese were once the innovators in the area of seafaring and navigation. They have contributed to other areas of science and medicine, and modern trends would lead us to believe that they will continue to play their part in embracing this new century, so long after opening up the old world to development.

Cinema (*o cinema*)

Portugal has never really had what could be termed national cinema with the same level of standing as the French, for example, although it has not lacked talented participants. Its history dates back to the first (silent) projections in 1896, through various silent films, to its first talking film in 1930, *A Severa*, about the life of the Fadista Maria Severa. The films that have been produced over the years do not have an identifying 'Portuguese' tag – they have tended to be more universal, dealing with themes recognizable around the globe and less with the specifics of 'Portuguese-ness'. However, this has led critics to think that in many ways it has created an open door for experimentation within the Portuguese film industry, which in turn has led to some brilliant productions, particularly over the past five years. Although there was a decline in cinema attendance from the mid-1980s for about a decade (for every 100 cinema-goers in 1985, only 38 were still attending by 1994), by 1995 the downward trend was being reversed, and has been steadily increasing since. Over the same period, Portuguese politicians have debated the extent of state involvement and financing in the film industry, with more openings now for public funding. But as the popularity of Portuguese cinema returns and the number of new films being produced increases, the Portuguese Government is still looking at ways of pulling in additional finance for commercial distribution of films, and a prop to local authorities' responsibilities towards building and maintaining cinema properties. Cinema attendance is very cheap in Portugal – a ticket costs a few *euros*. The return of the popularity of the cinema has also been witnessed in the enthusiasm for, and attendance at, a growing number of film festivals, such as the annual Fantasporto (in Oporto), the international festivals in Troia and the Algarve, and the more recent, innovative Festival de Cinema Gay, held in Lisbon. There has also been an increase in the number of *os Multiplex*, multi-screen complexes, with modern, non-smoking cinemas where queuing for tickets is a problem, given the huge crowds wanting to get in.

Well-known names

The most successful film director to date has been **Manoel de Oliveira** (1908–). Now in his nineties, he was nominated for a Cannes prize in 2000 for the reworked story of a 17th-century French novel (*The Princess of Cleves*) into the modern work *A Carta* (The Letter). Oliveira started his film career as an actor, but soon became more interested in production. During the 1920s he experimented with short films, and his first full-length feature film, *Douro, Faina Fluvial* (based on the Douro region) came out in 1931. This was to pave the way for a long, distinguished career in the film industry, and has included much recognition internationally, and particularly at the Cannes Film Festivals.

Of the old school of actors, three in particular stand out: **Vasco Santana** (1898–1956) came from a stage background and easily took to the theatre. As talking pictures arrived, he starred in a number of comedies, extending his fame beyond his native Lisbon, and many of these early films (now 70 years on) are still shown on Portuguese TV. Always portrayed as a sympathetic character, as seen in *A Canção de Lisboa* (the first complete sound picture in 1933), Vasco Santana represented a Portuguese Charlie Chaplin.

João Villaret (1913–61), also began his career on the stage in Lisbon where his family had well-established connections. An accomplished actor with a fine repertoire of skills, he appeared in many films (from drama to comedy) and also recorded poetry and prose readings. To many he is simply the most famous Portuguese actor of the 20th century.

Carmen Dolores (full name: Carmen Dolores Cohen Sarmento Veres) (1924–83) initiated a stage career at the tender age of 14. In 1945 she starred in *Amor de Perdição*, to great acclaim, and her film career then grew although she still enjoyed live theatre. In 1969 she travelled with the Casa da Comédia's production of Strindberg's *Dança da Morte*, taking her to Paris where she lived until her death.

Contemporary cinema

Since the 1980s Portuguese cinema has experienced a bit of a revolution, with a host of fresh, new talent emerging from the shadows of the greats of old. Directors, producers, and actors have all been making their mark on a progressively modernized domestic industry, and achieving international success with an ever-wider appreciative audience. There is a distinct air of confidence in the industry in Portugal, so much so that the Portuguese Film Institute (*Instituto de Cinema Audio e Multimedia* – ICAM) has started to back financially a number of productions which hitherto would have been struggling to raise money privately.

Recently, Paulo Branco, considered a real godfather figure in Portuguese cinema, opened a new production office in London. His list of productions run to over 100 over the past couple of decades, and he is largely responsible for the growing reputation abroad of Portuguese cinema. However, it is very obvious that despite this optimistic step, few Portuguese films seep through to foreign audiences. Some avid enthusiasts of film festivals, such as those run in arts cinemas in 'lucky'pockets of the world, are rewarded with a number of Portuguese productions, but these are rare. During 2000, a dedicated festival of Portuguese cinema was hosted in Bristol, in the UK. 'Sea Changes'was a collaborative attempt, backed by ICAM, to bring Portuguese work to wider audiences.

One of the most famous faces of the contemporary screen is **Maria de Medeiros**, and not only for her part in home-grown productions. She has also appeared in *Henry and June*, and *Pulp Fiction*. Born in 1965, daughter of a well-known composer, she studied philosophy at the Sorbonne in Paris, which is where she also first became interested in acting. By 1993 she was already winning acting awards – a 'Gold Lion'at the Venice Film festival for her part in *Três Irmãos* (Three Brothers). Since then she has not looked back, and her reputation as an international actress has steadily grown, and justifiably so. The climax of this success came in the 1997 Portuguese 'blockbuster'*Adão e Eva* (Adam and Eve), also starring another Iberian leading star – **Joaquim de Almeida**. No other film in Portuguese history has got as near to taking 1 million dollars, and creating such a stir at the cinemas. At the time of its release, it was benefiting from a better viewing average than most other competition, including the phenomenally popular Disney production *Pocahontas*. Around 250,000 people saw it in Portugal – a record for their domestic industry.

Other people involved in this new era of Portuguese film-making include director **Alberto Seixas Santos**, whose 1999 film *Mal* was on offer in some arts cinemas in the UK. Santos had work banned during the Salazar/Caetano regime because of its radical content; *Mal* is a dark, violent production exploring the situation of African immigrants, the urban poor, and the bitterness of ideas gone wrong, set against the backcloth of contemporary Lisbon. Santos himself had not wanted the film title translated, as *mal* means so many things in Portuguese. However, it was released under the translation 'Evil'.

The media

Television (*a televisão*)

There are 96.4 colour TVs per 100 households in Portugal (in the UK the number is 98.3, and in the US it is 98.1); far fewer own video recorders. The Portuguese are avid TV-watchers, particularly in the evening, to the extent that you even find wall-mounted sets in the majority of bars around the country (and not just for important sporting events on Sky, although, as you might expect, football does feature largely). If anything, the nation in general is hooked on soap-operas (*telenovelas*), many of them domestic productions, but the vast majority from the mecca that is Brazil. In global terms, Brazilians have been the world's leading consumers of TV soap-operas since the 1950s, when television drama took over from radio. In a recent *telenovela*, a long-awaited wedding scene attracted a staggering 100 million viewers, and was discussed on buses, at work and in cafés across the country. Although Portugal cannot compete with those sorts of numbers there is a variety of dramas to tune into, although Portuguese soap-operas are often overdramatic, verging on the farcical, as indeed is much of the national sense of humour. Whereas British comedy, for example, often uses clever word-play, even in its sit-coms, the Portuguese are more often entertained by ridiculous situations, and larger-than-life characters, usually led by 'all-knowing' buffoons.

The four terrestrial TV channels – RTP 1 and 2, SIC, and TVI (Canal 4), offer a varied diet of programming around the daily doses of *telenovelas*. Cable TV (*Cabo*) is also available on an increasing basis. The Algarve probably has the highest density of Satellite dishes in Portugal, so that its mainly ex-patriot community suffers no withdrawal symptoms from English (or other) – language programmes offered on Sky. All four TV channels show news and weather programmes, which follow the same format as English-language ones. RTP 1 and 2, and SIC are the main sports presenters (football is a common and important feature). RTP1 now shows the Portuguese version of 'Who Wants to be a Millionaire?', (*Quem quer ser Milionário?*) and tvi (channel 4), interestingly enough, has been showing Portuguese 'Big Brother', on some days four times during a day's viewing! It would appear that the attractions of big money, and posing on TV have now found a place in the homes of these hitherto unassuming people. The week's viewing also encompasses a range of films, mostly American, usually sub-titled, and a number of British imports such as *Sim, senhor Ministro (Yes, Minister)*. For the more intellectually oriented, Saturday mornings on RTP2 give you three hours of *Universidade Aberta*, Portuguese Open University programmes; there is no educational programming in the early hours. As an indication of the continued confidence in the future of home TV-entertainment, the biggest multi-media group (Valentim de Carvalho) has recently invested in the construction and equipping of Portugal's largest TV studio (1,500 square metres) in a huge complex near Lisbon, to service the terrestrial channels.

Radio (*a rádio*)

In 1977 it was estimated that there were almost as many radios as TVs in Portuguese households. Nowadays, despite the pulling power of television (regarded as one of the main leisure activities by the Portuguese), radio is still thriving with a number of varied stations, and including English-language programmes transmitting in the Algarve. The state broadcasting corporation, Radio Teledifusão Portuguesa, oversees both radio and TV. A popular independent station in Lisbon is Rádio Cidade, which has a Brazilian theme. Others include Rádio Comercial and Rádio Renascença. Portuguese men are often seen walking along listening to *a bola* – live football matches – on small transistor radios.

Theatre (*o teatro*)

Portuguese theatre was born with **Gil Vicente** (see p.56), whose farcical comedies set the scene even in those distant times, for a long tradition of satire still enjoyed today by its audiences. In its more recent past, the theatre has not been viewed as a 'cultural priority' by Portuguese governments, and subsequently suffered a lack of funding. Smaller theatres, and particularly travelling troupes, were most vulnerable, until a change in policy in the early 1990s allowed a higher level of funds to become available on a regional basis. It is inevitable, perhaps, that there is a concentration of professional companies in the capital; a pioneering development of theatre by the Évora Drama Centre has ensured the Alentejo has recently also come to the fore as a serious region for the art. International collaboration has been growing of late, resulting in a number of joint productions, and the appearance of Portuguese artistes in performances on a wider stage. Young, talented directors, such as **Eduardo Barreto**, whose 1998 London production *Nunca Nada de Ninguém* (translated as 'Never Nothing from No one') was highly acclaimed by the English press, are coming to the fore and staking a claim for Portuguese theatre.

While younger exponents of the theatre are keen to experiment and diversify, there is a core of theatre-goers who are still entertained by the traditional Portuguese farce, which is keenly illustrated in the popular *revistas* or 'reviews'. These are based on send-ups of recognizable politicians or other public figures, and depend very much on the generally well-educated, audience being well up on current gossip and scandals. One of the long-standing movers in this comedy genre has been **Herman José**, now a slick TV 'personality', popular with the masses; his sense of humour has to be acquired, but can now be done so through his own website: **www.hermanet.com**

The press (*a imprensa*)

A glance at the displays of newspapers and magazines at the street kiosks throughout Portugal will give you some idea of the range of publications on offer – not huge, but certainly substantial. From the daily and weekly journals to the glossy women's-interest magazines, sports, cookery, home decoration, and children's publications. Whilst the press suffered under Salazar, it is now flourishing, on a regional as well as a national level, and with many Portuguese versions of leading international publications.

Newspapers (*jornais*)

Although the kiosks appear to do a brisk trade in newspapers, statistics indicate that daily papers only sell around 75 copies per 1,000 inhabitants, compared with 99 in neighbouring Spain, 212 in the US, 216 in France, and a huge 332 in the UK. (As a point of extreme reference, the Hong Kong dailies sell a staggering 800 copies per 1000 people!) The main newspapers in Portugal are:

DAILIES	**Diários**	WEEKLIES	**Semanais**
Correio da Manhã	Popular tabloid, gossipy, large circulation	*Expresso*	Publishes from Lisbon on Saturdays
Diário de Notícias	Lisbon-based	*Independente*	'Quality' publication
O Público	Good comment on politics and social affairs		
Jornal de Notícias	Oporto-based		

NOTE: These days there is less political distinction between the main quality papers, with journalists of any political background working on all of them.

A Bola, a daily football paper is a best-seller, and there are a number of political papers in circulation, such as *Avante!* (Communist), *Revista V* (Monarchist), and *Zé Povinho* (protest).

Regional papers fluctuate in quality, but give a useful insight into local trials and tribulations. A number of English-language, German and Dutch papers exist for those in the ex-patriot communities who cannot read in Portuguese (or require information on car-boot sales, bridge tournaments or Alcoholics Anonymous meetings!), e.g. *Anglo-Portuguese News*.

Magazines (*revistas*)

Popular reading material includes good quality publications such as: *Visão* and *Focus* – weekly publications full of news, reviews and opinion, like *Time* and *Newsweek*.
Mulher Moderna, *Cláudia* and a host of similar women's magazines.

Magazines on a range of themes, many of which are Portuguese versions of well-known international publications dealing with homes, cooking, sports etc. *Readers Digest* magazines (*selecções*) are popular, as are crossword and puzzle booklets, and history magazines with free CDs or books.

Children's reading

Popular materials for youngsters includes translated comics (*bandas desenhadas*) of characters such as Donald Duck (*Pato Donald*) and Astérix. Children love collecting stickers (*autocolantes*), so many comics and books offer them as an integral part of the package. There are also children's supplements in papers, such as the *Diário de Notícias*, to which youngsters write poems and letters.

New media – Portugal on-line

Although information technology (*a informática*) came to Portugal relatively later than many European states, its popularity has been gathering momentum at quite a pace in recent years. EU subsidies for training and development in this area have poured into Lisbon, Oporto and a handful of other areas, offering students the opportunity to study technology-led courses, and companies to invest in equipment and know-how. However, while the numbers of subscribers to mobile phones is on a par now with the UK and the USA, access to Internet facilities is still paltry (9.6 Internet hosts per 100 people, compared with 10.8 in Spain, 32.4 in the UK, and a staggering 168.9 in the USA!). On a domestic level, very few households in Portugal possess a computer (8.1 per 100 people – the number is three times this in the UK, and over five times in the USA). However, in a survey in December 2000, results showed that 2.4 million people in Portugal have access to the Internet, but of these only 1.5 million actually make use of it, with email exchange being the facility used most. In the rural areas, computer technology will still remain a space-age concept, especially when you consider some places have only received electricity and running water in the last decade. The idea of people working from home, with their own 'technological office', is a strange one indeed.

The recent Green Paper on the Information Society in Portugal outlines in particular an initiative called 'Internet in Schools Programme', which aims to link schools to the Internet. Given the fact that many schools in Portugal suffer from a lack of tangible resources such as books, teachers and suitable accommodation, it remains to be seen to what extent, and how quickly, the Internet in the classroom becomes a reality, although early indications show that since 1997, 1800 schools have been *ligadas*. However, 'e-learning' is becoming more real for employees wishing to gain further qualifications by distance-learning via the Internet. Large Portuguese companies such as Portugal Telecom, and CTT (the Postal Service), are already reaping the benefits of on-line courses for their workers. Portugal Telecom has already ventured into the world of e-commerce, with a subsidiary Internet company. A study carried out on their behalf in 1999 suggested that increased access to the Internet in Portugal will lead to around 2.6 million users by 2003, with their spending rate growing by 26 times. An important development in Portugal's legal system has been the recent introduction of computers, which should help to speed up inordinately long administrative processes (see p.193).

Many Portuguese companies and organizations now have their own websites – a selection of those pertinent to areas covered in this book are given in each chapter. There is already a plethora of information sites on Portuguese-related topics: you only have to type in 'Portugal' to get an idea of the range.

Success in other areas

Science – the legacy

Por mares nunca dantes navegados
(Through oceans none had sailed before) – Camões

The Portuguese proved themselves innovators and craftsmen during the times of the early discoveries, and contributed to an understanding of the world through their nautical science and map-drawing skills. It was the Portuguese who led the field in the technical development of the art of war, particularly in ballistics, as far back as the 15th century. Portugal was the only country at the time that equipped its ships with heavy artillery, and were using flintlocks for 70 years before the French took them up in about 1610. Other weapons were advanced for their age, as was the armour of the time, and all intricately decorated by outstanding silversmiths and copper-workers.

Navigational aids

Although it was the Italians (Genoese) who were the leaders of the early nautical charts (called *portulano* charts), used in conjunction with a magnetic compass, in the 16th century, the Portuguese cartographers achieved phenomenal success in the development of map-making. As the navigators brought back more and more knowledge of the world, charts and maps became more detailed and elaborate.

Up to the first half of the 15th century, navigators relied on a compass ('needle') to calculate distance (the pilot relying on sight of land to fix the position of his ship), and a plumb line to check the depths of waters for safe passage. However, on some of the first Portuguese voyages down the coast of Africa, navigators discovered that winds and sea currents differed on outward and homeward journeys. Despite the unique sailing capacity of the *caravela*, whose large square-shaped sails allowed it to sail into the wind, it was decided that if the ships sailed out further into the seas, journeys would be longer, but quicker. However, losing sight of land meant

that the pilots had to rely on the stars and the sun to chart their position; this was the birth of astronomic navigation. It was not long after that two pieces of equipment were also invented, to aid calculation of latitude and longitude: the quadrant and the nautical astrolabe, and navigation was changed dramatically. The Maritime Museum in Lisbon has five nautical astrolabes – the largest permanent collection held by one institution. An astrolabe of Portuguese origin was sold to a museum in Virginia, USA, in 2000, for £110,000.

Astrolabe

The importance of those discoveries is summed up well by the author Jaime Cortesão: 'By discovering the oceans and the science of navigating them, the Portuguese did not just give civilization the best tool with which to govern the earth; they also opened the path for the unification of Humanity'.

It is also thanks to the Portuguese explorers that beautiful products were introduced to the West: bronze sculptures, ebony furniture from Africa, Persian and Indian carpets, tapestry-work and embroidery, silver-work, porcelain and lacquer-work from the Far East, and exquisite gold and mother-of-pearl decorations. All these, of course, in addition to the many varied foodstuffs they brought back.

Flying machines

The first flying machine was invented by **Bartolomeu Lourenço de Gusmão** (1695–1753) – **o voador** (the flyer). He invented the *passarola*; in 1709 it had its first flying experience, long before the French Montgolfier in 1783.

In 1922 the Portuguese aviators **Sacadura Cabral** and **Gago Coutinho** successfully completed the first aerial crossing of the south Atlantic from Lisbon to Brazil, in the hydroplane Santa Cruz. (The Spanish claim they were the first, in 1926, to fly to Buenos Aires, with their pilot Ramón Franco.) This courageous and adventurous feat of more recent 'navigators' is commemorated in Belém (Lisbon), with a life-size model of the plane. The two aviators were to continue their daring flights, in pursuit of aviation research, until Cabral plunged into freezing waters in northern Europe towards the end of 1924. The feats of these two had so touched Portuguese sentiment that, among many poets, Fernando Pessoa wrote of Cabral's disappearance:

Floriu, murchou na extrema haste;	He bloomed and died at the point of the stem;
Jóia do ousar;	A jewel of daring;
Que teve por eterno engaste	whose setting forever would be
O céu e o mar.	the sky and the sea.

Medical advances

António Egas Moniz (1874–1955) was a neurologist who invented the procedure of brain surgery called lobotomy, for which he shared the Nobel Prize for Medicine in 1949. He also invented cerebral angiography, a form of X-ray of the brain that allows blood vessels and other tissue to receive X-ray examination. The controversial procedure of lobotomy was carried out on the first human in 1936, although in fact it was Moniz's assistant who physically conducted the operation, as by then Moniz's own hands were crippled with gout. Between 1949 and 1952 some 5000 lobotomies were performed, in the pursuit of a calming effect for sufferers of acute mental distress. But the procedure of detaching the front lobes from the rest of the brain was outlawed in Portugal and with the development of drugs throughout the 1960s, was no longer required. Moniz was also an active politician, was ambassador to Spain, and later Foreign Minister.

Political 'firsts'

Portugal was the first country to abolish capital punishment in the 19th century, and can also boast the first woman Prime Minister in Europe, before Margaret Thatcher: Maria de Lurdes Pintasilgo.

The trend continues

With such a veritable legacy behind them – over 500 years of exploration and enquiry – it is not surprising that today's Portuguese have continued in the footsteps of those early discoverers. Science and technology are growing areas of expansion in Portugal. A high number of highly skilled graduates work in modern companies, especially in R & D (Research and Development), with research into the AIDS virus one high-profile area of medicine. The government has been investing in a network of science and technology parks, already hailed as centres of excellence, such as the Taguspark, just outside Lisbon.

(See also the chapters on education/business.)

GLOSSARY

a **tecnologia** *technology*
o **jornal** *newspaper*
o **diário** *daily paper*
a **revista** *magazine*
o **rádio** *radio**
a **televisão, a TV** *television, TV*
o **programa** *programme*
a **emissora** *broadcasting station*
o **cinema** *cinema*
os **telespectadores** *viewers*
o **controle remoto** *remote control*
navegar *to surf (the net)*
a **estréia** *debut, opening night*
tirar fotografias *to take photos*
a **navegação** *navigation*

o/a **cineasta** *film maker*
o/a **realizador/a** *director (film)*
o/a **encenador/a** *director (theatre)*
um **filme** *a film*
filmar *to film*
a **trilha sonora** *soundtrack*
o **cinéfilo** *cinema lover*
analisar *to analyze*
o **actor/ a actriz** *actor/actress*
o **canal** *channel*
a **antena parabólica** *satellite dish*
o **portal** *Internet gateway*
a **estrela** *star*
a **ciência** *science*
a **medicina** *medicine*

*The word for radio is masculine (o) when it refers to the wireless set, and feminine (a) when referring to the broadcasters.

Taking it further

Suggested reading

Reflections by Ten Portuguese Photographers, Amanda Hopkinson, features work by various photographers, Frontline/Portugal 600, 1996

Books by Professor Boxer, on the Navigations (See Chapter 1)

VIDA NOVA magazine (published in the UK for Portuguese communities), 106 Victoria Road, London NW6 6QB. Tel: 020 7625 5672

Places to visit/information

Information on technology: ICEP, Direcção de Investimento Internacional, Av.5 de Outubro 101, 1050 Lisbon. Tel: 790-95 00/ 793-01 03

Tagusparque, Núcleo Central 100, 2780 Oeiras, Lisbon. Tel: 21-422 69 31

The weekly magazine ***Visão*** has a pull-out section on entertainment, including theatre, cinema and TV

Portuguese Film Organization, Cinemateca Portuguesa, Rua Barata
  Salgueiro 39, Lisbon. Tel: 21-359 62 00
Bedeteca – Cultural centre dedicated to cartoons and caricaturists,
  Palácio do Contador-Mor, Rua Cidade do Lobito, 1800 Lisboa
Science Museum: Museu de Ciência, Rua da Escola Politécnica,
  56-58, 1250 Lisboa

Websites

Actors, **www.portugal-info.net/people/actors.htm**
Cinema, **www.cinemaportugues.net**
Big Brother, **www.tvi.iol.pt**
Cinema/science/radio/theatre, **www.citi.pt/cultura/index**
Annual film festival in Oporto, **www.caleida.pt/fantasporto**

Many newspapers are on-line; here is a selection:
  www.expresso.pt / **www.oindependente.pt** / **www.jn.pt**
  www.dn.pt / **www.publico.pt** / **www.euronoticias.pt**

Radio and TV stations are also available on-line; here are some:
  www.rdp.pt / **www.radiocomercial.pt** / **www.rtp.pt**

News site, **www.diariodigital.pt/matriz/htm**

On-line magazine for women, **www.mulherportuguesa.com/**

Cinema, **www.7arte.net**

9 POLITICAL STRUCTURES AND INSTITUTIONS

Os eleitores também gostam de consumir, mas não são parvos.
(The electors also like to consume, but they're not stupid) –
Visão magazine, February 2001, on the marketing of politics
as products

Portugal is a modern democratic republic presided over by an
elected president as head of state. As an independent country, it has
its own Constitution, freely held elections across a range of
political parties, and an administrative system for dealing with
local, regional and national bureaucracy. Since it joined the
European Union (then the EEC) in 1986, it has played an
increasingly integrated role in the EU set-up, taking presidency of
the Union during 2000. Portuguese citizens enjoy equal rights as
people living in the other EU member-states, and live a life
relatively free from constriction. However, this has not always
been the case, and the road to Portugal's current stable democracy
has been long and arduous.

The route to democracy

Monarchy

For a country with almost 900 years of independence, Portugal has
only experienced rule without a monarch for around 100 years.
From the first king, Afonso Henriques, in the 12th century, to the
last, Manuel II who was deposed in 1910, Portugal was ruled over
by a succession of monarchs, with varying degrees of success. (see
Chapter 1). During the 13th century Afonso III established local
assemblies of nobles, clergy and mercantile representatives, known
as the Cortes, which were consulted on questions of taxes and other

economic issues. Politics at this time were inextricably tied up with the intervening power of the Church, and the influence of groups such as the Knights Templar.

The final royal period, the House of Bragança, began in 1640 under João IV, and was to last until the imposition of the 1910 Republic. During its regime its rule was to suffer extreme swings in stability, not least during the three turbulent decades from 1801, a period of intense military struggle in the Peninsula. The British military occupation in Lisbon following their intervention against Napoleon began to rankle, undermining Portuguese self-determination, and gave rise to the Liberal movement, initially an underground group of discontents. In 1820 an uprising intended to bring about a constitutional government forced the return of João VI from Brazil, and pitted family and country into a power struggle between the Liberals (Republicans), represented by João, and then his son Pedro, and the Absolutists (Monarchists) led by Pedro's brother Miguel. Pedro's victory marked the last time absolutists held official power in Portugal. Under Maria II the first political parties were formed, and conflict arose between the Liberals (supporting the original 1822 constitution) and those known as 'Chartists'(adhering to the 1826 charter set down by Pedro, which provided for a parliamentary regime based on the monarch's authorization, and not popular will).

A stand-off between Britain and Portugal, over contended territory around the Zambesi in Africa, resulted in the English Lord Salisbury issuing the 'Ultimatum' in 1890 that Portugal should withdraw completely. The reverberations of such a message shook the Royal House in Portugal, as the old Anglo-Portuguese Alliance had hitherto guaranteed security for the ruling monarchists. Corruption and inefficient control of the empire resulted in a growing anti-monarch sentiment, and in 1908 Carlos I and his eldest son were assassinated in Lisbon. Although the second son, Manuel II, survived and claimed the throne, the House of Bragança and the monarchy, were overturned two years later.

Pretenders to the throne

Two figures stand out in Portuguese history as representatives of the hopes of the nation. One was the young monarch Sebastião, so fatefully lost in battle in North Africa, and in whose figure many since then have placed their hopes for a return to glory. 'Sebastianismo' is dear to the Portuguese sentiment of *saudade* and nostalgia, and over history has built up a cult status, although it is rejected by some intellectuals.

For others, in modern Portugal and elsewhere, Sebastião is seen to be embodied in the current Duke of Bragança, the very real pretender to the throne. The Royal House of Bragança has a solid following, not least from a group of Britons calling themselves 'The Association of St Michael of the Wing'. The name refers to an order of chivalry established after a vision of St Michael inspired the Portuguese to victory against the Moors in the 12th century. Although the order was short-lived, it was revived after the 1974 revolution, and has a thriving allegiance in both countries. Manuel II actually died in Twickenham, in London, but this group of monarchy enthusiasts staunchly believes he will not be the last king. Malcolm Howe, one of the group members, says: 'I've seen opinion polls with 70 per cent in favour of restoration. And the Duke of Bragança says there are more monarchists now than there were republicans when the Republic was implanted in 1910.' The current Duke, Duarte, married in the 1990s and now has a further heir to the seat. The family leads a quiet life on the Duke's extensive rural estate.

The republic

The first rumblings of socialist thought, led by a group in Coimbra known as the Generation of 1870, was suppressed by the government, but the rising tide of republicanism had sealed its victory by assassinating Carlos. In 1911 a liberal constitution was put into place, one of its most decisive actions being to separate church from state. The first President was Manuel José de Arriaga, who inaugurated what was to become a period of messy, ineffective rule. Between 1910 and 1926 there were no fewer than 45 different governments, most arriving in power by military intervention. The republicans failed to deliver promised financial reform and stability, and with the advent of the 1920s depression, their popular support slipped away. In 1926 a *coup d'état* brought General Oscar Carmona into power as President, and in 1928 he named **António**

de Oliveira Salazar as his Finance Minister. By 1932 Salazar had begun a stint as Prime Minister that was to last until 1968, and catapult him into the annals of history as dictator and leader of a regime from which the Portuguese are still recovering.

Dictatorship

The man

Salazar was the son of an austere, deeply religious and conservative rural family. As economics professor at Coimbra university, he was a talented and respected academic, and on appointment to the government he did an excellent job of straightening out the country's financial messes. His extreme views on religion, the nation, and a fatalistic streak, which he imposed on the country during his regime, were to curtail Portugal's development in many areas, alongside rapid advances elsewhere in Europe. He totally and fervently stood by his conviction of 'Nothing against the nation, all for the nation', and in effect cut Portugal off from all external influences. Salazar himself lived a relatively subdued life often outside the capital, with a housekeeper (thought by many to be his mistress) and two adopted daughters. In 1968 he suffered a stroke as a result of falling out of a deck-chair and hitting his head whilst in Estoril. He was never told that his position had been taken over, and he died still believing he was in control of his beloved nation.

The regime

Whoever you talk to in Portugal, you will always get an opinion on the regime. No life remained untouched by it – whether as a lucky beneficiary of its finer aspects, or as one of the very many who experienced (at first-hand or otherwise) its brutality. It is still too recent in the history, and the lives, of the Portuguese not to hold meaning for the majority, and the polemics of debate as to its pros and cons are as alive as ever. Salazar modelled his regime on that of Mussolini, and Spain's Primo de Rivera: his *Estado Novo* (New State) in fact had the trappings of a Fascist regime, under a republican government. Despite the respect for his idols, Salazar himself never assumed a dictator's title, unlike the Führer, Caudillo and il Duce – he simply remained Salazar. Despite numerous attempted coups, the country accepted (had no choice but to accept) the regime, as Salazar promised to protect the Portuguese from the quickly advancing technological age, which would erode their traditions and values. In 1933 Salazar endorsed a new Constitution. A growing Communist leaning had to bide its time over the next four decades before rearing its head and playing its part in the overthrow of the regime. For Salazar surrounded himself with cronies in the highest position – men who would not dare to oppose his ideals. There was only one political party allowed – The National Union, and total censorship of the press. Many liberal thinkers and intellectuals fled the oppression, and continued their expressions in France, the UK and Brazil.

Those who dared to stay ran the risk of confrontation with Salazar's feared and loathed secret police, trained by the Gestapo – the PIDE (Polícia Internacional e de Defesa do Estado), who had grown from an earlier section, the PVDE (the Vigilance Police). Many Portuguese people can still recall visits in the middle of the night, family and friends dragged away for interrogation for insurrection against the regime. Many of them never returned, or if they did they were never the same people again. Education was provided only for the chosen few – the staunch supporters of the Estado Novo, and most working-class people were denied access to it as it was the easiest way to avoid the spread of knowledge and, therefore, possible opposition. The grandfather of one of my close friends (who is half-Portuguese) ran a small school in Praia da Rocha in the Algarve. José Buisel was ordered to accept only those pupils recommended by the regime, but as a liberal thinker and educator, refused. He was lucky to suffer no more than to have his school closed down – defiance was usually dealt with in much more brutal ways. Other members of the family, though, were less fortunate. Other people may tell you that the regime brought its positive points; more security for example – people felt safe in their homes and on the streets; greater respect in the society; a feeling of strong leadership for the total good of the country. A number of people, of course, were untouched by the negative side of the dictatorship – these were the ones who found themselves fleeing the country when the regime cracked. It is impossible here to give more than a flavour of what the regime was like – a number of books are dedicated to the theme, some of which are listed at the end of the chapter.

Politically, Salazar stifled any opposition for a lengthy period, but he ran into all kinds of problems in the African territories, where his dominant moral value of the glorious empire blinded him to the stagnation of the Portuguese economy, bereft of financial stability due to the huge amounts of money pouring into the maintenance of the 'overseas provinces'. Soon Portugal faced the problem of mass emigration as people, particularly in the rural north, went in search of work (see p.247).

It was against this shaky background that Marcello Caetano took over as Salazar's successor, and maintained an iron-hand rule until discontent began to show through the ranks of the military.

The Carnation Revolution

The formation of the Armed Forces Movement (MFA – Movimento das Forças Armadas) in 1973 was the first solid step towards finally bringing down the regime. The combination of the now-strong underground Communist movement, thriving in the vast Alentejo region, and a group of young army officers (known as *Os Capitães de Abril*) who formed a junta gave impetus for the overthrow. At the same time, the chosen leader of this junta, General António de Spínola, had published a damning criticism of affairs in Portugal,

'Portugal and the Future', in which he advanced the recommendation for a military take-over. Caetano himself was worried by the publication, claiming later: 'I did not stop until the last page, which I read in the small hours of the morning. And when I closed the book I understood that the military coup, which I could sense had been coming, was now inevitable.' And come it did. With everyone in place on the evening of 24 April 1974, the warning signal of the song 'Grândola, Vila Morena' was played on the radio, and the advance on Lisbon commenced. By the next day, *o 25 de Abril*, it was all over, executed swiftly, efficiently and with

GOLPE MILITAR

"MOVIMENTO
DAS FORÇAS
ARMADAS"
DESENCADEIA
ACÇÃO
DE
MADRUGADA

**Newspaper headline
25th April 1974:**
*Military Coup
'Armed Forces
Movement' triggers
early-morning action*

minimal loss of life. Caetano and his officials took refuge at the barracks of the National Guard, from where they were later imprisoned. A restaurant that had been about to open that morning had asked for red carnations to be given to passers-by. Instead they were given to passing soldiers, who placed them in the barrels of their rifles as a symbol of a peaceful take-over – *A revolução dos cravos*. Political prisoners were released, and PIDE members locked up in their place, an interim government was sworn in, and many of those protected under the regime fled with few possessions, before lands and property were expropriated.

Tellingly, the front page of the newspaper *República* on 26 April carried a flash stating:

Este jornal não foi visado por qualquer comissão de ensura. (This newspaper has not been subject to censorship!)

Democracy

During the ensuing years, a series of upheavals in government added to the problems Portugal faced on its rapid withdrawal from its African colonies – seen by some as the most negative aspect of its recent history. Already experiencing catastrophic unemployment, Portugal now had to soak up both the returning troops and those peoples returning from Africa in the chaotic aftermath – *os retornados* (the returned ones). Despite this, positive steps were taken to move Portugal forward: the armed forces were reorganized, economic and social reforms began, some nationalization of industries and banks was started, and a constituent assembly backed by the socialists was set up. After a series of violent anti-Communist demonstrations which were particularly strong in the north, relative stability came in 1976, with the socialist prime minister Mário Soares. Soares, who many consider to have been the pivot in the transition to democracy, was dismissed two years later during extreme economic difficulties. In 1979 the conservative Democratic Alliance took power, in the figure of Francisco Manuel de Sá Carneiro. His leadership was short-lived; he died the next year in a plane crash, under circumstances still reverberating in Portuguese politics today (see p.192). Soares came back into power in 1983, becoming President in 1986 and guiding Portugal into the then EEC. He continued for another term of office until being replaced in 1996 by the socialist Jorge Sampaio, whose Prime Minister (António Guterres) was from the same party – the first time this had happened since 1974. In January 2001 Sampaio was re-elected President for a further term.

Portugal has come a long way since the dark days of western Europe's most lasting dictatorship. Its presence within the EU has been beneficial – poverty is being eradicated and many modern developments are heralding a new era. Some say the dictatorship was just as successful in improving living standards (which rose from around 30 per cent of the European average in 1965, to 56 per cent in 1974. It is about 70 per cent now). José Saramago, the Nobel writer and life-time Communist, recently remarked that 'Portugal would have arrived exactly where it has today if there had been no Revolution.' There are many who disagree!

The Portuguese Constitution

Portugal é uma República soberana, baseada na dignidade da pessoa humana e na vontade popular e empenhada na construção de uma sociedade livre, justa e solidária. (Portugal is a sovereign Republic based on the dignity of the human person and the will of the people and committed to the construction of a free and just society united in its common purposes) – Article 1, Portuguese Constitution

The 1976 Constitution aimed to reflect the hopes of those who had been directly involved in the 1974 coup. Their wishes were that the African colonies should be liberated, that resources (financial and human) should no longer be wasted in colonial wars, and a new social democracy be established. On this basis, the Constitution enshrined fundamental civil rights and freedoms, calling for the creation of what it called a 'classless state', with public ownership of land and resources. Censorship and the death penalty were written out of the statutes, and included for the first time were the right to strike and the right of assembly. Fascist organizations were made illegal, a move which for some time was a source of contention. Legislative power was assigned to the Parliament and Government and judicial power to the courts.

The post of presidency (elected by the people for a five-year term) is largely ceremonial, with few executive powers. As head of state and commander-in-chief of the armed forces, *o presidente* (the president) ensures the country functions smoothly and in accordance with the Constitution. His main roles are:

- to appoint the prime minister and ratify cabinet
- to proclaim parliamentary laws and decrees
- to commute prison terms or grant pardons
- to represent the country in international matters.

Day-to-day running of the country is the responsibility of the Government. In January 2001 the President, Sampaio, was reported as being *furioso* with his Government for abdicating its responsibility to him in the case of the dismissal of a leading General (Martins Barrento). Sampaio himself was in the middle of his re-election campaign at the time and could have done without the added distraction.

A Bandeira Portuguesa

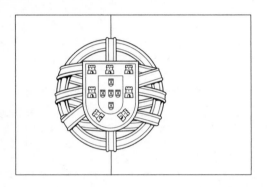

The left-hand side of the flag is green, representing the hope for prosperity and well-being, and the green fields of the homeland. The red panel on the right symbolizes the bravery and blood spilled by so many heroes in the Crusades, the discoveries and in the defence and expansion of the country.In the centre of the flag is a sphere which represents the voyages of the Portuguese explorers around the world, and in its centre is the royal coat of arms of Portugal – a large shield (*escudo*), with a smaller one within it. The larger, red shield is surrounded by seven castles, the fortified towns taken from the Moors by Dom Afonso III. The smaller, white shield encloses a further five, small blue shields, each one containing five white dots. These shields represent the five wounds of Christ, and the total number of white dots, added to the middle dot of each shield (in effect counted twice), recall the 30 pieces of silver gained by Judas in his betrayal of Christ, and the royal power to mint coins.

For the *Hino Nacional* (the National Anthem), refer back to Chapter 5, p.104.

Government

How the political system is structured:

Elected by the people
|
| Presidente da República |
|
nominates
| Primeiro Ministro |
|
nominates

Conselho de Ministros
(Government)
in the Assembleia da República (parliament)
Approx. 230 seats
Legislative power / Annual state budget / controls action of the
Government / ratifies international treaties

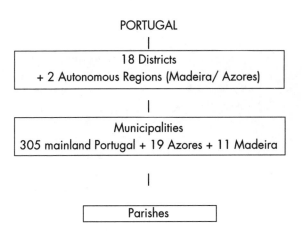

PORTUGAL
|
18 Districts
+ 2 Autonomous Regions (Madeira/ Azores)

|

Municipalities
305 mainland Portugal + 19 Azores + 11 Madeira

|

Parishes

Given that MPs are elected by proportional representation (i.e. all parties are represented in proportion to their voting strength), and the very real possibilities of non-majority parties, it is necessary for the prime minister to be appointed by the president. Once the results of a general election are declared, the president considers the make-up of parliament and chooses the most appropriate person to lead the country for the ensuing four years. This may result in coalition governments, as happened in the elections of 1979 and 1980, although it is rare. Once a prime minister has been appointed, a cabinet of ministers (*Conselho de Ministros*) forming the Government is chosen by that person and officially appointed by the president. While the prime minister can dismiss or appoint ministers at his discretion, the president must ratify any decisions affecting the running of the country.

Parliament

The Portuguese Parliament

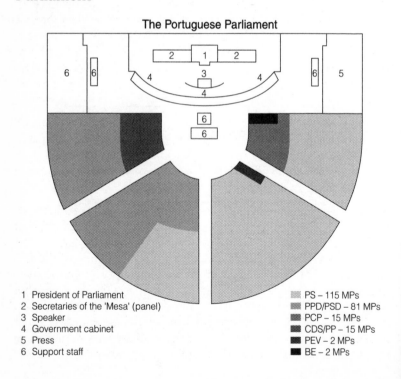

1 President of Parliament
2 Secretaries of the 'Mesa' (panel)
3 Speaker
4 Government cabinet
5 Press
6 Support staff

PS – 115 MPs
PPD/PSD – 81 MPs
PCP – 15 MPs
CDS/PP – 15 MPs
PEV – 2 MPs
BE – 2 MPs

The Parliament consists of one chamber, the Assembly of the Republic (*Assembleia da República*); there is no upper and lower house. There are approximately 230 members of parliament (*os deputados*) elected by the people every four years by proportional representation, around a fifth of whom are women. Portugal also has 25 members in the European Parliament. The Assembly meets in the Palácio de São Bento in Lisbon, where guided tours are available, in addition to three public plenary sessions a week. The Assembly elects its own leader, also known as a *presidente*, with a panel of secretaries, known as the Mesa.

Elections (*Eleições*)

Anyone over the age of 18 may vote, although the current Government wants to bring the age down to 16, but as the most recent presidential election showed, many Portuguese are simply not interested. At least that's what the exit polls suggested, with around 50 per cent of eligible voters not turning out. This level of abstention was unprecedented, and by the end of the campaign, Sampaio (the clear runner all the way through) had cause to declare to the people, 'vote for whom you like, but vote'. Politician Marcelo Rebelo de Sousa commented in the *Público* newspaper in January 2001:

> *Jorge Sampaio tem dois adversários: a abstenção e o espectro de Mário Soares, a votação que ele teve na sua última reeleição à volta de 70 por cento.* (JS has two enemies: abstention and the ghost of Mário Soares, the votes he had in his last re-election, around 70 per cent)

Many surveys and public polls in Portugal, announced in the press, highlight a very real problem with getting the general public to declare an opinion, or even an interest in, current affairs. When asked to comment on how well Portugal's presidency of the EU had gone, more than 50 per cent of people simply 'didn't know'. Surprisingly, a poll a few years ago about the Spanish revealed that 62 per cent of the Portuguese described them as 'our brothers'! People tend to voice their opinions more when it comes to local issues, and it is not uncommon for rural communities in particular to speak out against issues affecting their own way of life.

Political parties

The main parties are the Socialists (PS), Social Democrats (PSD), Centre Democrats (PP), and Communists (PCP), with a handful of less important groups, the most significant being the Left Block (BE). Proportional representation in the political voting system gives rise to a number of much smaller independent parties, but politics in Portugal are dominated by a small number of groups.

A esquerda (the left)

O Partido Socialista (PS)

The centre-left Socialist Party came to power in 1999 expecting to gain just enough votes for a majority. They fell one vote short, and have been surviving as a minority Government under the leadership of Prime Minister António Guterres, with 115 seats (or 42.9 per cent) in Parliament. Their situation means that they are always reliant on support for various laws from other parties – in return for favours, obviously! Guterres, who first came into power in 1995, defeating the Social Democrat Cavaco Silva, saw his personal poll ratings slip during 2000, and his government is now viewed with a modicum of scepticism. This is in stark contrast to the warm welcome Guterres' policies received at the beginning of his first term in office. He is dedicated to the fight against poverty and social exclusion.

O Partido Comunista Português (PCP)

The Communist Party has always had a strong following in the vast agricultural areas of the Alentejo, which played such an instrumental part in the 1974 revolution. It was here, from 1975 onwards, that large workers' cooperatives (*cooperativas*) were set up to protect those working the land on what had previously been the large estates, or *latifúndios*. Allied to the party is the United Democratic Coalition (CDU). The PCP currently hold 15 seats in parliament (around 7 per cent), with a further two seats being held by representatives of the 'Left Block', *Bloco de Esquerda* (BE). The Communist Party remains pretty orthodox, led by Carlos Carvalhas, and claiming that the French Party these days pays little more than lip-service to the cause, whilst at the same time praising the German Communists for their faith. A central figure of the old school is the ageing Álvaro Cunhal, returned from Moscow once the dictatorship fell, and still keeping an eye on his comrades' proceedings.

O Partido Ecologista – 'os Verdes' (PEV)

The 'Green' party has had a presence in Portugal since 1982, as an active ecological voice, and now with two representatives in Parliament. It is made up of regional groups, working to raise awareness of green issues, and has a section for younger members, called *Ecolojovem*.

A direita (the right)

O Partido Social Democrático (PSD)

The Social Democrats, currently led by José Manuel Durão Barroso who has been found to be the least popular of its figureheads, sits at centre-right of the political scale. After its heyday in the decade of government during the mid-1980s to its defeat by the socialists in 1995, the PSD has experienced problems with changes of leader and a drop in popularity. The party has not managed to submit a convincing alternative to the Government's programme, in part suffering the same problem as other right-wing parties in Europe: the socialists have moved towards the right! Senhor Barroso seems to want to blame everyone else for his party's lack of success, and has even been in talks with the more conservative Popular Party in an effort to combine forces.

O Partido Popular (PP)

The more right-wing Popular, or People's party, with its allied party, the Social Democratic Centre party (CDS), is particularly strong in the industrial and business areas of Oporto and parts of the north (traditionally always more conservative). It currently enjoys 15 seats in parliament, and is courted by the PSD. The leader of the PP, Paulo Portas (his own initials are a pure coincidence!), is a great campaigner and inspiring public speaker. He enjoys being out on the streets, in hand-shaking and baby-kissing mode. In 2000 the Government's budget was helped through by the PP, but only in return for higher state retirement pensions.

There is no National Front-type party, as it is forbidden under the Constitution. The controversial French politician Le Pen went to Portugal some years ago to inspire a small group of extremists, which has since almost disintegrated. Many of its members apparently seemed unable to recall Salazar!

Political scandals

No Government is devoid of scandal, on whatever level that might manifest itself, and Portugal is no exception. However, the very public denouncements of sexual impropriety as seen in the UK and USA in particular in recent years are quite rare in Portugal, although the Portuguese would probably relish them, while at the same time not condemning out of hand. What has been an on-going problem, and one that President Sampaio is rolling up his sleeves to tackle is corruption in politics. In what has recently been called 'a serious crisis for democracy', the main allegations in politics have been of a financial nature. It all came to a head in 1998 when the former chairman of the National Road Board claimed that politicians and parties were awarding works contracts to construction companies in exchange for payments. In a televised address to the nation, the Prime Minister instigated a number of measures to deal with the problems, and since then legislation on party financing has undergone a series of reforms. However, there are still calls for even more drastic means to make the financing of political parties totally transparent. At a time when political shenanigans are rife in the UK over party backers, and with memories of the problematic US elections in 2000 still reverberating, calls in Portugal for more modest political house-keeping is very apt. 'Names on cheques, not money under the table' suggested Sampaio recently.

On another scale, in 1999 the British newspaper *The Guardian* published an article linking the mysterious death of the Prime Minister Sá Carneiro in 1980 to a group of left-wing terrorists called the FP-25. The Portuguese Minister of Justice took action against the paper, but the investigation into the claims made in the article has since dissipated. The trials of members of the FP-25, who conducted various terrorist attacks in the 1980s, have created much public interest, no less so because among the accused was one of the most prominent figures of the 1974 Revolution – Captain Otelo Saraiva de Carvalho (who has always denied any involvement with the group). The case looks set to drag on, with details brushed under the carpets of some ministerial office!

The administration

Anyone who has ever had to deal with bureaucracy in Portugal knows just how drawn-out and excruciatingly frustrating it can be. Even the most simple paperwork processes can involve lengthy waits in lengthy queues, being sent from one office to another (and often back again!), being told you have not brought the correct documentation, everything in at least triplicate, and then another wait for the job to be processed. Documents are not valid after six months, so originals (birth certificates, etc.) are not accepted. And it's not just foreigners who are subjected to this ritualistic form of paper-torture; the Portuguese themselves live with it day in day out. It's absolutely no wonder one of the most commonly used expressions is a resigned *'Paciência'*! It is not surprising, perhaps, that many link this over-attention to detail with the years of the dictatorship, when a strict control was exercised in every facet of life. Add to this the very Portuguese trait of lack of urgency (fine when you're ambling through the mountains, not so when you need a birth certificate), and it's easy to see how it can all get so out of hand.

Central administration

Os ministros

The most important government ministries are the *Ministério de Estado* (State Affairs), *Ministério das Finanças* (Treasury), *Ministério dos Negócios Estrangeiros* (Foreign Affairs), *Ministério da Administração Interna* (Home Affairs) and *Ministério Público* (Public). There are 20 ministries in total. There is currently only one woman minister – for Health (*Saúde*). Each appointed minister in the cabinet chooses his (or her) own civil servants to run the office. The next level down from *ministro* is the *Secretária do Estado* (Secretary of State), posts Guterres and his Cabinet had problems filling in 2000. Most government offices are found in the splendid Praça do Comércio in Lisbon (by the riverfront, commonly known in English as 'Black Horse Square', or Terreiro do Paço by locals).

Local administration

A junta da freguesia

Each of Portugal's 4209 parish councils has an elected assembly and council, usually known as an *executivo*, and led by a *presidente*.

Os concelhos/ municípios

There are 305 municipalities on mainland Portugal, with an additional 19 in the Azores and 11 on Madeira. Central office is the town hall (*câmara municipal*) where the council meets, presided over by a mayor (*presidente da câmara*) who is elected by the local residents every five years. This is a paid position, and one endowed with a certain amount of local pride and esteem. The *assembleia municipal*, via its various *departamentos* and *gabinetes*, is responsible for the running of the local area, including raising local taxes on properties, car tax, and the granting of commercial licences.

Os distritos

For administrative purposes, the five mainland regions (which up until 1959 had in fact been 11 provinces – see p.6), are divided into 18 districts, the most important layer of local government. District governors (*governadores*) are appointed by the Minister for Internal Administration, and are answerable to the Government.

The two autonomous regions of the Azores and Madeira have their own *governo regional* headed by a *presidente* appointed by the prime minister in accordance with general election results. The two regions have powers assigned to them in the Constitution. A central government minister liaises between the regions and mainland Portugal.

Regionalization

Portugal's administrative set-up was one of the most centralized in Europe until 1974, and still remains pretty much so today. When the socialists came to power in 1995, one of their main campaign thrusts was to devolve power out to the regions, encouraging active participation of local citizens in political life, giving them a say in how the regions were developed and how public funds should be spent. Tellingly, though, after prolonged public debate closely reported on in the media, a referendum on *Regionalização* in November 1998 saw a rejection of the plan by more than 63 per cent of the voters. Few people in the agricultural regions of the north and centre could see how they would benefit from what they considered even more division of the country. They appeared more concerned with the very real issues affecting their ways of life, such as farming subsidies and employment. A few thought the plan would draw attention to the plight of poorer regions, but in the end the idea has been consigned to the back burner again. One priest was quoted as saying:

> *Inclino-me para o não. D. João II fez um esforço enorme em unir o País.* (I'm inclined to vote No. King John II made such a huge effort to unite the country!)

And, perhaps more typically, from the mouths of a group of old farmers:

> *Não compreendemos o que isso quer dizer.* (We don't know what it means)

The legal system

The Portuguese legal system is based on the *Code Napoléon* established in France following the Revolution there. The 'Code' itself was a unified arrangement, pulling together essentially northern, Germanic law, with the Roman law of the south. The Code Napoléon is hailed as a perfect example of simplicity and clarity; unfortunately in Portugal interpretation and the carrying out of a judicial matter is convoluted and can take an inordinate amount of time.

Crime, trial and punishment

The vast majority of crimes in Portugal involve the bouncing of (or not honouring) cheques, and theft. Serious traffic offences account for around 2500 cases a year, and drug-related crime (theft and assault) has now found its place in an otherwise relatively safe country. However, violence in and around nightclubs has increased alarmingly since 1995; in a recent survey 48.6 per cent of people interviewed in Lisbon and Oporto said they were afraid to go out at night. The main causes cited were alcohol and drugs leading to the threat of assault and theft. The types of heinous crimes (sexual, against children, shootings) which sadly have become the norm in the UK, USA and elsewhere, are still very rare in Portugal. Unfortunately though, modified hand pistols are now filtering through the black market, and have been used in a number of recent assaults. According to the police:

Adquirir pistolas é quase tão fácil como comprar um electrodoméstico. (Getting hold of pistols is almost as easy as buying a domestic appliance)

At the beginning of 2001 there was an outcry in Portugal when seven British paedophiles were sent to prison for trading images on the Internet. Why? Because it was thought the sentences of 12 to 30 months was far too lenient. One of the photographs found in their possession is thought to be that of Rui Pedro, a young Portuguese boy who went missing three years ago. Although this type of crime is extremely rare in Portugal, a case of child abuse is currently being heard in Madeira, involving a group of men including one Portuguese. Under Portuguese law the possession of child pornographic material is not considered a crime, and the case in Funchal is testing public emotion to the limit.

Common contraventions of the law at a less serious level usually involve traffic-related offences (particularly parking). These are usually simply dealt with by an on-the-spot fine payable at the local police station (*esquadra*). Cases taken to court are usually dealt with by three judges, with the accused opting for an additional jury if required. Judges are appointed for life, which is just as well really, considering the huge number of cases taking up to three years to reach court. Every citizen has the right of access to the judicial system, as laid down by the Constitution. Courts are autonomous and are bound only by the law of the land and the demands of the Constitution.

Supreme Court

The High Court – sits in Lisbon,
can judge on civil, criminal, commercial cases

|

Courts of Secondary Jurisdiction

Act as Courts of Appeal. Cases over a certain limit
can appeal to the Supreme Court

|

Courts of Primary Jurisdiction

|

County Courts	**Admin Courts**	**Tax Courts**
General cases, criminal, family, minors, labour cases. Court's decision final in cases under a certain value. Over this threshold you can appeal to the Courts of Secondary Jurisdiction	Local and national government matters	Tax cases

---

Although figures for crime have dropped over the last decade, cases brought to court have increased by around 6 per cent a year. Portugal's 50 or so prisons are full to capacity, with about 10,000 people languishing in cells, of which only about 500 are women. The most severe punishment is 25 years. A debate on *pena de prisão perpétua* (life sentence) is going on in Portugal now – it currently does not exist in Portuguese law, and there is no capital punishment. International law is currently being incorporated into the statutes to provide for life sentences.The death penalty was abolished in 1867. In late 1999 the Minister of Justice, António Costa, announced measures to encourage parties to settle their litigation in amicable, out-of-court agreements. This came as an attempt to counteract the laborious nature of the legal system, but would probably employ even more court officials to set it up!

The police

Most Portuguese people do not trust the police, regarding them as corrupt and, often, simply incompetent, which in many cases has been found to be true. There are a number of police forces in Portugal: the *Guarda Nacional Republicana*, (GNR), and the Public Security Police, *Polícia de Segurança Pública* (PSP), both with almost equal numbers of employees. The GNR are quite austere-looking, in grey uniforms, and are military-led. The PSP wear dark blue uniforms, are armed (as are their GNR counterparts), and deal with general policing matters, and traffic. There is also the *Polícia Judiciária* (Criminal Investigation Unit), *Brigada de Trânsito* (Traffic Brigade), *Guarda Fiscal* (Customs and Excise patrols) and the *Polícia Marítima* (Coastguard). There have been recently highlighted cases of police brutality in Portugal, with some of the victims claiming that it harked back to the PIDE days of Salazar's regime. The police certainly do not suffer fools (or foolish foreigners) easily, and have been accused of picking on blacks. However, they also sometimes turn a blind eye to teenage criminals who know their area better than the police themselves!

GLOSSARY

o **dictador** *dictator*
o **regime** *regime*
o **rei** *king*
a **rainha** *queen*
real *royal*
o **presidente** *president*
o **primeiro ministro** *prime minister*
a **democracia** *democracy*
a **política** *politics*
o **político** *politician*
o **partido** *party*
o **discurso** *speech*
o **golpe** *coup*
o **exército** *army*
detido/a *under arrest*

exercer o cargo de *to hold the office of*
o **mandato** *mandate, term*
a **sessão** *sitting of parliament*
a **campanha eleitoral** *election campaign*
a **intenção de voto** *which way you'll vote*
votar *to vote*
a **abstenção** *abstention*
o **chumbo** (col.) *failing*
o **tribunal de justiça** *law court*
o **juíz/ a juiza** *judge*
o **advogado** *lawyer*
declarar-se culpado *to plead guilty*
declarar X inocente *to find X innocent*
o/a polícia *police (officer)*
o/a preso/a *prisoner*

Taking it further

Suggested reading

A Small Death in Lisbon, crime novel by Robert Wilson, Harper Collins, 2000, gives good background to the Salazar regime, including relationships with Britain and Germany during the War, and police investigations

Portugal: 50 Years of Dictatorship, António de Figueiredo, Harmondsworth, 1975

Insight on Portugal: The Year of the Captains, *Sunday Times*, Andre Deutsch, 1975

Portugal: the Impossible Revolution?, Phil Mailer, London, 1977

Portugal: Birth of a Democracy, Robert Harvey, Macmillan, 1978

Portugal's Struggle for Liberty, Mário Soares, Allen & Unwin, 1975

Places to visit/ information

Biblioteca/Museu da República e Resistência (Contemporary history), Estrada de Benfica 417/9, 1500 Lisboa. Tel: 774-24 02/3

Websites

Politics, **www.citi.pt/cultura/index**
The site of the Contemporary Portuguese Politics and History Research Centre (cphrc) Dundee University, Scotland has good information and links, including music of the revolution

Politicians, **www.portugal-info.net**
All the Portuguese ministries have links under, **www.pcm.gov.pt**
Law, **www.jurinfor.pt**
'Citizens shop', **www.lojadocidadao.pt**
Information on the municipalities, **www.anmp.pt**
The president, **www.presidenciarepublica.pt**
Parliament, **www.parlamento.pt**
Government cabinet, **www.primeiro-ministro.gov.pt**

10 BASICS FOR LIVING

A vida para uns é mãe, para outros é madrasta (Life for some is a mother, for others it's a stepmother) – *Proverb*

Education

Educação is one of the top priorities of the current Government in Portugal, and one seen with a certain amount of urgency in terms of its advancement. Educational reform has been a buzz-term since the 1974 revolution, when it was obvious that the state of play was dire, with fewer than 40 per cent of 14-year-olds in school. Between then and 1986 various developments took place, albeit very cautiously, and by the 1990s between 57 and 91 per cent of 14-year-olds were receiving education of some sort, and numbers of students attending higher education rose from around 4000 in 1974 to more than 70,000 by 1992. In 1986 the *Lei de Bases do Sistema Educativo* (Comprehensive Law on the Educational System) established a solid, general framework for the re-organization of the system. Under this Decree, all citizens have a right to education, and equal access to school and also success at school is guaranteed. While the state plays no part in directing education in any particular 'philosophical, aesthetic, political or religious' way, it does take very seriously its role of democratization of education, and in order to achieve its aims, education is now the principal item of expenditure in the national budget.

The changes that have taken place so far have been fundamental, particularly in reducing illiteracy among young people (although it still persists in the older generations: in 1991 just over a million illiterates, 12 per cent of the population over 15, in 2000 87 per cent of the population over 15 is considered literate). Other positive moves have been to increase school attendance at both pre-school age, and in the 13 to 23 age range (which has gone up from 56 per cent in the 1980s to 66 per cent a decade later, and continues to rise steadily). Portugal has taken advantage of subsidies and EU programmes to shore up and develop education across a much broader spectrum than ever before, and most particularly in the area of *formação profissional* (vocational and technical training). Since the beginning of the 1990s, Portugal's spending on education has remained at around 5 or 6 per cent of GDP, in 1999 5.8 per cent, compared with 6 per cent in France, 5.3 per cent in the UK, and 5.4 per cent in the USA.

There are still many problems facing everyone involved in the progress of education in Portugal: increasing still further the numbers of youngsters in school, and making sure they leave school with a qualification and training to ensure they are prepared for work; improving resources – many school buildings are in need of repair, and schools lack equipment and books; better working conditions and pay for the teachers (a primary teacher can expect to earn about 1000 euros a month, and a secondary teacher about 1250 euros). One university teacher, Maria Filomena Mónica warns:

Temos um sistema de ensino que destrói ambições e nivela por baixo. (We have an education system that destroys ambition and brings everything down to a low level)

The problem looks set to run and run.

Schools

Although the Ministry of Education has overall responsibility for education – its development and funding – it is the municipalities who oversee construction of school buildings and their maintenance, equipment and operational expenses, as well as providing some funding for school transport and extra-curricular activities. Compulsory education is free, and pupils in cases of hardship also receive free books, transport, meals and, sometimes, accommodation. However, at secondary level token tuition fees are charged and books must be purchased. Most pupils attend state-run schools, but a number may choose to go to a private institution

The Portuguese education system

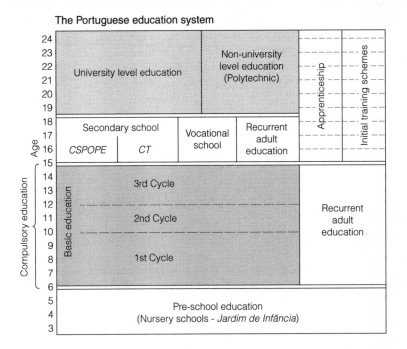

which receives equal benefits as state schools if it follows the same national curriculum. There are a growing number of international schools in Portugal, reflecting the increasing numbers of foreign residents. Some of these follow a British or American curriculum, but others also cater for the Portuguese market, with a dual system in place. They benefit, in most cases, from enhanced facilities, and an interesting mix of nationalities, and may be seen by some middle-class Portuguese families as a beneficial option. However, there have been reported cases of establishments run by fraudsters, especially in the Algarve, where businesses can appear and disappear in the bat of a sunburnt eyelid!

Children between the ages of three and six usually attend optional pre-school education, in the form of a nursery (*Jardim de Infância*) run either by the Ministry of Education, in which case it is free, or at a school under the auspices of the Ministry of Employment and

Social Security (MESS – some might say an unfortunate acronym for a ministry!), where parents share costs according to their income. MESS schools provide social assistance in addition to educational training. The numbers of children in pre-school groups have increased dramatically since 1974 (when 42,500 were enrolled), to almost 122,000 in 1989, and by now approximately 50 per cent of all three- to six-year-olds are in nursery school. In groups of no more than 25, children attend nursery for five hours a day (MESS schools provide a longer service), and educational guidelines dictate that they should learn to express themselves 'through movement, and dramatic, visual and musical expression, learning the mother tongue and mathematics'. Emphasis is on fun, creativity and social skills, and Portuguese youngsters certainly appear lively and expressive.

Teachers (*professores*)

All teachers in state schools are civil servants (*funcionários civis*).

Nursery teachers undergo three years' training at institutions of HE and achieve a degree (*bacharelato*).

Teachers in basic and secondary education are subject specialists, and undergo training depending on which level, or 'cycle' they will teach:

- 1st cycle – a three-year bacharelato degree
- 2nd cycle – a three-year bacharelato, plus one or two years higher diploma or a *Licenciatura* (university) degree
- 3rd cycle/secondary – five or six years leading to *licenciatura*.

Compulsory education is divided into three *ciclos*, corresponding to primary (taught in an *escola primária*), preparatory (*escola preparatória* or *secundária* – up to the age of 12), and the third *ciclo*, up to school-leaving age at 15. Throughout this time Portuguese youngsters are taught a range of subjects, including one or two foreign languages, personal and social education. Many schools operate a 'shift' system to their timetable, as resources can only allow pupils to attend either in the mornings (from 8–1) or afternoons (1.15–6.15). Some may attend school in the evening. The most common method of teaching is 'chalk and talk', with all the pupils sitting facing the front of the classroom, although there have been changes in recent years, as new ideas from other countries have been incorporated. However, it is still the old pre-revolution doctrine that prevails. Many schools subscribe to innovative schemes in place throughout Europe, such as the 'Science Across Europe' programmes, with pupils keen on potential links with other schools and countries.

Ensino secundário

For any youngsters going on to secondary education, up to the age of 18, they can choose between the regular secondary system, a vocational school or an art education course. *Ensino secundário* itself offers two strands of courses: general courses usually leading on to further study, or technical-type courses, such as civil construction or computing. All pupils receive instruction in general subjects, which are:

- Portuguese (*Português*)
- philosophy (*filosofia*)
- one or two foreign languages (*línguas estrangeiras*)
- physical education (*educação física*)
- personal and social development/ moral and religious education (*desenvolvimento pessoal e social/ religião*)

Vocational schools were set up in 1989 as a practical alternative to normal secondary schooling, most offering three-year courses leading to vocational qualifications; specialist art schools exist for people wishing to enter the worlds of dance, music, or the visual arts. Figures in 1993 showed that there were around 313,000 pupils on general secondary courses, 31,000 on technical courses, and around 22,100 at vocational schools. A further 31,000 pupils attended evening courses. All who pass the 12th year are awarded a school-leaving certificate. In general, Portuguese schools are very like other countries – though the vast majority are in modern buildings, often lacking in inspiration. Pupils do not wear uniform apart from at some private, or church-run schools, they talk loudly, carry around brightly coloured rucksacks with their books and a multitude of coloured pencils, pens and rubbers, and swamp the streets at home-time. Bullying is rare – there is no adequate word in the Portuguese language for 'bully'. Most children eat in the school *refeitório*.

Further and higher education

Higher education (*ensino superior*) is split between the more traditional university (*universidade*) providing established courses rooted in critical analysis and thinking, and the polytechnic schools (*escolas politécnicas*), which began in 1979 but really started to develop in the mid-1980s. The prestigious universities are in Coimbra, Lisbon, Porto, the Minho and Évora. There are four private universities, and around 70 private higher education colleges (*escolas superiores*), as well as the independent Catholic University (*Universidade Católica*). Access to all higher education establishments is dependent on successful completion of the 12th year of schooling, a series of tests (aptitude and course-specific), and is subject to 'numerus clausus', i.e. the number of places is set annually. The high numbers of pupils failing or leaving school early over the last decade may have reduced the pool of those wishing to apply to HE, but this has not held them back: over the last 30 years numbers have increased tenfold, and in 1996, 338,000 students enrolled in higher education. However, the numbers actually graduating tell a different story: in 1996 only 39,000 students graduated. The most popular courses since the early 1990s have been management engineering, economics and computer science. Courses at universities last from four to six years and lead to a *licenciatura* degree; those at polytechnic schools tend to be for three or four years and lead to the *bachelarato*, or *licenciatura* after extended study. Many university graduates go on to study for a masters' degree (*mestrado*) or doctorate (*doutorado*), often at overseas establishments. In Portugal you can call yourself *dr.* (*doutor/doutora*) when you have a first degree, you do not have to have taken your doctorate!

Portuguese students are just as vociferous as elsewhere when it comes to staking a claim to their rights. There was a famous case in the 1990s when a lecture hall in Coimbra with only 40 seats was provided for a lecture for 400 students! Lack of facilities, overcrowding and lack of interest by the tutors (who can make more money in the private sector) have all led to unrest. In the current *contestação* over planned reforms, students have demanded new methods of teaching, adequate training of teachers and better facilities, among other things.

A different area of training which Portugal has been developing and investing in since the early 1990s is the apprenticeship system, and initial training schemes for young people. These all have a practical leaning, and currently benefit from solid EU funding. The Institute of Employment and Vocational Training has an extensive network of training and careers advice centres across the country, and in 1993, 20,320 young people enrolled on apprenticeship schemes alone. The Portuguese government sees these schemes as a positive step towards enabling the less academically oriented to prepare themselves for the real world of work. One social group particularly keen on vocational training is the young gypsy population, seeing it as the key to escape their social misery, with some aspiring to become doctors and lawyers. A survey in 2000 of young gypsies (aged 16–25) in Lisbon found a large number unable to read or write, but with a keen interest in vocational training. With the second largest EU gypsy population after Spain, this is a sector not to be ignored. Interestingly enough, the parents wanted their sons to become lawyers in the main, whilst for the girls, dressmakers, housewives and street traders were the proffered choices!

Health

The Portuguese can expect to live, on average, to 72 if they are men, and 79 if they are women. This compares favourably with countries such as the UK (75 and 80) and the USA (73 and 80), but is slightly less than their Spanish neighbours, at 75 and 82 years respectively. Portugal could be classed as a 'quasi-Mediterranean' country in terms of its diet, which is predominantly a healthy one, or at least it has been until recent years. Now, a preponderance of saturated fats and fast-foods has started to encroach and cause widespread concern among nutritionists with regard to the growing health problems related to the diet. On the surface, it would appear that the Portuguese are generally a healthy nation, however, the latest findings from the National Health Observatory indicate grave areas of concern. The headline on the cover of the March 2001 edition of *Focus* magazine ran: *Estamos mais gordos e feios!* (We are fatter and more ugly!) See following section on diseases.

Of course typical problems such as the common cold, and other viral infections spread as in any other country, but are often treated with herbal tea infusions, especially in the rural areas. A full range of pharmaceutical products is available, but many people prefer traditional remedies for viruses and stomach upsets. For most illnesses the first stop for the Portuguese is their local pharmacy, where the *farmacêutico* often diagnoses problems and advises on remedies, as well as dishing out pills and *xaropes* (cough mixtures). The traditional Portuguese pharmacy, which still exists where it hasn't been replaced by a modern equivalent, is a real experience. Entering one is like stepping into a Victorian apothecary: walls are lined with beautiful wooden panels and glass display units, there are sets of intriguing miniature drawers, and a real air of elegance and deference. Voices are rarely raised, service is slow, but the presence of the pharmacist (often quite severe-looking) exudes comfort and confidence. Some shops have a ticket system for being served – similar to what you would see at some supermarket fish or deli counters. Paying for your articles can sometimes be lengthy, as some packets of products require a section to be removed and stuck into the pharmacy books for tax purposes. This is usually carried out with such care and precision that time allowances must be made for pharmacy visits.

Doctors and dentists

Doctors are treated with great respect throughout Portugal – as are other 'professionals'(see p.261), and are always addressed as *senhor Doutor/senhora Doutora*. With three doctors for every 1000 inhabitants, the Portuguese actually enjoy a better access to the profession than the British, who only have 1.6 per 1000, and the Americans, who have 2.6. There are also an increasing number of private medical practices, especially in the capital and the Algarve – in Portugal you pay for a consultation with your doctor, even under the state system. It's not really surprising, then, that health-insurance companies are also plentiful: the general cost of health care can be expensive, although certain costs can be claimed against tax. Increasingly, the Portuguese are consulting their doctors for preventative diagnoses, but it seems that, while they wait for results of tests, they cannot desist from the vices of food, tobacco and alcohol.

One of the main problems the Portuguese have is dental hygiene. It is no wonder when you consider their penchant for sweet cakes and the number of sugar packets emptied into a single gulp of coffee! Visits to the dentist (*o dentista*) are not cheap, which could be one of the factors deterring people from doing so. Another reason may be the bewildering range of dental practitioners, all with varying degrees of experience and competence, from the *estomatologista* who will have had six years in medical school plus three years hospital dentistry, to the *odontologista*, technicians, who are often self-trained. In the middle of the bunch there are a high number of Brazilian dentists (around 3000, compared with 2–3000 Portuguese dental doctors with six years' training). With no national board of dentistry, it seems that sorting out teething problems can be 'hit or miss'.

Main diseases

Apart from the high incidence of injury and death from road accidents (Portugal has the worst record in Europe for road safety – see p.216), the latest findings from the *Inquérito Nacional de Saúde* (INS) in 1999, reveal that the Portuguese lead a more sedentary lifestyle than before, that obesity has become an increasingly worrying problem, and that smoking and drinking remain a cause for concern. These, in turn, are leading to more premature deaths from heart disease (*doenças cardíacas/coronárias*), problems with the liver (*fígado*) and lungs (*pulmões*). Men, it seems, continue regularly to consume alcohol, whilst older women are suffering more than ever from obesity, high blood pressure and diabetes. The younger generation is eating less and smoking more. These ailments reflect the growing number of people prevented from carrying out routine activities due to medical complaints. Although fewer people may be confined to bed, many more are having to stay at home because of illness. Many of the 5000 taking part in the survey admitted they could not bend down to pick things off the floor with ease, or found going up and down stairs difficult.

A obesidade

Although the problem of weight has not reached the proportions it has in some countries, it is slowly becoming an area for concern in Portugal. Since the last inquiry in 1996, the number of people with the 'ideal' body weight has decreased, reflecting an increase in the numbers of overweight individuals (as also in the numbers of underweight, or anorexic people). One of the problems would appear to be that the Portuguese are spending more of their leisure time in front of the TV, or in other seated activities. Although the situation is exacerbated in old age, there is concern that women over the age of 25 are averse to physical exercise: only 40 per cent of those interviewed claimed to participate in a sport.

Excess weight	Men		Women	
	1998	**1999**	**1998**	**1999**
Extremely low	0.8	1.8	2.4	3.0
Low	3.3	2.8	7.5	7.4
Desirable weight	66.3	62.0	61.0	57.8
Excess weight	19.3	20.6	16.5	16.8
Obese	10.3	12.9	12.6	15.0

(Figures represent the percentage of the population aged 18 or over.)

O alcoolismo

The INS survey found the typical 'alcoholic' in Portugal was male, a specialized worker or unemployed, middle-aged, living in the north, and a passionate wine-drinker! Seventy-five per cent of those in the north interviewed said they had drunk daily in the week leading up to the survey. As a general rule, it was found that the leaning towards drink decreased as the level of education increased, although men of university-level education also admitted to high levels of drinking. The figures have changed very little since 1996, and although there is very definitely a cause for concern, experts believe the problem is under control. The main area of worry is with the consumption of alcohol among youngsters: 10 per cent of boys and 5 per cent of girls between 15 and 17 confess to drinking 'várias vezes por semana' (several times a week).

O consumo de tabaco

A very worrying trend is in the increase in numbers of women smokers. Since the INS carried out a survey in 1987, the number of women smoking has increased from 5 to 7.9 per cent. Interestingly, there has been a slight decrease in the number of men smoking, and since the late 1980s the number of people who have stopped smoking has gone up, from just over 20 per cent to 26 per cent. Anti-smoking campaigns are now in full force, backed by the *Conselho de Prevenção do Tabagismo*, with slogans such as '*Sou livre, não fumo*' (I'm free, I don't smoke).

Percentage of smokers in the Portuguese population

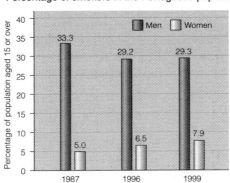

A toxicodependência e a SIDA

Drugs have become an increasing part of Portuguese life, particularly among the inhabitants of the shanty areas and the poorer parts of Lisbon. *Haxixe* – hashish (cannabis) – is the most easily available and consumed drug, mostly coming in from North Africa via the Algarve. Ecstasy and other types of amphetamine are also now within access of clubbers, and heroin is in circulation within the marginalized groups of society. In Portugal, as in Italy and Luxembourg, 40 to 60 per cent of people detained by the police have been involved in the consumption or trafficking of heroin. Most crime (assault and theft) in Portugal is now drug-related. Among those addicted to drugs, and especially those using needles, the level of AIDS is now the highest in Europe, and continues to rise. Whilst levels among drug-users in other EU countries has fallen since 1994, only three countries remain with a serious problem: Italy, with 15 cases per million inhabitants, Spain with around 40, and Portugal with 60 per million.

The health service

Portugal spends 7.9 per cent of its GDP on health, compared with 6.8 in the UK and 13.9 in the USA. The health system is run by the *Ministério da Saúde*, through a series of local centres (*administração regional de saúde*) and the health centres (*centros de saúde*). Treatment in a state hospital (*hospital civil*) is free, as is vital medication, whereas you have to pay to be treated at a *centro de saúde*, or a *hospital* or *clínica particular*. It is surprising (or perhaps not in the circumstances) how many people make the pharmacy their first port of call for less serious illness, as the pharmacists themselves dole out good, free advice on treatment.

The Portuguese health system has been criticized for its lack of facilities, lengthy waiting times and lack of care and attention to patients. Despite various reforms, the modernization process will not come quickly enough for many sick people, especially those who live away from the larger cities. Most local hospitals are small and outdated, and some towns only have a *centro de saúde*, which cannot possibly cover all treatments, thereby necessitating transfers of patients to the nearest suitable location. However, the number of hospital beds in the country is not too different from other 'advanced' countries; you are just as likely to get a bed in Portugal, with 4.1 beds per 1000 people, as you are in the UK (4.5 beds), the USA (4) and Spain (3.9). Medical staff themselves are dedicated people, qualified professionals, working against the odds within a system which is not doing them, or their patients, any favours.

Serviços de emergência – emergency services

Portugal benefits from an excellent national emergency service, operating in Portuguese, French and English. The number 112 gives access to *a polícia, o hospital, o serviço de ambulâncias* or the fire brigade. *Os bombeiros* are usually *voluntários*, although some are regular '*companhias*'.

Alternative medicine

Alternative forms of treatment, such as homeopathy, aromatherapy and others, have been slow to take off in Portugal, although there have always been *curandeiros* and *ervanários* (healers and herbalists). There are some practitioners in Lisbon, and the Algarve has a number of mainly foreign-led services. Perhaps it is viewed as too 'New Age' for this still conservative people, which is surprising given the pagan-type practices still carried out in some northern rural towns, where the local *curandeira* may be called on to cure sickness. Other terms, sometimes used perjoratively, for those involved in 'magic healing' are *bruxa* (witch) and *feiticeira* (magic woman).

Housing

As was mentioned in Chapter 4, the style of domestic architecture varies from north to south, and from the cities to the rural regions. In rural areas most people live in small, basic houses which may be terraced in the town centre, or detached cottages and farmhouses. Dwellings are likely to be old, with few facilities, although the women of households in the Alentejo and Algarve take pride in their regular white-washing of the exterior walls, to such an extent in some areas that it brings out a real competitive streak in the senhoras! Bright exteriors, meanwhile, often mask the reality that many people in Portugal live with – no central heating, humidity and damp, and for some there are still no inside toilets (in the Alentejo for approximately 20 per cent of households). In the winters, which can be harsh, families sit around a table whose tablecloth hides an electric fire underneath. The *braseira* is a common feature of many homes; you place your feet and legs under the cloth and warm yourself at meal times. There may be open fires, and heavy shutters at the windows, but little else to keep out the cold. Women often wear thick *xailes*, and lots of sweaters indoors, and people sleep under many layers of blankets, with the typical hand-woven wool rugs (*colchas de tear*) on top. The lack of adequate heating and, in many cases, ventilation, means that most Portuguese houses also have a problem with damp – the majority of bathrooms never eradicate the black mildew from the walls and ceiling.

In larger towns and cities housing is much more modern, apart from the old city centres themselves, where families still live in traditional apartments in old, brooding-looking or interesting buildings. Living conditions are usually cramped (extended family and students may typically live at home), and the buildings often suffer from a lack of maintenance. This is due in the main to the fact that by law rents are fixed for life, and so subsequently landlords have found it increasingly economically unfeasible to look after their properties. A walk around Lisbon, for example, will illustrate the number of once-elegant buildings in shady tree-lined avenues with flaking façades and dingy interiors. Some are undergoing face-lifts right now, in an attempt to spruce up the capital (an initiative instigated for the 1998 Expo), but much remains to be done.

Rental prices in Lisbon and Oporto, for families wishing to move, are now so exorbitant that most people simply stay put and endure the conditions around them. On the outskirts (*nos arredores*) of the cities, and the urban sprawl of many larger towns in the countryside, most people live in modern housing, almost 70 per cent of which has been built since 1960. The 1970s were a boom decade for housing – mostly apartment blocks and even today around 70,000 new buildings are constructed each year. Around 40 per cent of the population live in an apartment of some description – be it in a small block in a country town, or one of the high-rise council flats outside Lisbon or Oporto. Although council rents are low, some of these estates suffer the same problems as elsewhere in the world – a conglomeration of the most needy, isolation from each other, lack of facilities, decay and deprivation. One step beyond are the outlying shanty towns, (*bairros de lata*) corrugated huts mostly inhabited by gypsies and immigrants.

The Algarve's housing is a mixture representing its tourist trappings. Whilst the Portuguese there live in mostly typical old houses or more recent flats, the high-rise luxury holiday apartments and villa complexes mushroomed out of control during the 1980s. It looked as though Portugal was going the same way as Spain's Costas, until the PROTAL law of the early 1990s declared that no more new massive construction could be undertaken on land that did not have prior building consent. This curbed expansion to a certain extent, but not totally: some development has been allowed on protected green areas, the building sites, cranes and placards are a constant reminder of the increasing number of people who wish to visit this region. The exclusive villas are mostly holiday or second homes of foreign visitors or residents, as a glance at the name-plates will reveal.

Wherever the Portuguese live these days, the vast majority now benefit from electricity and piped water (although for some these have only come in the past couple of decades). Piped gas is still relatively rare; the majority of households rely on bottled gas (*garrafas de gás*) for all their needs. Ownership of domestic appliances has risen steadily over the last decade: in 1998 97 per cent of households had a fridge, compared with 94 per cent at the start of the decade, washing-machine ownership went up from 68 per cent to 85 per cent over the same period. Fewer houses possess a freezer (55 per cent), dishwasher (15 per cent) or microwave (15 per cent).

Social security

Portugal's *segurança social* covers health care, unemployment benefits, housing, pensions, and a number of family allowances and payments to widows. The workforce contributes to the system through salary deductions, with employers paying 24 per cent to every employee's 11 per cent of gross salary. Many working people also pay into a separate, personal scheme, especially to cover medical costs. For the really needy, there is help from one of the world's oldest charitable organizations: the *Santa Casa de Misericórdia*, originally set up by Queen Leonor in 1498, to give 'spiritual or corporal' help to the needy, and 'to alleviate the poverty and suffering which befall our bretheren in Christ'. The *Misericordias* spread across the globe with Portuguese expansion in the 15th and 16th centuries, opening hospitals, and acting as a social services network. Initially sponsored by the Crown, the *Santas Casas* today receive money from the National Lottery and other state support, and continue to help the less advantaged in life.

Transport

The principal forms of transport in Portugal are the same as in most countries, with the addition of the tram network in Lisbon, and the trolley-buses in Oporto. It is rare to see someone on a bicycle, save for a few older men in the countryside or youngsters at play. In the rural areas farm trucks and carts are still a common sight. City centre traffic is a huge problem, and Lisbon is a prime example of how it can all go wrong, despite an expanding network of public transport.

Roads

There is a good network of highways/motorways (*auto-estradas*), and main roads (*estradas nacionais*), designated by EN plus a number, such as the well-known EN125 across the Algarve. These main highways link the Algarve to Lisbon, and northwards to Oporto, with cross-routes inland to the Spanish border and beyond to the main Spanish cities. Upgraded EN roads are now known by an IP (*itinerário principal*) number. Roads in general are not good quality, with pot-holes, crumbling roadsides, and a lack of warning signs, which, given the high rate of car accidents (Portugal has more car accidents than any other European country), doesn't help matters. There are approximately 800kms of motorway, with another 1000 planned and under construction, with money from the EU. This is still very much less than in Britain (3000km) and France (9000km), however the Portuguese use their road network much more than other European countries or the States. Many *auto-estradas* are now toll roads (*portagem*), and a recent innovation to speed up movement through the payment booths is the *via verde* card and electronic strip, which allows cars to 'swipe' themselves through the green line (*linha verde*) and payment is deducted automatically from the driver's bank account.

Whilst massive investment continues to be made in the construction of highways, other areas of infrastructure are left in precarious situations. No more evident was this than in the disaster in March 2001 in the Douro valley, where the Castelo de Paiva bridge collapsed, plunging 80 people to their deaths in a bus. The mayor of the small town had been asking the Government for improvements to the bridge for three years, before Portugal's biggest disaster of this kind. The horrendous event, which was projected around the world on news programmes, prompted two days of national mourning, and the immediate resignation of the Minister for Public Works, Jorge Coelho. Two weeks later a second road disaster occurred when a bus came off a well-known danger road near Viseu, crashing down a ravine and killing 14. It has been a black time for the reputation of Portugal's roads.

The most notorious road in Portugal (for all the wrong reasons) is '*A Marginal*', which runs along the edge of the river Tagus along from Lisbon out to Cascais and the west. This stretch has the highest accident rate in Europe, and despite newly installed speed reduction traffic lights along the way, the accidents, many of them fatal, keep on happening. Portugal is rated 21st in the world for deaths on the roads – the highest placed European country. So, what exactly is the problem?

Cars

Although there is no recognizable national Portuguese car, 60 per cent of the population own a vehicle, the most popular being the small cars seen in the rest of Europe. There has been a long history of car manufacturing in the country; Ford was there in 1932, followed by General Motors in 1959. New cars have huge taxes levied on them, making them an expensive commodity. Cars have been traditionally taxed according to the size of the engine, and over the years governments have reaped huge revenues from this, which have been invested in the rapidly developing motorway system. In recent years there has been an influx of diesel cars such as BMW, Mercedes-Benz and Volkswagen, to combat the tax rules. An attempt within Government in 1999 to win favour with the public, by promising to terminate this system has so far come to nothing; the cost of road development now exceeds the receipts for annual car tax, so the revenue is vital for progress in this area. Still the roads are inundated with vehicles, and town centres become rat-runs, with cars parked in all manner of inhospitable places. City centre parking is often under the auspices of *arrumadores* – young men who will help you find a space for a fee, and if you choose to ignore their services you may well run into even more problems!

Although the bad quality of many of the roads may well be a contributing factor to accidents, one of the major problems when many Portuguese get behind a steering wheel is that they become Jekyll-and-Hyde characters, not appearing to think consequentially: they do not see the possible repercussions of a certain action carried out here and now. What else can explain overtaking on blind bends, or on the inside, great speed even in built-up locations, or simply not keeping their eyes on the road? Another problem in the past has been the availability of the *carta de condução* licence to paying would-be drivers, who have had very little practical experience. Despite years of vigorous campaigns, and hefty punishments, drinking and driving is still a big problem, and so many get away with it, often excusing themselves by saying 'I've not had that much'. In 1998 a 'Zero Tolerance Maximum Safety' campaign was introduced in an attempt to deal with Portugal's horrendous record of accidents. Within just one year, fewer people died on major roads and the accident rate also decreased. It will still take a long time for figures to return an average more in line with the rest of Europe.

Motorbikes (*motocicletas*) and mopeds (*motorizadas*)

One thing you cannot fail to hear when you are in a town or a sleepy village is the rough roar of two-wheeled vehicles, usually with no silencer. Portuguese youths (with enough money) enjoy screeching through town on motocross-style motorbikes, whilst it seems as if many of the older generation are happy to put-put along on ancient mopeds. Often these have a wooden box attached to the back for transporting produce to market. A more deluxe model is a small three-wheel vehicle, half-van half-bike, sometimes with an open trailer back. It is common to see mother, father and child all perched precariously on these machines. Old helmets are in situ but rarely fastened!

Public transport (*os transportes públicos*)

Buses and coaches

Buses (*autocarros*) are extremely efficient, serving all parts of towns and cities; they are cheap, and run on time until they hit the rush hour (*a hora de ponta*). They can become overcrowded, particularly in the larger cities, and with all the Portuguese enjoying a chat – very noisy too. You enter a bus at the front, and usually have to take a ticket from the driver and punch it in a little machine (*obliterador*) just behind him. Doors at the back of the bus let you off. In many places tickets can be bought in multiples, saving money. These *módulos* are on sale at little kiosks near the main bus routes.

The Portuguese Coach Network, *A Rodoviária Nacional*, was recently privatized, thus allowing a rapid expansion and competition from a number of other companies. Services around the country have subsequently improved, and now you can get a coach (*camioneta*) to most parts of Portugal, for a very low fare. The older coaches, from companies such as the distinctive orange-liveried EVA, and *Rede Expressos* in the north, are a more basic style and tend to get overhot in the summer. Increasingly, however, investment is being made in new, state-of-the-art luxury coaches, with air-conditioning, and some with hostess service for drinks and snacks.

Trains (*comboios*)

The railway network, *Caminhos de Ferro Portuguêses* (CP), is a state-owned company, running a system of approximately 3000km (1998) of track. Trains are very reliable, cheap, and a great way to see Portugal; unfortunately the network does not reach very far through inland areas. In fact, in recent years a number of lines have been closed, especially some narrow-gauge lines in the north. In particular, a popular line to Bragança was shut down, despite vehement protests from the Mayor of Bragança in defence of a vital lifeline for his people. Happily, since 1999, the CP has been working with the Tourist Board to reopen a number of small lines in the Douro valley.

Despite these cases, a modernization plan is currently underway for the whole network, and there are already new high-speed (*alfa*) trains linking Lisbon and Oporto (314km) in around three hours. Plans are afoot to link the Lisbon–Madrid route on to Barcelona and Paris, with the acclaimed AVE/TGV trains. The ordinary trains are huge, silver machines, whose steps are very difficult to climb up. Inside the carriages, the bench-seats are comfortable, and high up so you have a great view, but you will often share your journey with a number of locals, who will nod and smile at you, so it's a good opportunity to talk to people. Children under four travel free on public transport, and there are good discounts for those aged 4 to 12, students and anyone over 65.

Transport in Lisbon

All transport in the capital, apart from the metro, is run by the state-owned company Carris. Their kiosks are seen all over the city, selling tickets and a variety of travel cards for the different zones of travel, or four and seven-day tourist passes. Lisbon also now offers a special 'Lisbon card', with access to all public transport, and free entry to some museums and monuments. Lisbon is a spectacularly busy city, although it never seems as overbearing as London or New York. One of the novelties of getting about are the trams (*os eléctricos*), built originally in Sheffield, in Britain, pre-World War I. The older ones trundle through the downtown streets (*a baixa*) and up the hills at either side, to the districts (*os bairros*) beyond. More modern styles have been introduced, with two carriages joined together with flexible rubber so they bend round corners, and a mechanized voice informing you of each stop. Trams are popularly used by many Lisboetas, which makes it all the more surprising to hear that the demise of many routes has been mooted in an attempt to give the main streets back over to traffic. One form of transport not to be missed, and essential for weary legs, are the funiculars and elevators, taking people up and down the steepest slopes. The *Elevador de Santa Justa* was built by an apprentice of Eiffel at the turn of the century, and stands 32 metres of neo-Gothic splendour.

The underground (*o metropolitano*)

The metro is a small, but expanding system in Lisbon, whose entrances are marked above ground by a large red M. The original system had just three arms to it, but was extended in preparation for Expo 98. The Oriente station, at the Expo site, is an example of beautiful modern architecture, with expanses of tiled surroundings. Stops hitherto unreachable under the ground have now opened up, with a system that is swift and efficient, albeit uncomfortably crowded at peak times.

Ferries (*os barcos*)

The other main feature of Lisbon transport are the trans-Tagus ferry-boats (*os cacilheiros*), carrying people to and from work in the capital from the southern side of the river. They are a much better way to get across at rush hour when the bridges can be spectacularly jammed with vehicles. The ferries are also often used as a means of connecting with buses going to the popular beaches at Caparica, and as far as Sesimbra, round the coast. The port at Sines is also set to become one of the biggest container ports in Europe, another sign of positive investment in Portugal.

Air transport (*transportes aéreos*)

The three international airports are in Oporto (Pedras Rubras), Lisbon (Portela) and Faro, with internal flights available interconnecting the three. Regional airfields at a number of locations provide smaller domestic services. Over the past five years massive improvements and expansion have already taken place at Lisbon and Faro, and another new airport has been approved for Lisbon, at the cost of two thousand million US dollars; it should be ready by the middle of this decade.

GLOSSARY

o **aluno** *pupil*
estudar *to study*
ter boas/más notas *to get good/bad marks*
a **bolsa (de estudo)** *grant, scholarship*
o **sistema educativo** *education system*
o **ensino** *teaching*
ensinar *to teach*
aprender *to learn*
viver em *to live in*
alugar *to rent*
o **dono/proprietário** *owner*
a **casa** *house, home*
lar doce lar *home sweet home*
a **imobiliária** *estate agency, real estate*
os **subúrbios** *suburbs*
o **apartamento** *apartment, flat*

estar bem de saúde *to be well*
sentir-se mal *to feel ill*
o **primeiro socorro** *first aid*
o/a **especialista** *specialist*
o **médico** *doctor*
o **consultório** *doctor's surgery*
a **receita** *prescription*
ser tratado *to be treated*
o **carro/automóvel** *car*
conduzir *to drive*
a **carta de condução** *driving licence*
o **terminal** *bus station, terminus*
a **paragem de autocarros** *bus stop*
a **estação de caminho de ferro (CF)**
   railway station
a **rede nacional** *the national network*

Taking it further

Suggested reading

Structures of the Education and Initial Training Systems in the European Union (Portugal), European Commission: DGXXII, Education, Training and Youth

Portugal Matters! (photocopiable resource on all aspects of Portugal), from Education Matters, 29 High Street, Halberton, Tiverton, Devon EX16 7AF

Portugal: Basic Data, and *Portugal: the Infrastructures* (booklets produced for potential investors), available from ICEP, the Portuguese Trade and Tourism Offices

Notes and advice on driving in Portugal, and residence, available from your nearest Portuguese consulate

Living and Working in Portugal, Sue Tyson-Ward, Second Edition, How To Books Ltd, 2000

Information

Ministry of Education – Secondary Department: Departamento do Ensino Secundário, Av.da Boavista, 1311 – 5, 4100 Porto. Tel: 02-600 26 10 / Higher Education Department: Departamento do Ensino Superior, Av. Duque de Ávila 137 – 4, 1050 Lisboa. Tel: 01-354 72 70.

Science across Europe scheme: The Association for Science Education, College Lane, Hatfield, Herts AL10 9AA, UK. Fax: 0707-266532

Employment and Training Network: Instituto do Emprego e Formação Profissional (IEFP), Av. José Malhoa 11, 1070 Lisboa. Tel: 01-727 31 23

Websites

Education, **www.educare.pt**
Family medicine, **www.come.to/medicodefamilia**
Portuguese Railways, **www.cp.pt**
AA (Cars), **www.acp.pt**
General Highways, **www.dgv.pt**
Portuguese Embassy in London – various links,
  www.portembassy.gla.ac.uk
Open University (Lisbon), **www.univ-ab.pt**
Portuguese Ministry of Education, **www.min-edu.pt**

11 | THE PORTUGUESE AT WORK AND PLAY

Não se tem sem trabalho (You don't get anything without work) – *Proverb*

Although Portugal is still very much a rural country with many communities depending on small-scale agriculture to eke out a living, over the last decade the country has moved forward in many ways. It now has the economy of an industrialized country. Despite its continuing dependence on EU subsidies for sectors such as farming, and training schemes within education and employment, there is a growing air of confidence in the country's capabilities. Heavy investment in infrastructure and facilities, and a keen drive for quality and professionalism, has attracted major foreign investment in areas such as car assembly (and components production), electronics, and computer technology. The culmination of this recent success was seen by many to be the triumph of Expo '98, with Portugal's modern image projected to the world. But whilst the country pushes its foot into a modern, advanced world, beyond the capital and environs and the Oporto region, people rely on tourism (increasingly) for a living, or still live off the land.

However much working practices may have changed for some people, the Portuguese still find time to relax. Usually this translates into spending time with the family (at home, strolling outside, or on holiday), which remains the constant pivot in the lives of many. More people now participate in active leisure pursuits, although this depends very much on availability in certain pockets of the country. Television may play a large part in the enjoyment of spare time, but other trappings of the modern world, such as video or computer games, are far less prominent.

Portuguese youngsters are more likely to be out kicking a ball around, or gossiping in the local square. Village and community dances and festivals still feature strongly as opportunities for enjoyment, but what the Portuguese also do to a fine art is simply to sit and chat – sometimes over a coffee – and observe the meanderings of the world beyond.

The economy

Portuguese society and the economy have been changing at an alarming speed, over a relatively short time since the end of the Salazar/Caetano regime. When it joined the (then) EEC in 1986, it had been struggling to get its economy (and politics) on an even keel. Its GDP per head (in terms of parity of purchasing power) was only 53 per cent of the EU average. In the last 15 years the gap in living standards between Portugal and the rest of Europe has been halved, and GDP currently stands at 75 per cent of the European average, an average annual growth of 2.3 per cent from 1990 to 1998. By all accounts Portugal's transformation from those initial, difficult years in the EEC, to one of today's first 11 Euro countries has surprised economists, and probably many of its own inhabitants too. The upbeat comments of Prime Minister António Guterres ('We have proved we can do it') are echoed by the director of Portugal's most influential financial group, Espírito Santo: 'These are all steps in a confidence-building process in a country that was tragically lacking in confidence for many years.' However, some international observers have noted that, in the midst of this undoubtably feel-good era, there is still a discernible gap in living standards, not just in relation to the rest of Europe, but internally too. Old and new, wealth and poverty, are seen side by side in the larger cities and there are stark differences from region to region, and between generations. António Barreto, Director of the Institute of Social Sciences at Lisbon University, widely commented recently that, 'in New York or London there are pockets of poverty. You have to say that Portugal is poor with pockets of wealth'. No room for complacency, then.

The state and the economy

After the 1974 revolution, the government enjoyed a stake in over a quarter of the economy. Since 1989, and with two constitutional amendments to permit it, it has gradually been privatizing industry and the financial sector, hence reducing the state's holdings in these areas. Former state monopolies have been opened up to private enterprise in sectors such as public transport (bus and coach services), steel, oil and gas production and distribution, and banking and insurance, among others. The state has gradually released hold on the national electricity service (Electricidade de Portugal), and has sold all but a few shares in Portugal Telecom. By as early as 1993, 29 state-owned companies had already been sold off. The government retains 'golden shares' in a number of companies, which allow it to veto mergers. By opening up so many sectors to private businesses, the Portuguese people are starting to benefit from the effects of competition. Some of the sectors still remaining under state control are not enjoying a similar situation: RTP (the broadcasting corporation), and some railway companies have accumulated huge debts, and, according to insiders, the Lisbon metro is bankrupt. Strangely enough, despite the off-loading of so many state-controlled companies, the public-sector payroll has somehow increased since 1995 to around 680,000!

The sectors

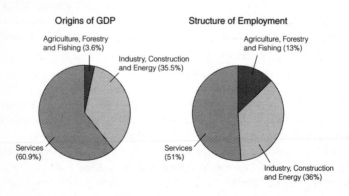

Source: Economist World in Figures 2001

Services sector

Just over half of Portugal's labour force now works in the services sector, in financial institutions, teaching and health, retail, and the huge growth areas of tourism and its ally, catering. This represents a leap of around 15 per cent from the early 1980s. Portugal has, over that same time, grown in popularity as a holiday destination, and as a suitable location for investment by foreign companies. As more have set up business in the country, the more need there has been for all the accompanying services. Whilst the obvious signs of expansion are in the Algarve, where visitor numbers have increased year on year, from 2.95 million in 1993 to just over 4.5 million in 2000, Portugal has witnessed an overall increase in visitor numbers to just over 27 million in 1999. These visitors spent 5.1 thousand million dollars in Portugal in 1999, 6.3 per cent more than in the previous five-year period.

To a great number of the Portuguese, particularly those in isolated rural communities, little will have changed in their daily lives. Many of them still buy their produce in small, local shops, or at the market. The consumer world of gargantuan shopping malls (*centros comerciais*) is far removed from their lifestyle. Without a doubt, though, the face of retailing has been changing in larger towns, with a mushrooming of super- and hyper-markets, and modern all-encompassing shopping centres. And, are the Portuguese tempted by the hype? Well, when the latest, Colombo Centre opened in Lisbon in 1999, as the biggest shopping mall on the Iberian peninsula, more than 2.2 million people visited it in the first month, an average of 70,000 a day. Estimates of 18 million visitors in its first year were well on target to be exceeded.

Industry

As Portugal's economic structure has evolved over the past 20 years, so too the nature and number of industries have changed to meet the demands of a more industrialized society. Whereas 21 per cent of the labour force worked in industry, construction and energy back in 1982, now that figure has risen to 36 per cent. What were once the backbone of Portuguese industry, the traditional shoe-production, fish-canning, textiles and cork-related business, have slowly been giving way to 'new industries', such as car and component production, plastics, agro-chemicals and technology-led business. That is not to say that the old faithfuls have disappeared completely – some have been regenerated with modern techniques for production, such as the shoe industry. In a recent interview with the head of a Portuguese trade association, a journalist was firmly put in his place after referring to the 'traditional' shoe industry, and was shown (via modern technology) images of a computer-controlled new factory.

Now, the Portuguese workforce are being put through training schemes, and taken on by some of the many foreign companies implanted in the country. Foreign direct investment in Portugal has risen from US$4.375 billion in 1992, to an incredible $25.934 billion in 1997, and now 'big names' such as Shell, Siemens, Nestlé and IBM are all providing employment for people who would previously have been engaged mainly in agriculture. The decision by Ford-VW in the late 1990s to develop its AutoEuropa car plant near Lisbon has given jobs to over 10,000 people. It is one of the most advanced car plants in the world, producing three different models on the same production line.

Agriculture

The success stories of the other sectors is not mirrored in agriculture, forestry or fishing, which have declined as the others have evolved. Since the beginning of the 1980s the number of people working in this traditional sector has been halved; now it represents only 13 per cent of the workforce. In the 1960s 44 per cent of working people were employed on the land – traditionally Portugal relied on this resource when employment fell in other areas – the people could always go back to the land (or emigrate, which they did in large numbers from the north particularly – see next chapter). During the dictatorship, the large farming estates, *latifundia*, of the vast Alentejo region employed thousands of people working the land, with few or no rights to holidays, decent wages or working conditions, or prospects for improving their lot. With 1974, came the impetus to depose the (largely) absentee landlords, of their lands, and in their place workers' cooperatives (*cooperativas agrícolas*) were established. Despite the euphoria that followed this take-over of the land, workers have found that even with European subsidies, a life in agriculture, with a lack of modern equipment, has been rife with difficulties. Since 1995, subsidies in rural development have totalled around 2.3 billion escudos.

Even the strong cork-processing industry is feeling the pinch as a number of wine bottlers have been turning to plastic corks to avoid loss through tainting of the wine. Portugal has always been the world's largest producer of cork (about 150,000 tons a year, 60 per cent of the world market) but that, too, may now be affected. In the north, people are still employed in grape-producing areas by varying sizes of wine estates (*quintas*), from the family-run, to the large, well-known groups such as Dow and Taylor Brothers. The work is tough, poorly paid, but to some it's all there is. For some families, many generations may have been involved in grape-picking, and although many young people now choose to break from tradition, a number stay put in difficult conditions and continue in this old industry.

The plight of Portuguese fishermen is no brighter. The hardy characters, descendants of the courageous sailors of old, have had to face a demise which many other countries have also felt. Declining fish stocks in the North Atlantic, fewer EU subsidies, and the younger generations rejecting the family business for greater things, have all contributed to a shrinking industry. Those who are left (around 28,000 fishermen today, compared with 40,000 in 1990) struggle with old boats and equipment, and receive pitiful financial recompense in return for their bravery and hardship. Fish may be one of the staples in the Portuguese diet, but different eating habits are also reducing the reliance on this resource; as youngsters are brought up in an increasing burger and pizza society, what chance has the mere sardine in comparison? Traditions linked to fishing remain strong, however, with brightly painted boats, the use of oxen to pull them ashore, and many religious festivals, particularly in the north.

Despite the downward trend in this whole sector, Portugal still has proportionately the largest farming sector in the EU.

Artesanato

Many people in Portugal earn a living from small, cottage craft industries, hand making various products for sale mostly to visitors. They are helped through a number of craft centres and associations for craftsmen. You may be tempted by some of the following, often being made in your presence:

> *azulejos* – tiles   *barro decorativo* – decorative earthenware products
> *bordados* – embroidery   *cestaria* – basketware
> *colchas de tear* – woven bedspreads
> *estanhos e cobres* – pewter, copper and brass products
> *figurado/ estatuetas* – colourful painted figures
> *filigrana* – gold and silver filigree work
> *tanoaria* – barrel-making   *tapetes* – hand-made rugs
> *vitrais* – stained glass windows   *couro* – leatherwork

Working practices

The workforce

Portugal's working population of approximately 4.6 million (almost half the total population) are hard-working, flexible and increasingly highly educated. A survey undertaken by the Institute of the German Economy, in 1997, found that only the Americans worked longer hours. With significant investment in training programmes, the greater part of the workforce is well prepared for the transitions Portugal is experiencing. Many managing directors of foreign firms now operating in Portugal have praised the workers, including the MD of Siemens: 'Portugal provides one of the best workforces in Europe. It is experienced, and can learn and adapt quickly.' Certainly, the labour force gets on with its work: Portugal has one of the lowest levels of union membership in Europe, despite having a choice of around 400 different unions to join. It is rare to see strike action in Portugal, although recent cases have included teachers and lecturers. Portugal loses only 29 working days a year (per 1000 employees) through strikes, compared with 308 in France, 51 in the USA, and 19 in the UK.

In 1994, only 94,000 Portuguese workers were involved in strikes, compared with 5.5 million in Spain, and over 2.5 million in Italy.

Within companies, the Portuguese Constitution provides for workers'committees, which not only represent the employees' rights, but also play an active role in what the company is doing. There are national associations, known as *ordens*, representing professionals in varying fields such as the legal, engineering, and medical. There are two federations of trade unions:

- UGT – *União Geral dos Trabalhadores* (General Workers' Union), covering primarily the service sector, and aligned with the social democrats/socialists.
- CGTP – *Intersindical*, representing industrial workers, and linked with the Communists.

Employers are represented by the *Confederação de Indústria Portuguesa* (Confederation of Portuguese Industry), and the *Associação Industrial Portuguesa* (Portuguese Industrial Association). It is not compulsory to join any union in Portugal.

Women at work

Women constitute over 40 per cent of the labour force. During Salazar's rule, women needed their husband's permission to take a job, and in 1960 only about 20 per cent of women of working age were in paid employment. That is now 63 per cent, on a par with any advanced European country. With freer access to higher education than ever before, today's young Portuguese women enjoy an independence not experienced before. Women have now gained a foothold in hitherto male-dominated professions – finance, business management, journalism, medicine – although most work hierarchies are still male-dominated, as is the case elsewhere (see also Chapter 12). An interesting thing to note when you go into a Portuguese bank: you are more likely to be dealt with by a male bank clerk than a female. This is the complete opposite of the situation in the UK.

Working hours and holidays

The average working week is between 35 and 44 hours, with eight hours a day constituting the legal maximum. Many companies operate a five-day week, but a great many Portuguese work far beyond the designated level, especially the self-employed, those still involved in farming, and those employed in tourism. Portugal is high up on the table of comparative effective annual work hours round the world, at 1876 hours per person per year. The USA is slightly better, at 1912 hours, but the Portuguese work harder than the British (1777 hours), the French (1771) and the Germans (1579). Even the fanatical Japanese work fewer hours, at 1848 each.

So, are the Portuguese compensated for their labours? They are rewarded with 22 official working days' holiday annually, although, of course, this number may fluctuate according to the level of seniority in a company, or with self-imposed limits for those in family-run businesses. A recent European survey on work and leisure patterns in six countries, highlighted that, whilst two-thirds of the Germans enjoy between 16 and 35 days' holiday a year, a fifth of the Portuguese do not have a single day's holiday. In Spain the figure is even worse, with almost 30 per cent of the people not having a holiday at all.

Pay

It is little wonder that so many foreign firms have found investing in Portugal such an attraction, as the country has the most competitive labour costs in Europe. This, in part, is due to the level of wages, where the Portuguese earn around a third of the EU average. In manufacturing, for example, taking into account base salary and any benefits applicable, a Portuguese worker is likely to be earning around $5.3 dollars an hour, whereas his counterpart in the UK would be on $12.3, in the USA $14.5, and the lucky Germans on $25.7 an hour. The poorest workers are those employed in agriculture and fishing, whereas high-flying finance and business workers and those involved in the computer and technical industries can earn very comfortable incomes. The minimum wage is around $90 a week, although some people supplement their low earnings through other means, not all of them legitimate. Salaries are fixed as monthly amounts and employees usually receive 14 payments a year – the two extra being at Christmas and as a summer holiday subsidy.

Tax and social security

The Portuguese are taxed on all their assets held worldwide at rates between 15 and 40 per cent. There are a number of allowances, such as health and education expenses, which are gladly taken advantage of, given the level of payments easily expended in these areas. They pay less in taxes than any other European. Employers contribute to the *Caixa* or National Insurance, at a rate of 24 per cent of salary, with workers making up a further 11 per cent themselves. Although the *Caixa* gives access to a range of benefits under the *Sistema de Segurança Social* (Social Security System), an increasing number of companies are offering their employees the option of additional private cover. This is readily taken up by those who can, as a precaution against the continuing problems in quality and speed of service, and costs of medical and dental care and education. Tax evasion, on the other hand, goes on at a higher rate than the rest of Europe, with many people claiming much lower incomes on their tax returns. It was reported that in some cases, self-employed lawyers and architects had claimed to earn less than waitresses or construction workers. A tax 'amnesty' in 1997, offering people the opportunity to pay arrears without any penalties, provoked such long queues at tax offices, that the current Government is now looking into ways of improving tax collection, and spreading the burden of tax more fairly.

Unemployment

For many years Portugal has had the lowest rate of unemployment in Europe. It currently stands at 5 per cent of the workforce, compared with 12 per cent in France, 6 per cent in the UK, and in the USA around 4.5 per cent. After its initial (and sustained) rocket in its economy, the inevitable slowdown is likely to cause a slight rise in unemployment, and, as with elsewhere, restructuring of industries and technological advance will result in more people relying on *segurança social*, or relocating. At the moment Portugal has full employment, and more women in the workforce than many other European countries. Its population is also ageing less quickly, hence a surfeit of young people ready (and increasingly able) to step into positions. For those who choose not to try their luck elsewhere, as many thousands did during the lean years of dictatorship (see emigration p.247), the state system of benefits will take care of them. In addition to general social security benefits, unemployment payments are available, in some cases for up to 30 months. There is also now a job start benefit, for young people seeking their first job. Portugal has developed a large network of modern job centres (*centros de emprego*) around the country, offering careers guidance, help with job applications, and training.

Holidays

When they are not conscientiously hard at work the Portuguese who can get away eagerly relish their freedom. With 13 national days off during the year, they already have a good start on many countries when it comes to spending a day away from work. Like the French, they also take the opportunity to add a day or two on either side of a bank holiday, to *fazer a ponte* (make the bridge) when an intervening weekend gives the possibility of a short break. Hence, a day off on a Thursday gives rise to a four-day holiday by also missing the Friday! August is traditionally the month when everyone takes their summer break. It is almost impossible during this month to do anything involving administration, as most public-sector offices become ghost corridors. This is the time of the year when most Portuguese living outside the country make their annual pilgrimage back home to visit family and soak up enough of *a terra* (the land) to sustain them through the subsequent 11 months of nostalgia. Given that August is also the peak month for visitors from abroad to land on Portuguese shores, it's easy to see why travel and services become overstretched for this short, frenzied period.

Holiday destinations

The Portuguese love the beach (*a praia*) and all the trappings of relaxing (or active) days in the sun. With a coastline of over 800km, they have little need to seek out foreign locations to enjoy themselves. What foreign visitors have been discovering over the past 20 years or so, the Portuguese already knew about. In line with other southern European countries, most Portuguese spend their holidays in their own country – few have the money for exotic far-flung trips, and most just want to pass the time with their families, relaxing. Fifty-three per cent of them prefer to stay on their homeground, although their second choice is to go to Spain. However, whereas over half of foreign visitors make for the Algarve, the Portuguese are just as likely to grace the beaches in the north, on the Costa de Prata in particular. Whilst 54 per cent of foreign holidaymakers head for the Algarve, only 27 per cent of the Portuguese make for the south, compared with 21 per cent who spend time around Lisbon's coast and 15 per cent who languish on the Costa Verde. Only 7 per cent of foreign visitors visit the northern coastlines. Beaches such as the long, white stretches in Nazaré, Figueira da Foz, or Peniche become a chaotic multitude of Portuguese bodies and sunshades during the summer. Families set up camp, often within reach of a wind-shield (which can be rented), as the Atlantic coastline has its shortcomings, despite the magnificent beaches. A day out on the beach usually involves a cool-box filled with picnic and drinks, ball games, and plenty of sun protection. The Portuguese wisely sit **under** their shades while everyone else burns to blisters!

The nice thing about Portuguese beach habits is that, quite often, whole generations spend the day together, with grandparents in deck-chairs and toddlers playing in the sand. Young Portuguese people spend most of their summer holiday in and around the beach, in groups of friends, topping up their tans or engaging in more active pursuits, such as beach-tennis, or surfing. Recent findings show that the Portuguese prefer to spend holidays as a family rather than alone or in organized groups, unlike the Germans, 16 per cent of whom are quite happy to travel on their own.

Although the beach is a mecca in Portugal, the Portuguese may also spend time inland, more often than not if they are visiting family. In this case, time is spent enjoying meals together, strolling outside, and catching up on news in relaxing circumstances. Young people may go off on camps (either organized through school, or just within friends), or youth-hostelling. Those who are left behind to bake in temperatures of up to 40° make for local municipal swimming pools (*piscinas*), parks or just the nearest café, to gently

Holiday companions

Source:12/01/FOCUS - Infografia Impala / Ema Gonçalves

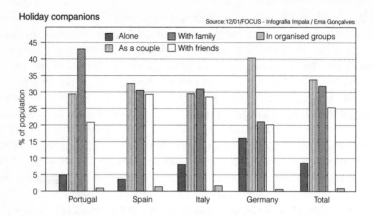

while away the holiday. At night they are likely to be out and about (often meeting at ice-cream parlours – *gelaterias*) and dancing the night away in small clubs and discos.

The activities most enjoyed by the Portuguese on holiday include: visiting family and friends, resting, eating well, going to the beach, and looking after their bodies. They claim they would like to try out adventure sports, professional development activities, domestic hobbies, go to sporting and musical events, and use the computer, but rarely get round to these. For most people, holidays at Easter and Christmas are linked with festivals and family. Few people take a winter holiday away. Almost 55 per cent of the population say they prefer to take their holidays all in one go, and preferably in the summer.

In pursuit of leisure

After Italy and Spain, Portugal is the country where work is considered more important than leisure. Only 11.2 per cent of the population takes advantage of 'free time'. In the home the Portuguese are more than likely to relax in front of the television, or over family meals. In a survey called *O uso do Tempo em 1999* (the use of time in 1999), it was found that the TV was the great unifying force of the nation: on average the Portuguese spend 1 hour and 56 minutes a day in front of it, and that was even before the impact of 'Big Brother'. Ninety-four per cent of those interviewed claimed they watched TV every day, leading the government to feel concerned about the effect of *voyeurismo* on its people. More people tuned in to what was happening in various soap-operas than the reality of presidential elections this year. It prompted the magazine *Visão* to ask, '*Estamos a ficar cretinos?*' (Are we becoming cretins?). It has not been the custom to engage in a range of hobbies or crafts, and there are few places where people can go and join leisure classes or clubs. Clubs which do exist are usually social meeting places dominated by men, similar to the British working men's or ex-servicemen's clubs. The cinema has once more become a popular (and cheap) place for entertainment, and for those with access to other cultural venues there is a good choice of theatrical and musical events, supported particularly well in Lisbon and Oporto. However, the overall picture would suggest that Portuguese families spend only about 6 per cent (1992) of their total budget on cultural consumption. This is far less than in many countries; in France, for example, the figure is nearer a quarter. It would also appear that, in Lisbon, many local inhabitants have either never heard of several of the city's cultural amenities or never visited them. The number of visitors to national museums has dropped from over one million in 1995 to around 990,000 in 2000. Many cultural initiatives also go unnoticed, or are sparsely attended. This is surprising, given the otherwise widespread enthusiasm for festivals and community dances, or *bailes*.

In terms of overall spending on leisure activities, two-thirds of the Portuguese dedicate about 15 per cent of their family income on enjoying themselves, while almost 11 per cent spend nothing. The vast majority (86.3 per cent) are not prepared to reduce the working day or salary in exchange for more free time.

One location which did pull in the crowds was the Expo 98 site of attractions, which attracted over 8 million visitors during six months in 1998. The site, now renamed *o Parque das Nações*, still attracts people to Europe's largest oceanarium, a 700-boat marina, and Expo Urbe development.

Sport

Portugal still lacks good local sports and leisure facilities in many areas. Some people may have limited access to swimming pools, tennis courts or football pitches, but indoor recreational and fitness facilities are few and far between. Although a number of towns may have a small fitness centre (*ginásio*) offering some dance and exercise classes (and in the capital and the Algarve there are more private health clubs), there is not quite the same obsession with fitness and the body beautiful as there has been in other countries. This may be partly to do with the fact that the Portuguese are able to spend much time out of doors, due to the climate, and see less need for body-sculpting indoors, but also because many simply do not take an active interest in healthy activities. Spectator sports have always been popular, especially football, and particularly on TV. Portuguese men also carry around a small transistor radio to pick up matches while promenading at the seaside, in the park, or simply in the street. Organized sport is less attractive – the Portuguese much prefer to get something going spontaneously, although many belong to a sports club. That is not to say they are not competitive – they have produced some world-class sports people over the years, as the list on p.242 illustrates.

Football (*a bola*)

There is no doubt that *futebol* (football, soccer) is the nation's favourite sport, where passions run high, though violence at matches is rare. The Portuguese also follow British football avidly on TV. Portuguese spectators at matches are vociferous, and often accompany their support with fireworks, drums, and other noisy accoutrements. There may be three *ligas* (leagues) in Portugal, but the three most important teams are Benfica (recently reported as having fallen into bankruptcy) and Sporting (both in Lisbon), and Porto FC. Over the years Portugal has produced outstanding players, such as the world-renowned Eusébio, part of the glorious Portuguese team who reached the semi-finals of the 1966 world cup. Many have appeared in British line-ups: Luís Boa Morte for Arsenal, then Fulham, Abel Xavier at Everton, Dani once played at West Ham, and many have turned to other big clubs in Europe where they can earn far more than in the domestic game at home. Goalkeeper Vítor Baía has since made a welcome return to his beloved FC Porto from Barcelona, where he will earn far less than some of his counterparts, but is reported to be happy to be home. The football transfer market was rocked by the fee paid for Luís Figo on his move from Barcelona to Real Madrid in 2000. At £37 million it made him the world's costliest player. However, it won him few friends in the Spanish city he left behind – on recent return fixtures between the two clubs he has been bombarded with abuse and missiles. Portuguese players may lack some of the flair of their famous Brazilian cousins, but they are skilful tacticians and deservedly respected in Europe.

Other ball games

The Portuguese enjoy watching tennis, but whereas good facilities for playing exist mostly in the Algarve and in Lisbon, where World Tennis Masters championship matches have been held, elsewhere (and particularly for young people) there has been a pull towards basketball (*basquetebol*), volleyball (*voleibol*) and handball (*andebol*), in which the national university team reached the finals of the World University Championships in 2001. Roller skating is also popular in Portugal, and Lisbon allowed an area to be set up a couple of summers ago for youngsters to practise their *patinagem em linha*. The Portuguese have a strong ice hockey (*hóquei em patins*) team which usually does well.

For those who prefer to play with a smaller ball, Portugal is undoubtedly regarded as a world-class golfing destination. Some of its 20 or so top courses are around Lisbon, but the Algarve boasts the majority with 11 of its courses in the world's top 100. In 1999 the Algarve was declared worldwide golf destination of the year by an international panel. The Portuguese Open is one of the highly rated circuit competitions, and new courses are being developed to keep up with keen demand. Unlike in Spain, there are no well-known Portuguese golf stars.

In rural areas a kind of pitching game with horseshoes (*ferraduras*) is played, where the horseshoe is flung towards a metal spike in the ground. Whoever gets the most shoes around the spike wins. Competitiveness is rife, as the stake may be a prize pig!

Watersports

Apart from swimming (*nadar*) done for leisure in town pools or at the beach, or competitively, the Portuguese coastline and aquatic conditions are ideal for a range of activities. In the long summer months Portuguese youngsters love to surf and wind-surf. The rolling waves of the Atlantic favour the sport, and along the coast from Lisbon, the beaches at Guincho and Praia das Maçãs, play host to the daring young – for pleasure, and in international *surfista* competitions, where Portugal ranks among the very best in Europe. Sailing (*a vela*) and scuba-diving (*o mergulho*) are pursuits of the better-off or foreign visitors, but there are numerous marinas and yacht clubs around the coastline.

Cycling and equestrian pursuits

Despite the fact that, generally speaking, the Portuguese are not a cycling nation in terms of an everyday means of transport, there is great enthusiasm for the sport of *ciclismo*. There is an annual *Volta a Portugal*, now in its 62nd year (2001), which attracts international riders. With 14 days, and over 2,000 km of sometimes harsh terrain, it's as good a test as any of the riders' mettle. There is a separate prize for the mountain stage – *o Prémio da Montanha*. Portuguese riders often do very well in the midst of tough competition. Other events include the *Volta ao Algarve*, and more recent 'BMX Freestyle' competitions.

Changing wheels for hooves, horse riding (*o hipismo*) is becoming more popular, particularly country trekking. Dressage has always been a traditional art in Portugal, mainly in the Ribatejo region, where horses have been bred as part of bull-fighting establishments. Portuguese horsemen are very skilled, their *Lusitano* horses probably even more so. Equestrian pursuits, however, have never really been of great interest to the general public. Show jumping, horse races, Pony Clubs, gambling, are not a preoccupation of many. Now, however, at least the better-off in society have access to Portugal's first polo club, opened in 1991 by the wife of the famous Argentinian player, Horacio Heguy. The *hipódromo* (racecourse) at fashionable Quinta da Marinha resort in Cascais is a mini-version of the Campo Grande complex in Lisbon, where the fine art of training horses, or *haute école*, has been carried out for generations. In the 1948 Olympics, in London, Portuguese riders won the bronze medal.

Country pursuits

In such a rural environment it is hardly surprising that hunting and shooting are common pursuits. Pigeon, pheasant and partridge are popular targets, but in some areas wild boar are also pursued. Although the typical hunter has been the local countryman, or farmer, more recently *caças* (hunts) have been set up for the wealthy enthusiasts on large estates. This is attracting visitors from overseas too; unfortunately targets have also included song-birds – the Italians are enthusiasts of the sport they get from shooting thrushes – their desires pandered to on these private estates.

Hunting foxes (*raposas*) is also a pursuit dating back to the Duke of Wellington, who is reputed to have imported hounds for entertainment when not fighting the French on the Peninsula. Hunting traditions are just as they are in Britain, with red jackets and masters of the pack, or *Equipagem*. There is only one hunt club, the Santo Huberto, based 75 miles east of Lisbon, but you get the feeling they are there to stay. 'Despite the revolution and the Common Market, we are still here,' remarked their Master in an interview for a Portuguese edition of *Country Life*.

The other very popular open-air leisure activity is fishing (*a pesca*). Both freshwater (in rivers and lakes) and sea-fishing, including beach-casting. It is a common sight to witness Portuguese anglers perched precariously on rocky ledges on cliff faces, casting into turbulent waters below. Fishing licences are very cheap, and there are many participants.

Motor racing and gambling

Portugal is home to the Estoril Grand Prix circuit (*Autódromo do Estoril*), where various motor racing (*automobilismo*) activities take place. This, along with car rallying (*ralis*) and go-karting (*kartismo*), is a popular spectator sport. *Motociclismo* (motorbike racing) also attracts a high level of interest.

When it comes to gambling, the Portuguese have little to lose their shirt on, so people risk their money on the National Lottery (*A Loteria*) draws – *totoloto* and *totobola* – tickets for which are sold at news-stands, or by registered agents in the streets. The numbers are drawn on TV on Saturdays amid great excitement. Scratch cards (*raspadinhas*) are now popular too.

Famous Portuguese sports people

Carlos Lopes	Marathon runner	Gold Medal	1984 Olympics
Rosa Mota	Marathon runner	Bronze Medal	1984 Olympics
António Leitão	Athlete (5000m)	Bronze Medal	1984 Olympics
Fernanda Ribeiro	Athlete (10,000m)	Bronze Medal	1984 Olympics
António Pinto	Marathon winner		
João Rodrigues	Sailing	World (1995) and European (1997) Champion	
João Gomes	Fencing	World and European Level (1997–8)	
Miguel Almeida	Judo	European Champion (2000)	
João Rebelo	Shooting	European Champion (2000)	
José Couto	Swimming	3rd best 200m breast-stroke in world (2000)	

GLOSSARY

trabalhar *to work*
a indústria *industry*
a pesca *fishing*
a barragem *dam*
a empresa *firm, business*
a fábrica *factory*
a terra *the land*
cultivar *to grow, cultivate*
a quinta *farm*
o agricultor *farmer*
o subsídio *subsidy*
modernizar *to modernize*
a indústria de automóveis *the car industry*
a gerência *management*
os trabalhadores *workers*
o funcionário público *civil servant*

o turismo *tourism*
o turista *tourist*
visitar *to visit*
jogar futebol *to play football*
passear *to stroll, go for a walk*
ver a televisão *to watch TV*
as férias *holidays*
passar as férias no campo *to spend holidays in the countryside*
um dia de folga *a day off*
um feriado *national day's holiday*
bronzeado *sun-tanned*
os espectadores *spectators*
participar *to take part, participate*
practicar um desporto *to play a sport*
a equipa *team*

Taking it further

Suggested reading

Portugal – A Profile (booklet aimed at investors available from ICEP)

Atlantic Spain and Portugal (Guide for yachtsmen), RCC Pilotage Foundation, Imray, 1988

Living and Working in Portugal, Sue Tyson-Ward, How To Books, New Edition, 2000

Places to visit/ information

Information sheets on fishing and yachting in Portugal available from ICEP – Portuguese Trade and Tourism Offices

Portuguese UK Chamber of Commerce – 4th floor, 22/25a Sackville Street, London W1X 1DE. Tel: 020-7494 1844

Portuguese Industrial Association: Associação Industrial Portuguesa, Praça das Indústrias, Pavilhão da FIL, 1300 Lisboa Codex. Website: **www.aip.pt**

ICEP Information on business opportunities: ICEP, Direcção de Informação, Av.5 de Outubro, 101, 1050-051 Lisboa. Tel: 21-790 9500. Website: **www.icep.pt**

General Sports Council: Direcção Geral de Desportos, Av.Infante Santo, 74-4, 1300 Lisboa

Portuguese Equestrian Federation: Federação Equestre Portuguesa, Av.Duque D'Ávila 9 – 4, 1000 Lisboa

Golf Federation: Fed.Portuguesa de Golfe, Rua Almeida Brandão 39, 1200 Lisboa

Tennis Federation: Fed. Portuguesa de Ténis, Estádio Nacional, Caxias, 2480 Oeiras

Websites

If you type in the Portuguese word for any sport or leisure activity, you will come across many sites. Many of the English-language general sites on Portugal also have links to work and leisure themes.

www.citi.pt/cultura/index/desporto

Leisure, **http://lazer.publico.pt**

Beaches, **www.infopraias.com**
Businesses, **www.empresas-negocios.com**
The two main workers' unions, **www.cgtp.pt** and **www.ugt.pt**
General sports info, **www.infodesporto.pt**
Football newspaper on-line, **www.abola.pt**
Secretary of State for Sport, **www.sedesporto.pt**
FC Porto, **www.fcporto.pt**

12 THE PORTUGUESE PEOPLE

Dum modo geral, creio que somos pessoas com quem é fácil viver. Não somos excessivamente orgulhosos, não somos arrogantes, não temos qualquer ideia duma superioridade rácica... (Generally speaking, I believe we are people with whom it is easy to live, we are not excessively proud, we are not arrogant, we don't have ideas of racial superiority...) – José Saramago, 'Discovering Portuguese' BBC

Portugal has fought long and hard throughout history to establish a free, independent nation. Its sons have been pioneering explorers, and later, brave and hardy fishermen. The country, whose economic basis has always been the land, is now in transition to a more industrialized nation. Despite the developments taking place, Portugal maintains a reputation of being one of the safest countries in the world (in a recent study, only Japan and Denmark were found to be more secure places to live). Its people are rightly proud of their tolerance, their ability to form firm friendships, and their place in the shaping of world history. Their self-acknowledged *brandos costumes* (soft customs) have won them many friends the world over, and although their tardiness and helpless resignation sometimes frustrate the brisk hi-tech visitor, their honesty and politeness prevail. They have their darker side: a melancholy and fatalistic acceptance of events, often illustrated in nostalgic talk of the past, and clearly evident in the fado songs, and traditions and rituals.

But, here at the doorstep of the 21st century, what are the Portuguese really like? Who really is *zé povinho* (the man on the street)?

The population

	Population in 2000 (in millions)
Portugal	9.9
Spain	39.6
France	58.7
United Kingdom	58.7
United States	274.0
Source: Economist World in Figures	

Portugal has the slowest-growing population in the European Union, its average annual growth over the last decade was merely 0.01 per cent, compared with 0.08 per cent in Spain, and 0.22 per cent in the UK. The US growth came in at 0.91 per cent. Over the next 15 years predictions show that the growth will slow even further, marginally more than in Italy and Spain. Its older people (65+) account for about 16 per cent of the population, on a par with most EU countries, and women now have an average of 1.4 children, compared with much larger families right up to the revolution. Reasons for this decline in the size of families include greater freedom for women to choose different lifestyles (such as a career and financial independence), less reliance on family members to work the land, and a wider access to contraception.

Portugal's population density is calculated to stand at 107 people per square kilometre, the same as France, less than half that in the UK (241), and over 3 times that of the USA (30). In Spain the figure is also far less, at 79. With only a few major cities, and a predominantly rural landscape, where do the people live? You can travel for hours in the vast expanses of the Alentejo and only come across a handful of homes and 'one-horse' towns. If you look at a detailed map of the country, you can see quite easily the difference in density between north and south. Surprisingly, two-thirds of today's population live in an urban environment, although with only the Greater Lisbon and Greater Oporto areas with a population in excess of one million, the vast majority of the people live in smaller towns and villages (Lisbon proper has about 900,000 and Oporto around 400,000). The majority of the population lives either in the northern regions, or around the Lisbon and Tagus Valley.

Emigration

Emigration from Portugal began in force from about the 1870s, rising significantly around the years of the newly established Republic in 1910, then peaking in the 1970s. It is estimated that between 1855 and 1973 just over 3 million people left Portugal legally, with probably around another million departing without the necessary paperwork. The vast majority have left in search of a better life; they are still doing so today.

In the early years, people chose to go to Brazil – once slavery had been abolished there in 1888, and with openings in the cotton and coffee industries, it attracted 85 per cent of Portuguese emigrants. During the first quarter of the 20th century, the focus turned from Brazil to the USA, although the South American mecca still absorbed large numbers. The impoverished years of Salazar's dictatorship resulted in a mass exodus from the countryside, where there was little work or opportunities, to northern European countries who needed manual labour to rebuild infrastructures following World War II. Thus it was that France, Germany and Switzerland in particular played host to many thousands of Portuguese workers. Today, over a million Portuguese are still living in France, and a total of about five million live in other countries around the world. Important Portuguese communities include Venezuela, South Africa and Jersey (UK Channel Islands).

The employment situation grew worse in Portugal after the 1974 revolution, when the country's population was swollen by troops returning from the newly liberated African colonies, plus tens of thousands of people leaving Angola, Mozambique (etc.) in search of a better life back in the homeland. Additionally, between 1980 and 1990 an estimated 35,000 people a year have been returning to Portugal for reasons such as homesickness, wishing their children to be educated in Portugal, or unemployment. The numbers exacerbated employment problems back in Portugal, and those who have returned (*os retornados*) have encountered other difficulties such as a lack of professional qualifications to equip them for new industries, and hostility from locals where they have taken up residence.

Northern Portugal, where poverty is particularly acute for the rural masses, is still experiencing emigration. It is often the young men who choose to go and work in either catering, or in manual labour, often leaving behind their families, including young children. Villages become ghost-towns run by the women and old people. Their only chance of reunion comes with the annual return home for a month in August. It is a difficult choice, but for some it is the only way to find a means to survive. Working abroad ensures a higher level of income, which is sent home to waiting families. Those who do emigrate often live in paltry conditions in order to save up what they can. They form their own communities, in some cases members of the same families all working together in the same place. This happens frequently in the large hotels in Switzerland, where some 22,000 Portuguese work regularly. Most emigrants desperately want to return to their homeland, missing the calm way of life, and traditional values, but while conditions on the land remain precarious back home they continue to content themselves with their adopted destinations.

The family (*a família*)

The family has always been the rock in Portuguese society, and despite recent developments and trends towards modern lifestyles, family values remain one of the solid fundamentals of Portuguese life. The extended family, with grandparents, aunts and uncles, and cousins, has always played its part in the nurturing of younger family members, and in influencing decisions pertinent to the well-being of all. Whilst the average number of inhabitants per household may no longer reflect the tradition of generations living together (at 2.7 people per dwelling it is on a par with Spain, the UK and the USA), families maintain strong ties, and live close whenever possible. Young Portuguese people stay at home longer than their counterparts in Anglo-Saxon countries, usually for economic reasons. The majority of students attending universities, for example, are at home during their studies, and even when they find jobs they may choose to stay in the family nest a bit longer. Family traditions are easily observed when the Portuguese are out celebrating birthdays and anniversaries in restaurants: the whole family comes out in force for a unified celebration and get-together. Tellingly, the Portuguese word *parentes* refers to 'relations', and not 'parents' (*pais*).

Typical names

The most common names in Portugal are Maria (almost everyone answers to this!) and José – perhaps not totally surprising in a country still predominantly Catholic. What some people find strange are combinations such as Maria José for a woman or José Maria for a man, but this is common right across the Iberian peninsula. Jesus as a first name is far more common in Spain, whereas in Portugal it is more likely to form part of the middle or surname. Other common female names include Ana, Isabel, Catarina, Sofia and Joana, and popular male names include Fernando (Nuno), João, Paulo, Francisco, Miguel and Carlos. Names do not fluctuate much with the times – there are no Chelseas, Britneys or Brooklyns in Portugal!

The most popular surname in Portugal is Silva, with other common names being: Pereira (Pear tree), Oliveira (Olive tree), Ferreira, Gomes, Conceição (also a female Christian name), Fernandes, and Lopes. (Note that the Spanish spelling of some of these is with a final –z (Gómez, López, Fernández etc.) so you can tell easily if the footballers you are watching come from Spanish or Portuguese backgrounds).

The Portuguese, like the Spanish, have the tradition of keeping their mother's surname and incorporating it into their new name when they marry, hence Maria da Silva marrying Paulo Lopes would become Maria da Silva Lopes, and their offspring may well maintain both names, such as Nuno da Silva Lopes. The father's surname comes last, unlike in Spain. In practice, in everyday use, many will simply use a single surname, that of the father.

Marriage

Despite the emphasis on family values, since the 1960s the number of marriages has been decreasing. Although Portugal still has the highest rate of marriage in Europe, outside the UK, more young people are likely to live together before getting married than in previous generations, following a general trend elsewhere in the world. In the 1960s nine out of ten couples opted for a church wedding; the figure today is more like two out of three. People in the still-traditional north are more likely than their southern counterparts to choose a full Catholic church ceremony. More children than ever before are being born outside marriage, and often by choice. Almost one in five births today is to an unmarried couple, in the 1970s only one in 14 babies was born under these circumstances. In the 1950s, 1960s and 1970s unmarried women found to be pregnant would be deemed to have brought great shame upon their families, and would have been persuaded to give up their babies for adoption. Even Portuguese men found to have sown their seed to foreign visitors experienced difficulties explaining to their family a possible bi-national offspring. In many cases the women simply returned to their own country and had their babies adopted. Nowadays there are fewer taboos, and less stigma of illegitimacy, except perhaps in the staunchly conservative rural north.

Divorce

Before the revolution, and under Salazar's family-conserving laws, only a few hundred divorces a year were allowed. Now, almost a fifth of all marriages in Portugal end in *divórcio* (divorce), around 14,000 a year. This seems to be rising, as in 1999, there were 69,000 marriages in Portugal, and 18,000 divorces. This is the second highest rate among southern European countries (France is higher, but the UK is even higher, as too is the USA). Spain, Italy and Greece all have much lower rates. Developments in modern living can erode the traditional make-up of relationships, and Portuguese women have more freedom than ever before to break bonds once considered sacrosanct. Most divorce cases are initiated by wives, although more marriages are ending by mutual consent (in 1999 15,500, up 22 per cent on the previous year). A higher number of divorced men tend to remarry than women. Women tend to be given the responsibility of raising any children, although since 1995 couples have been able to opt for co-rights after divorce.

The role of the sexes

Women

O casamento baseia-se na igualdade de direitos e deveres dos cônjuges (Marriage is based on the equal rights and obligations of the husband and wife) – Article 1671 Civil Code, Equal Rights for spouses

Before 1974, marriage was based on inequality of the spouses, as Portuguese wives had very few rights. They needed their husband's permission to work, to be educated beyond normal schooling, and to be issued with a passport. Only a handful of professional women were allowed to vote. In 1960 only about a fifth of women of working age actually earned money in a job, the lowest rate of any of the EU countries at that time. This figure rose though, during that decade, as most young, able men were absent as soldiers stationed in the African colonies. With the revolution came universal suffrage, and life for Portuguese women has since changed more dramatically than in most other western European countries. Nowadays, more women work while married, more are increasingly taking better positions in work, and have the choice (which they are taking) of having fewer, or no, children. Now, 63 per cent of women work, a figure which is now nearer the upper range in Europe. Over the last 40 years the number of women going to university has more than doubled, and fertility rates have dropped from around the highest in Europe to among the lowest. This is a picture similar to that of Spain, Italy and Ireland, and due in the main to better education, wider access to contraception and the freedom of choice of lifestyle.

But while women in Portugal are still the mainstay of the family, (which they themselves consider the most important institution in their lives) and have a highly increased life expectancy than ever before (and better than their husbands: 79 years for women, 72 for men), not everything is rosy for the average Portuguese woman.

While feminism is viewed with considerable reticence, and rejected by many (men and women), it has, nevertheless started to open up debate, which may, ultimately lead to improved social conditions. The *Comissão para a Igualdade e para os Direitos das Mulheres* (Commission for the Equality and Rights of Women) in Lisbon, has recently highlighted areas for concern.

- In most cases women have to juggle their working life with that of family responsibility, which may include not only children and sick or less-able bodied family members, but also the older relations. Although many women are happy to shoulder these tasks, the fact remains that women are also the providers for these families, with 46 per cent of paid work carried out by them.
- Despite large numbers of women in employment, many are still in lower paid work (as is the general case in Europe). 70 per cent work in the textiles and footwear industries, teaching, health and social services, and in domestic work. In 1993 the average monthly salary for a woman was only 76 per cent of her male contemporaries, a figure that has not changed much today. It is still far easier for a Portuguese man to have a career.
- A discussion in Parliament in 1998, focusing on whether women should be able to request a termination of pregnancy up to ten weeks led to a vote on new legislation. At the time abortion was still only sanctioned in three circumstances: rape, foetal malformation, and danger to the woman's life. Although Parliament had voted to support the new law, the church stepped in when a public referendum was underway, and the decision was narrowly defeated, and ideas to amend the situation abandoned.
- Despite public feeling towards equality for women in the church and armed forces, in reality the conservative echelons of the decision-makers in the Catholic Church find the idea abhorrent. In the armed forces the dominant attitude is that women should adapt to the masculine culture therein.

In spite of persistent problems for women in Portugal, you still get the impression that they are a force to be reckoned with, the pivot of family life, and certainly no fools. A possible explanation for this is that, over the centuries, women were left behind while their men went off to explore or fight overseas, therefore requiring them to fend for themselves and keep the household running smoothly.

Men

A direcção da família pertence a ambos os cônjuges, que devem acordar sobre a orientação da vida em comum, tendo em conta o bem da família e os interesses de um e outro. (The management of the family belongs to both spouses, who should agree upon the orientation of common family life, bearing in mind the well-being of the family and the interests of each other) – Article 1671, Civil Code: Equal Rights for spouses

Although it is the woman who has traditionally managed household affairs and the education of children, the Portuguese man has always fulfilled the role of figure-head, provider, and role-model for his family. Old attitudes prevail, and the concept of 'new man' does not yet sit comfortably in hard-working Portuguese masculine society. Despite changes in the make-up of family life, with more women at work, Portuguese men are brought up in the blinkered belief that they are the providers and protectors of the family. Many still do not equate women with 'rights', few participating in *as tarefas de casa* (household chores). But, undoubtedly, they work hard, and take a keen interest in family life, often being the disciplinarian in the home. Attitudes among the younger generations are slow to show signs of change, as they do not know any different, but as more young Portuguese people become mobile in the global work market, and come into contact with other cultures, perhaps Portuguese man will come to learn how to use an *aspirador de pó!*

Love and sex

In keeping with the majority of southern European people, the Portuguese are outwardly demonstrative when it comes to their affections. Young people hug and kiss in the streets, and park benches play host to many exchanges of love. And it's not just the young! In general the Portuguese are a tactile nation, exhibiting less of that Anglo-Saxon prudery still lingering since the Victorian ethos of 'cover up and don't mention it'! That's not to say that they go as far as their French cousins in how much they willingly display to all and sundry. Although lithe, tanned Portuguese girls and women may don flattering (sometimes skimpy) swimwear, topless sunbathing is very rare. In fact the only beach where it is acknowledged is on the Costa da Caparica (over the Tagus south from Lisbon), where there is a *praia nudista*, a dedicated stretch for nude bathing, a long way down from general bathers. Elsewhere, (in the Algarve for instance) any fleshy expanses on show are more likely to be foreign. It's interesting that, while displaying many southern traits, the Portuguese still maintain this modicum of restraint.

Portuguese men, in particular, are prime examples of Latin, red-blooded males. At the mere whiff of a potential conquest, the majority will try their chance. They are great *apreciadores* of the female form. However, whereas in Spain and Italy a foreign female may have to put up with lurid comments whilst passing in the street, Portuguese man is more likely to demonstrate his interest via a lingering glance, or a not-too-subtle smile or nod.

There is a typical double standard in play in Portugal: it's absolutely fine for men to flirt and have flings (and affairs) to their ego's content, but women (girlfriends, wives) should be at home, maintaining total fidelity. It is little surprising to learn that men have far more partners than women during their lifetime. They have a much more cavalier attitude to contraception, and often show scant regard for safe sex (although that, at least, is changing now among the younger generation). Whilst they cannot be regarded as a promiscuous society, the incidence of AIDS is continuing to rise, particularly among the male population, although at a far lower rate than in neighbouring Spain, except among the drug users (see Chapter 10).

Open displays of homosexuality are rare, especially outside the capital. In Lisbon, certain bars and sectors of the city are famed for their homosexual leanings. A stroll down the main Avenida da Liberdade will take you past one of the 'colourful' parts of the city, where a whole host of characters hang out looking for playmates of any persuasion. Here, as in other, select districts of the city, a number of *pensões* (guest houses) are more famed for their nocturnal activities than the breakfasts they may provide! Elsewhere in the country, lesbians and gay men are regarded with puzzlement, or simply just ignored. It is not illegal in Portugal to indulge in a homosexual relationship, and in 1997, gay rights took a step forward, with Lisbon backing a Gay Pride and Film Festival, and opening a Gay and Lesbian Community Centre. There are few attacks on gay people, although some may encounter discrimination in the workplace, but all now have access to a number of support groups, such as *Gay Opus Associação*, gay newspapers (*Diferente/ Lilas*), and a dedicated website.

Young and old

Youth

Portuguese children, in the main, are brought up in a family-oriented environment, where respect and good manners are paramount. As a result, they are well-adjusted and generally well-behaved. They are allowed a certain freedom of expression, and are subsequently lively, and sometimes boisterous. Both sexes tend to go around in groups together, enjoying each others' company at the beach, at cafés and at discos.

While Portuguese students may not be as vociferous as those in France, when it comes to voicing their indignation over unfair conditions in education, they, too, are not afraid to protest. In February 2001, in an outraged protest at the Government's recent faltering over the right to sex education in schools, secondary-school students marched on parliament giving the 'middle-finger' salute as an obvious indication of their feelings! University students also express themselves in protest, as revealed in Chapter 10.

One particular bone of contention among young men is the continued existence of military service (*o serviço militar*), which is obligatory for all men aged 18 (as it is across Europe, apart from Britain, Belgium and Holland). At 18 young men will be called to an *inspecção militar*, and once accepted as fit, will spend 18 months in service – either in the *Exército, Marinha* or *Aviação*. The subject is emotive and controversial in Portugal, with many young people and politicians calling for abolition, and a step towards making it a paid profession for young people. You can opt out and do civil work, if you are a genuine *objector de consciência*, although the process is arduous. Girls are not obliged to do service, but may offer themselves as volunteers. The singer Rui Veloso expresses the feelings of many about military service, in his song '*Máquina zero*':

Não me façam guerreiro eu nunca fui audaz
Sou um gajo porreiro só quero viver em paz...

Don't make me into a fighter, I've never been daring
I'm a great lad, I just want to live in peace...

Youth crime is still less of a problem in Portugal than in other parts of Europe, probably as a result of the reasonably consistent strong family upbringing. In a recent European-wide School survey (1999) among teenagers, Portuguese youngsters were less likely to have dabbled in illicit drugs than those in the UK, France, and many others. They were in fact, in 21st place in the league. Portuguese youth appears among the very least susceptible to this temptation, a figure also evident for daily smoking at the age of 13 or younger (Portugal lies 22nd in the list). When they reach adulthood these figures may alter, as the Portuguese smoke on average 4.5 cigarettes a day. Portuguese teenagers' relationship with alcohol is also one built on respect – they do not feature at all in the 'top 10' teenage alcohol hot-spots (Denmark has the worst problem, followed by the UK and Greece), although some admit to having a drink on a regular basis. This is an interesting reflection on how alcohol is viewed by the young, as the Portuguese are the world's third biggest consumers of wine, at 53.2 litres per head annually, and the 2nd biggest drinkers of pure alcohol (11.2 litres each). Only Luxembourg and France feature any higher. The Portuguese also drink an average of 64.6 litres of beer each, but that's a mere drop in the barrel compared with 99.4 litres in the UK, or 94.5 in Australia. This attitude to alcohol, where you do not need to be 'tanked up' for a night out, may go a long way to explaining the relatively low level of juvenile delinquency and crime incited by alcohol. Young Portuguese people do not go round in groups terrorizing their neighbourhoods, joy-riding in stolen cars, or generally making a nuisance of themselves. Of course, they are not all paragons of virtue, and without a doubt, there are problems, in the capital in particular. These usually originate from the youngsters living in the shanty boroughs, or *bairros de lata* (tin districts). In most cases, though, the low unemployment situation, and enormous training opportunities currently on offer, mean that Portuguese youngsters have less to feel aggrieved about than in many places.

Youth culture is influenced by American and British rock and pop. The young live in jeans, except for family occasions, listen to Anglo-Saxon music, and aspire to great things. They also maintain an enthusiasm for home-grown entertainment, with a good choice of Portuguese bands to listen to.

Old people

The over 65s in Portugal account for almost 16 per cent of the population, a situation very similar in France and the UK, but higher than the figure in America and Australia, both around 12 per cent. As their life expectancy has increased over the last decade, Portuguese elders can expect to enjoy a full life up to the age of 72, for men. Women can count on a further seven years (see p. 251). This is certainly less than in many other EU countries (by two to three years on average), and may be explained by an, as yet, underdeveloped health system, or by the high incidence of traffic fatalities, and other accidents, and health problems highlighted earlier. As the seniors of the family hierarchy, *os idosos* (the aged) are treated with great respect, and are often integrated into extended-family situations, either living with, or very close to, other family members. The concept of retirement homes, or 'old-folks' homes, is not readily taken on board, although a small number of *lares para os idosos* do exist. Retirement, (*a reforma*) usually comes at 65 for both men and women, at which age a small state pension is payable. Pensioners receive a Christmas bonus, and a '14th payment' in July. Retired people are known as '*reformados*' with an implication that they have finally got to reforming their lives!

Religion

Although the vast majority of the Portuguese are Roman Catholic (97 per cent), it is also true to say that the influence of the church is less now than at any other time in its history. Northern Portugal remains the stronghold of the church, with its ecclesiastic heart in the city of Braga, an important religious centre for many centuries. There is a saying that goes: '*Porto trabalha, Lisboa desfila e Braga reza*' (Oporto works, Lisbon parades and Braga prays). Women, especially older ones, are the most devout, attending church with more regularity than the rest of the population, who now tend to attend church mostly for special celebrations. Easter and Christmas still draw families, as do weddings, baptisms and funerals, but regular attendance at Mass has decreased.

People enjoy the religious festivals throughout the year, often in celebration of a local saint, or specific day, and the whole family, including youngsters, participate in processions and church services. For many, though, the draw is more secular than devotional. On the other hand, the shrine at Fátima remains a major magnet for the pious, attracting thousands (up to 100,000 on each date) on their annual pilgrimage.

There are few other religious groups in Portugal. The only two of any note are small gatherings of the Jewish and Muslim faiths. The Jewish community was once strong in Portugal, especially based around the Alentejo (Évora, Castelo de Vide, Marvão), as around 60,000 had been expelled from Spain in the 1490s and taken refuge in Portugal. However, in the 15th century they had to either convert to Christianity (becoming known as *Marranos*, or New Christians), or flee the country. Their persecution and expulsion in the 16th century, and during the Inquisition, was finally apologized for by Mário Soares in 1989. For the many who had carried on their own religion privately while outwardly converted to Catholicism, deathbed confessions were a potential threat to the continued community. In the Trás-os-Montes region friends and family would 'silence' the dying to safeguard the secret, a practice which continued up to the 20th century, and which is described in the story '*Alma-Grande*' in Miguel Torga's *Tales from the Mountains*. During World War II, Portuguese diplomat Aristides de Sousa Mendes helped over 200,000 Jews escape from France with false passports, despite incurring the wrath of Salazar. His story has finally come to light, many years after his death (see suggested reading on p.267). Although numbers today are only around 2000, there is an active Israeli community in Lisbon, a Portuguese Jewish Student Association and a Jewish Studies Association.

There are around 15,000 Muslims in Portugal, mainly from Mozambique, and of Indian and Pakistani origin.

Portugal's long-established links with the church are evident in the number of churches the length and breadth of the country. Despite its strong Catholic bent, it is a tolerant society, particularly in the southern regions, where the power of Catholicism is felt less. So far, few inroads have been made by less conventional religious cultures and sects, although Lisbon is home to the country's first Church of Christian Scientist, and *Igreja Universal do Reino de Deus*. There are a healthy number of *astrólogos* and 'faith healers', as a browse through any daily newspaper will reveal.

Social relationships

Immigration and racism

Portugal has never been a country with a perceived problem of immigration, although the mass arrival there of many thousands of immigrants from the former African colonies after 1974 certainly put employment and housing under strain. The number of immigrants in Portugal has grown in recent years, but officially registered foreigners make up barely 2 per cent of the resident population. The largest ethnic minorities continue to be of African origin, including Cape Verde, the largest group at around 40,000, and Angola. During the 1990s the number of Asian immigrants increased slightly, and in the last few years a higher number of Eastern Europeans have arrived in Portugal, fleeing atrocities in Kosovo and the former Yugoslavia. In addition to immigrants entering the country as ethnic minorities, Portugal is also home to the second largest gypsy population in Europe after Spain. Some 40,000 gypsies enjoy Portuguese nationality: they have been in the country since the 15th century, but, as in many countries, they live in the poorer shanty areas and are viewed with suspicion by the majority.

Portugal does not suffer the same racial tensions as many other countries. The Portuguese have always been a tolerant people, and perhaps as a result of their very early exposure to so many different cultures around the world, they are far less prone to xenophobia. Clashes, where they do arise, are more likely to be isolated conflicts of racial origin, and not as a result of widespread racism, unlike in many other countries. Only around 3 per cent of the people claim to be 'avowed racists', compared with 8 per cent in the UK and a huge 22 per cent in Belgium. However, a report in May 2001 highlighted an alarming number of Portuguese extreme nationalist websites. Social differences between the immigrant people and other sections of Portuguese society are not particularly marked: good levels of employment, and current socio-economic conditions in the country allow for participation in society. That is not to say that there are no problems. Many people from ethnic backgrounds tend to end up living in the poorer areas of Lisbon and Oporto, or in the shanty towns, and working on building-sites or in menial work. So far, action and pressure groups involved in the rights of immigrants have yet to emerge with any conviction. However, the situation is slowly changing, and politicians are realizing that they should play a more interventionist role in furthering the integration of immigration communities. With this in mind various measures have recently been put in place:

Help for immigrant communities

- extraordinary amnesty procedures for illegal immigrants
- 1991 – setting up of the Co-ordination Unit for Multicultural Education Programmes
- 1993 – Intercultural Learning Project – for primary schools in areas of high ethnic minority density
- 1996 – High Commission for Immigration and Ethnic Minorities set up. Municipal Electoral Law gives the right to vote and stand in regional elections, on the basis of reciprocal arrangements with the country of origin
- Pressure groups and associations gaining a voice

Status

The middle-class Portuguese, in particular, have a tendency to preoccupy themselves with appearances, manifested through status symbols. The emphasis on someone's standing in society is observed in the use (some might say overuse) of professional titles, such as *'senhor/senhora doutor/doutora'* (for those in the medical profession, but also for anyone known to be university-educated). *Engenheiro/a* and *professor/a* are similar devices to demonstrate professional standing. Some Portuguese get carried away with the phenomenon, and continue to use the titles in English outside Portugal, where for instance the title 'doctor' may suggest the person has a university doctorate, when what they really have is the equivalent of a bachelor's degree. Education in general is a concern for the more affluent and some will go to great expense to send their children to certain private schools, especially in Lisbon.

Large houses in well-off districts of towns are external signs of wealth, as are cars, furnishings and home appliances. The Portuguese in general are smart dressers, but the middle-classes are particularly well-polished, with not a hair out of place, even for a stroll in the evening, when they will be on display. It's interesting to note that the expression for keeping up appearances is *'(só) para (o) inglês ver'* (just for the English to see)!

Animals and the environment

As a whole the Portuguese are not a nation of pet-owners. A few may keep small dogs (*cães*) (often as status symbols, and there is an equivalent of Crufts in the upmarket resort of Estoril), but usually dogs are viewed as working animals and are either the domain of shepherds and farmers, (such as the Portuguese web-footed water-dog, or the Serra da Estrela sheepdogs, reputed to have wolf's blood in them) or are kept chained up outside as guard-dogs. In the Algarve there are a large number of street dogs, who quite happily live off scraps doled out by butchers or passers-by. They are not a threat, although they can get tetchy in the warmer months. It is rare for cats (*gatos*) to be kept as pets (again there are large numbers of feral cats not considered a problem), and rabbits (*coelhos*) are considered fair game. What you may come across, though, are cages of small birds (*passarinhos*), canaries, fixed on the exterior walls of houses and apartments. Animal rights issues, as in most southern European countries, are not considered a priority by the majority, although there are a few organizations, such as the *Liga para a Defesa dos Animais* working to oppose animal cruelty. For, while the Portuguese may not be as bloodthirsty as their Spanish neighbours, they still indulge in a range of activities which would be considered cruel by other nations' standards. We have already explored the themes of bull fighting and hunting in earlier chapters; other practices (usually linked with local traditions) include pitting bulls against each other until the death of the weaker and the sacrifice of chickens for ritualistic reasons. Having said this, systematic cruelty to animals such as the sort witnessed so often elsewhere, is probably not as widespread.

Attitudes to the *ambiente* (environment), and behaviour towards the beautiful country they inhabit, both leave a great deal to be desired. You will not drive for very long in the Portuguese countryside without passing dumped domestic appliances rusting into the earth, litter scattered at will, and abandoned vehicles. This problem appears to stem from a lack of suitable recycling and dumping sites, and an underdeveloped system for raising awareness of environmental issues among the people. But even where tips have existed, problems have still occurred. In January 2001 a small parish near Lisbon discovered that a tip (*lixeira*) which had been closed and sealed with earth over a year before, was starting to become eroded, allowing contaminated earth to slip down the huge mound towards nearby houses. Responsibility for the situation has been passed from parish to local council to local politicians, and still the danger to health persists. This is by no means an isolated case of disregard for the health of people, and ignoring the impact on the environment. Many of Portugal's rivers have been polluted by industry, sewage, and oil spills, and there are high levels of damage to the environment through air pollution, chemical use on the land, and heavy construction works, which have been a prominent feature of Portugal's development in recent years.

The latest controversial project in the Alentejo, is the construction of the Alqueva dam, which will flood an area of vital environmental interest. The area is home to the rare, and threatened Iberian Lynx (the most endangered big cat in the world), as well as rare birds, including Portugal's only pair of golden eagles. The creation of the biggest artificial lake in Europe (160 square miles) is almost complete, as the Government has gone ahead, with EU funding, against much criticism from bodies such as the Iberian Birdlife Study Centre, and the League for the Protection of Nature, which claim that if the dam were filled by just a few metres less, half a million trees and important habitats could be saved. There is growing concern now that certain important areas in Portugal are being sacrificed for lucrative leisure projects, such as 'high-quality' tourist villages.

The natural environment has also recently come under threat from the increase in the use of plastic wine corks. More wine bottlers have been abandoning the traditional cork, as a result of 'tainted' drink, indiscriminately (it would seem) blamed on the quality of the cork. As the world's largest producer of cork, the effect of a move away from this product would mean that the land would probably be used for alternative crops, such as sunflowers (*girassois*) or the fast-growing eucalyptus (*eucalipto*). These, however, suck the life out of the soil and use up large reserves of water, causing problems for wildlife and people. The RSPB (Royal Society for the Protection of Birds) is campaigning in Britain to get supermarkets to label their wine according to the type of cork, to allow customers an environmental choice.

Despite the very many negative aspects of environmental damage in Portugal, there are also examples of good works in progress:

- Environmentally friendly office and apartment blocks in Lisbon, in a project by the *Co-operativa Verde* and a 'green' group of architects. '*A Torre Verde*' (the Green Tower) is being developed with environmentally sound materials and structures.
- The Friends of Monserrate are working to preserve and develop the beautiful gardens at the Palace near Sintra. This has resulted in the creation of a safe haven for the endangered Schreiber's Green Lizard.

- Eco-development and promotion in the Mértola area of the Alentejo, through educational programmes for young people.
- Foz Côa Valley in the North of Portugal has been declared a UNESCO world heritage site, after the find of one of the biggest and most important monuments of open-air Palaeolithic rock art in the world.
- An extensive network of protected National Parks and Reserves which preserve the natural environment and promote an interest in wildlife and habitats. The largest, and oldest, park is the *Parque Nacional de Peneda-Gerês* in the far north.
- Development of wind power, particularly on the south-west Atlantic coast. Solar power is already well-utilized.
- Initiatives such as the *A Rocha* Field Study and Bird Observatory on the Alvor Estuary in the Algarve. Although established (after many trials and tribulations) by a group of English Christians, many Portuguese have eventually come to value its presence, although its existence is constantly under threat from development in the area.

The tide of opinion does seem to be turning in Portugal, with the latest polls suggesting that the majority of younger people are particularly concerned about environmental issues, such as overdevelopment on the coasts, urban rubbish, protection of the countryside, and a reduction in hunting. Many people give great importance to the protection of the wolf, which is in risk of extinction in Portugal. The areas of gravest concern are considered to be forest fires and water pollution. Only 1 per cent of people surveyed thought that nuclear energy was a good thing, and more than 70 per cent thought the state should close down factories found to be adding to pollution problems. More than 75 per cent of people believe that the situation will get worse in Portugal over the next decade.

Comparable recycling (*reciclagem*) figures

Glass – Portugal 44 per cent / Germany 79 per cent /
New Zealand 36 per cent

Paper – Portugal 40 per cent/ UK 40 per cent / Germany 70 per cent /
USA 41 per cent

(1997 figures)

Portugal and the Portuguese

This final section has been put together drawing on opinions of a number of people surveyed for this publication, and from interviews published in *Portugal Matters*.

The Portuguese on the Portuguese

■ I'm proud to be Portuguese, Portugal is the oldest country in Europe and in this sense, I feel a real European.

■ We enjoy our peaceful existence in our calm country, living amongst a gentle people that have played an important role in world history.

■ Being Portuguese feels good. It's a quiet country with no wars.

■ Portugal would be a cleaner country if people threw less litter around.

■ Portugal's a poor country but we're an open society.

■ People are changing, they are more aggressive and materialistic now. I much prefer the way we were in the old Portugal.

■ The Portuguese living in Portugal usually underestimate themselves and their country: foreign is always better than national. The Portuguese living abroad normally overestimate their country (especially food, climate and people).

■ The Portuguese are trusting people who don't normally suspect others (apart from the Spanish!).

■ From other times and from other places they brought *saudade*, a mixture of western mythology with the remote tradition of Zen.

■ Portugal is a poor country because it lacks organization and pragmatism in its oversized state and government institutions.

Foreigners on the Portuguese/Portugal

■ They are polite, proud of the country and language. Cultured. Melancholic.

■ Friendly, laid back, trustworthy, dignified.

■ Maniacs in cars.

■ The countryside is beautiful.

■ Annoyingly slow with lots of red tape.

■ Not too pushy but could be more friendly on first acquaintance.

■ The Portuguese make space for the people they meet; they are ceremonious in greetings/farewells and tolerant of interruptions. But they are correspondingly neglectful and inconsiderate of persons not present.

■ The first thing that struck me about the Portuguese was their gentleness... I also think of the devotion they show to their young and old...I love their laid-back attitude to life epitomized in expressions such as 'don't worry' and 'no problem'.

■ They are dignified and proud, especially in poverty. They differ temperamentally from the other peoples of southern Europe, notably their near neighbours the Castilian Spanish. It has always been a different ball game facing the challenges and opportunities of the wild Atlantic with all its vastness rather than the cosy, introspective Mediterranean of the other southern European nations.

GLOSSARY

o **povo** *the people*
a **cidade** *town, city*
o **campo** *countryside*
viver *to live*
o **habitante** *inhabitant*
a **família** *family*
o **bilhete de identidae** *ID card*
(o **índice de**) **natalidade** *birth rate*
a **fecundidade** *fertility rate*
diminuir *to decrease*
aumentar *to increase*
o **racismo** *racism*
a **violência** *violence*
as **raças** *races*
a **perseguição** *harassment*

nascer *to be born*
casar-se (com) *to get married (to)*
morrer *to die*
o **imigrante (ilegal)** *(illegal) immigrant*
imigrar *to immigrate*
o **meio ambiente** *the environment*
proteger/ defender *to protect/defend*
a **poluição ambiental** *environmental pollution*
caçar *to hunt*
lixos industriais *industrial waste*
melhorar/piorar *to improve/get worse*
a **religião** *religion*
a **igreja** *church*
cátolico/a *Catholic*
os **fiéis** *the faithful*

Taking it further

Suggested reading

Under the Bright Wings, Peter Harris, Hodder & Stoughton, 1993 (tells of the setting up of *A Rocha* reserve in the Algarve)

Tales and More Tales from the Mountains, transl. Miguel Torga Carcanet, 1995 (for insight into the people of Trás-os-Montes)

The Last Kabbalist of Lisbon, Richard Zimler, Arcadia Books, 1998 (Jews in 16th century)

A Good Man in Evil Times, José-Alain Fralon, transl. Peter Graham, Viking, 2000 (story of Aristides de Sousa Mendes and saving of Jews in the war)

Bem-vindo, Lidel, 1998 (Portuguese language coursebook, contains many interesting passages about attitudes of young Portuguese people)

The Portuguese: The Land and its People, Marion Kaplan, Penguin, 1991

Places to visit/ information

BBC 'Discovering Portuguese' television series, six programmes
  with interviews with the Portuguese
Quercus, environmental group, Associação Nacional de
  Conservação da Natureza, Bairro do Calhau, Parque Florestal de
  Monsanto, 1500 Lisboa. Tel: 01-778 84 74. Email:
  quercus@mail.telepac.pt
Ecology/Friends of the Earth, Assoc. Portuguesa de Ecologia e
  Amigos da Terra, Calçada Marquês de Abrantes 10, 3/f Lisboa
Adopt-a-wolf scheme, Centro de Recuperação do Lobo Ibérico,
  CRLI, Apartado 61, 2665 Malveira
Animal Rights League, Liga Portuguesa dos Direitos dos
  Animais, Rua José Costa Mamede 9, 2775 Carcavelos. Tel: 01-
  458 18 18
Lesbian and Gay Centre, Centro Comunitário Gay & Lésbico de
  Lisboa, Rua de São Lazaro 88, Lisboa. Tel: 01-887 39 18

Websites

Ministry for the Environment, **www.min-amb.pt**
Quercus (see above), **www.quercus.pt**
National Statistics, **www.ine.pt**
Amnesty International, **www.amnistia-internacional.pt**
SOS Racismo, **www.terravista.pt/nazare/1064**
SAPO, for up-to-date news and views about Portugal and the
  Portuguese

POSTSCRIPT – PORTUGAL IN THE WORLD TODAY

The view most visitors to Portugal have has changed very little over the last 30 years: a gentle country with an easy approach to life, welcoming people, and an idyll of rural backwardness. Be this as it may, if you look closer you will now observe a nation in transition, a nation dipping its big toe in the warm waters of this modern, technological era. In embracing this new age (for good or bad), Portugal has had to reassess its relationships in the global market, and take its place again in the world it once dominated.

Portugal in Europe

Since joining the (then) EEC in 1986, Portugal has played an increasingly active role in the European Union, culminating in its presidency during 2000. It currently has 25 members in the European Parliament. Portugal is also a member of many organizations, such as NATO and the UN, fully playing its part in international affairs. As a poorer member of the EU, it obviously benefits from a wide rage of subsidies, many of which have been highlighted throughout this book: education and training in particular are improving through EU-backed initiatives to train young people for work in a technical environment; business and industry have enjoyed help to provide financial incentives to large companies to invest in the country.

Interestingly enough, a Euro-survey conducted in Autumn 2000 on whether EU membership was considered a good thing by its citizens, showed that whilst only 28 per cent of the British and 48 per cent of the French thought it was good, 61 per cent of the Portuguese decided it was a positive move. Similarly, 69 per cent of the Portuguese could feel the benefits of membership, compared with only 30 per cent of UK citizens and 46 per cent in France.

Attitudes to the Euro are divided: Portugal was amongst the first wave of countries to sign up to the common currency, but although 59 per cent of people surveyed think it was right to sign up, 69 per cent also believe Portugal will lose an important symbol of its sovereignty.

On the subject of Spain, despite the history of hostility between the two nations over the centuries, both countries enjoy amicable relations these days. Whilst the Portuguese may not travel too much to Spain, Spanish visitors account for 6.9 per cent of all visitors to Portugal, the third largest group after the British and Germans. Portuguese border towns often receive Spanish TV channels, and the inhabitants can usually communicate in both languages (although the Spanish struggle to understand Portuguese). Nevertheless, it is still easy to offend a Portuguese person by assuming you can simply speak to them in Spanish, and surveys still reveal mixed feelings towards their Iberian 'brothers'.

Portugal and Britain

Portugal and Britain formed a strong link of comradeship in the 12th century, their respective armies fighting alongside each other in the Crusades and on numerous occasions subsequently. They have never turned their weapons on each other (although when Portugal was under Spanish rule the ships of the Armada set sail from Lisbon), and the two nations enjoy the world's longest-standing friendship treaty. Today, the citizens of both countries treat each other with respect and friendship, and it is hardly surprising that such a high number of British people visit Portugal – and the number continues to rise. High-profile celebrities own villas there, such as the English singer Sir Cliff Richard, who has just launched his own brand of wine, cultivated on land he has recently transformed into vineyards in the Algarve.

Around 40,000 Portuguese have made a life for themselves in Britain, some of the millions of Portuguese emigrants around the world carving out livings for their families in the hope of a better standard for their children. In Britain, and mainly in London and the Channel Islands, many of them work in catering, hotels and domestic work. The UK has been introduced to the taste of Portugal through the expanding chain of Nando's – a restaurant/

take-away chain specializing in chicken piri-piri. Its range of sauces is now available in many supermarkets.

British citizens who have set up lives for themselves in Portugal (an estimated 9,000 have settled there, mostly in the Algarve), can also claim to work in the services industry – opening bars and offering services such as building, swimming-pool maintenance and satellite-dish installation to the mainly expatriot enclaves.

Portugal and the USA

Links were established with the USA in the 19th century, when American whaling ships used the Azorean islands (also whaling communities) as stopping-off points. In more recent times the islands were used as re-fuelling bases by the US Air Force in World War II. They now serve trans-Atlantic commercial airlines. Large numbers of Portuguese have been making their homes and lives in the USA since the very early stages of emigration from Portugal. Large communities can be found particularly around New England and Connecticut, where some parishes are almost totally Portuguese-speaking. It is estimated that about half a million Portuguese now live in the USA. The American influence can be felt to a certain extent in Portugal, although mainly in larger cities, where McDonald's, for example, has now become part of the fixtures and fittings in 100 locations.

American films are popular on TV and at the cinema, shown in the original with Portuguese subtitles, although it is the mighty Brazilian soap-opera which reigns supreme in Portugal. Music, fashion and style all pick up influences from the States. However, Portugal still maintains a distinctly national feel to its identity.

Portugal and its former Empire

Although 200 million people in the world may speak Portuguese, less than 5% actually live in Portugal. It is important to remember this in context of the whole Portuguese-speaking world, as it illustrates the sort of scale of influence such a small country as Portugal has had in the world. Whilst all the Portuguese-speaking communities may be inextricably linked by their language and histories, more recent events have pulled them in various directions, and away from the homeland.

In the aftermath of the Revolution in 1974, the African colonies were given Independence, but during the ensuing civil wars, particularly ravaging in Angola and Mozambique, the vast majority of Portuguese who were living there returned to Portugal. As the world has witnessed for many years, the problems have not been solved. Princess Diana and other celebrities in her wake have highlighted the horrors of land-mines in Angola and in Mozambique disasters of a natural type have rocked the world with images of despair and waste. Portugal has decried and mourned the atrocities along with the international community, and has welcomed ex-colonial peoples to its shores, helping them to integrate into Portuguese society.

Portugal has felt helpless in relation to the genocide in its ex-colony of East Timor. When Portugal removed its presence from there in 1975 it was aggressively invaded by Indonesia, which has since waged running battles there, consequently costing the lives of around 250,000 Timorese. According to Amnesty International, about a third of the population has now been brutally killed. The problems have been well-documented of late, international attention once more being brought to the area in 1997, when the Nobel Peace Prize was awarded to the leader of the Fretilin Independent Movement, José Ramos-Horta, and the Bishop Carlos Belo. Portugal has consistently deplored the fact that the international community has done little to react to the horrendous situation on the island.

Despite these obvious areas of concern in the former Empire, Portugal does work closely with its ex-colonies where it can, to look for solutions to the problems. There are many positive ties, too, on cultural levels, and in the case of Brazil, in areas of business and commerce. Elsewhere, once-Indian strongholds have long-since been reclaimed, such as Goa, where Portuguese influence today can be seen mainly in architecture and some traditions. As many Goans have remained Catholic they celebrate Christmas with a Midnight Mass and fado! The Portuguese influence in Sri Lanka is now only kept alive through the names of some of its people: the test cricket team has one Aravinda da Silva, for example. Macau, back in Chinese hands since 1999, is now a 'Special Administrative Region' of China. The territory, first reached by Portuguese explorers in 1514, was handed over in an atmosphere considered much more amicable than that of Hong Kong from the British. It is thought by many observers that the Portuguese heritage and influence will remain vital to the territory, not least because it will provide an important stepping-stone for the Chinese for trading links in Brazil and Africa.

Portugal has undoubtedly been a dominant force in the opening-up of the world, since the first tentative steps of its navigators, some 500 years ago, to its continued presence across the continents. The writer José Saramago once said that the world simply cannot ignore a country such as Portugal, with such a long, important history, with so much culture, and with a language spoken by so many people; if Portugal were to be ignored by the world, he declared:

Não é porque sejamos invisíveis, é porque o munde é cego!
(It's not because we are invisible, it's because the world is blind!)

INDEX

TEACH YOURSELF

BEGINNER'S PORTUGUESE

Sue Tyson-Ward

Do you really want to learn Portuguese? Do classes terrify you and other coursebooks overwhelm you? Then *Teach Yourself Beginner's Portuguese* is for you!

Sue Tyson-Ward has written a friendly introduction to Portuguese that's easy right the way through. It's written in two parts: the first teaches you the basic grammar you'll need, with lively dialogues, explanations and vocabulary. In the second you move on to practising what you have learnt in a range of real-life situations. *Beginner's Portuguese* is ideal for you because:

- Everything is explained in simple English
- There are hints throughout to make learning Portuguese easy
- What you learn is useful right from the start
- Key words are listed at the back of the book
- There's a key to all the activities

TEACH YOURSELF

PORTUGUESE

Manuela Cook

This is a complete course in understanding, speaking and writing Portuguese. If you have never learnt Portuguese before, or if your Portuguese needs brushing up, *Teach Yourself Portguese* will give you a thorough grounding in the basics and will take you onto a level where you can communicate with confidence.

The very successful original *Teach Yourself Portuguese* has been completely revised and updated, with stimulating new dialogues and new, authentic material. Dr. Manuela Cook explains everything clearly along the way and gives you plenty of opportunities to practise what you have learnt.

The course contains:

- graded units of dialogues, culture notes, grammar and exercises
- a pronunciation guide
- tables of regular and irregular verbs
- a Portuguese–English vocabulary
- an English–Portuguese vocabulary
- special reference to Brazilian Portuguese forms

By the end of the course you'll be able to communicate effectively and appreciate the culture of Portuguese speakers.